OSCAR WILDE

VISIONS AND REVISIONS

Irish Writers in their Time

Series Editor: Stan Smith

This innovative series meets the urgent need for comprehensive new accounts of Irish writing across the centuries which combine readability with critical authority and information with insight. Each volume addresses the whole range of a writer's work in the various genres, setting its vision of the world in biographical context and situating it within the cultural, intellectual, and political currents of the age, in Ireland and the wider world. This series will prove indispensable for students and specialists alike.

1. Patrick Kavanagh
(Editor: STAN SMITH)

2. Elizabeth Bowen
(Editor: EIBHEAR WALSHE)

3. John Banville
(JOHN KENNY)

4. Jonathan Swift
(BREAN HAMMOND)

5. James Joyce
(Editor: SEAN LATHAM)

6. W.B. Yeats
(Editor: EDWARD LARRISSY)

7. Oscar Wilde
(Editor: JARLATH KILLEEN)

Oscar Wilde

Edited by
JARLATH KILLEEN
Trinity College, Dublin

IRISH ACADEMIC PRESS
DUBLIN • PORTLAND, OR

First published in 2011 by Irish Academic Press

2 Brookside,
Dundrum Road,
Dublin 14, Ireland

920 NE 58th Avenue, Suite 300
Portland, Oregon,
97213-3786, USA

www.iap.ie

British Library Cataloguing-in-Publication Data
An entry can be found on request

978 0 7165 3074 9 (cloth)
978 0 7165 3075 6 (paper)

Library of Congress Cataloging-in-Publication Data
An entry can be found on request

Printed in Great Britain by the MPG Books Group, Bodmin and King's Lynn

Contents

List of Contributors

Bruce Bashford is the author of *Oscar Wilde: The Critic as Humanist* (Fairleigh Dickinson University Press, 1999). He is Associate Professor of English at Stony Brook University. He teaches courses on literary theory and the history of criticism, the art of rhetoric and Oscar Wilde.

Sos Eltis is a fellow and tutor in English, Brasenose College, Oxford. She is the author of *Revising Wilde: Society and Subversion in the Plays of Oscar Wilde* (Clarendon Press, 1996). She is currently preparing a book on the fallen woman on stage from 1850 to the present. She teaches nineteenth- and twentieth-century literature and has a special interest in drama.

Noreen Doody lectures in English Literature at St. Patrick's College, Drumcondra, a college of Dublin City University. Her research interests are in Irish Studies and nineteenth-century literature, focussing on the work of Oscar Wilde and W.B. Yeats. She has published widely in this area.

Michael Patrick Gillespie is the Louise Edna Goeden Professor of English at Marquette University. He has written or edited nineteen books and over fifty articles on the works of James Joyce, Oscar Wilde, William Kennedy and Samuel Beckett. He has also published on chaos theory and on Irish Film. His latest book is *The Myth of an Irish Cinema* (Syracuse University Press, 2008).

Jarlath Killeen is a Lecturer in Victorian Literature in Trinity College Dublin. He is the author of *British Gothic Literature, 1824-1914* (University of Wales Press, 2009); *The Fairy Tales of Oscar Wilde* (Ashgate, 2007); *Gothic Ireland: Horror and the Irish Anglican Imagination in the Long Eighteenth Century* (Four

Courts Press, 2005); *The Faiths of Oscar Wilde: Catholicism, Folklore and Ireland* (Palgrave, 2005).

Anne Markey is the Postdoctoral Fellow on the IRCHSS assisted Early Irish Fiction project in Trinity College Dublin, where she also teaches. She has published on Irish writers including Yeats, Wilde and Beckett and her edition of Joseph Campbell's translations of Patrick Pearse's stories was published by UCD Academic Press in 2009. She has co-edited a new edition of *Vertue Rewarded; or, the Irish Princess* with Ian Campbell Ross (Four Courts Press, 2010). She is currently working on a monograph on Wilde's fairy tales.

D.C. Rose was director of the Oscar Wilde Summer School in Bray, Ireland, and edits the online journal, OSCHOLARS. His chief area of interest is *fin de siècle* Paris and Wilde's accommodation within it. He is now engaged in an extended study of *Pelléas et Mélisande* and also researching the representation of Paris in English literature.

Florina Tufescu, lecturer with the Dalarna University Centre for Irish Studies in Sweden, originally from Romania, specializes in English and comparative literature and criticism, in particular *fin de siècle* and intertextual theory. She is the author of *Oscar Wilde's Plagarism: The Triumph of Art over Ego* (Irish Academic Press, 2007).

Anne Varty is Emeritus Professor at Royal Holloway College, University of London. Her research interests focus on the literature, theatre and journalism of the Victorian period and her work is often interdisciplinary. She also has strong interests in contemporary and late twentieth-century British theatre. She is currently working on a stage history of folk and fairy tales on the nineteenth-century British stage, the literature of British involvement in the opium trade, and the history of illustrated editions of Wilde. She is editing a forthcoming volume of essays on Liz Lochhead. She is the author of *Children and Theatre in Victorian Britain* (Palgrave Macmillan, 2007), shortlisted by the Society for Theatre Research for the Best Theatre Book of 2007; *Eve's Century. A Sourcebook of Writings on Women and Journalism 1895-1918* (Routledge, 2000); *A Preface to Oscar Wilde* (Pearson Education, 1998).

Acknowledgements

My first thanks go to my contributors for their generosity and openness during the editorial process. My thanks also to Lisa Hyde of Irish Academic Press. She commissioned this volume, helped to keep it on time, and was immensely supportive through the whole process. A special thanks to Darryl Jones, who listened patiently to my tales of woe.

My love, as always, to Mary Lawlor and our daughter Eilís.

Oscar Wilde: A Chronology

1851 November	Marriage of William Wilde and Jane Francesca Elgee.
1852 September	Birth of William Charles Kingsbury Wills Wilde.
1854 16 October	Birth of Oscar Fingal O'Flahertie Wills Wilde.
1855	Wilde family move to Merrion Square.
1857 April	Birth of Isola Francesca Emily Wilde.
1862–64	The Mary Travers affair.
1864–71	Wilde attends Portora Royal School in Enniskillen.
1867 February	Death of Isola Wilde.
1871 November	Death of Emily and Mary Wilde.
1871–74	Wilde attends Trinity College Dublin.
1874–78	Wilde attends Magdalen College, Oxford.
1876 April	Death of Sir William Wilde.
1877 June	Death of Henry Wilson Wilde.
1878 June	Wilde wins the Newdigate Prize for poetry with his poem *Ravenna*.
1880 September	Wilde's first play, *Vera; or the Nihilists*, printed privately.
1881 June	*Poems* published.
December	Wilde begins his lecture tour of the United States and Canada.
1882 November?	Wilde starts writing *The Duchess of Padua*.
1883 November	Wilde becomes engaged to Constance Lloyd.
1884 May	Wilde and Constance Lloyd marry.
1885 January	The Wildes move to 16 Tite Street, Chelsea.
June	Cyril Wilde born.
1886	Wilde meets Robert Ross.
June	Vyvyan Wilde born.
1887	Wilde becomes editor of the *Woman's World*.
1888 May	*The Happy Prince and Other Tales* published.
1889 July	'The Portrait of Mr. W. H.' is published.

1890 June	*The Picture of Dorian Gray* is serialized in *Lippincott's Magazine*.
1891	Wilde meets Lord Alfred Douglas.
February	'The Soul of Man under Socialism' published in the *Forthnightly Review*.
April	*The Picture of Dorian Gray* published.
May	*Intentions* published.
July	*Lord Arthur Savile's Crimes and Other Stories* published.
November	*A House of Pomegranates* published.
	Wilde writes *Salome* towards the end of this year.
1892 February	*Lady Windermere's Fan* opens.
June	*Salome* banned by the Lord Chamberlain.
1893 April	*A Woman of No Importance* opens.
November	*Lady Windermere's Fan* published.
1894 February	*Salome* published.
1894 June	*The Sphinx* published.
October	*A Woman of No Importance* published.
1895 January	*An Ideal Husband* opens.
14 February	*The Importance of Being Earnest* opens.
28 February	Wilde is handed the Marquess of Queensberry's card accusing him of being a 'posing Somdomite [*sic*]' at the Albemarle Club. Wilde decides to seek for the prosecution of Queensberry for libel.
5 April	Queensberry is found 'not guilty'. Wilde is arrested for 'gross indecency'.
26 April	First prosecution of Wilde opens.
1 May	Jury cannot agree and a new trial is ordered.
25 May	Wilde is convicted, and sentenced to two years' hard labour. He moves from Newgate to Pentonville to Wandsworth to Reading Gaol.
1896 February	Death of Lady Wilde. Wilde is told of her death by his wife Constance.
1897 Jan.–March	Wilde writes letter to Lord Alfred Douglas that will become basis of *De Profundis*.
19 May	Wilde released. Moves to the European continent.
1898 February	*The Ballad of Reading Gaol* published under the pseudonym 'C 33'.

	April	Death of Constance Wilde.
1899	February	*The Importance of Being Earnest* published.
	July	*An Ideal Husband* published.
1900	30 November	Wilde dies in the Hôtel d'Alsace, Paris.

CHAPTER ONE

Introduction:
Wilde's Aphoristic Imagination

JARLATH KILLEEN

Will there never be an end to books devoted to Oscar Wilde? Given that this is yet another of them, the answer to this question is obvious: not any time soon. The sheer volume of critical material on Wilde has necessitated four book-length bibliographical guides to help students and other readers through the morass, and these guides only go up to about 2001[1] – since then the critics have been anything but silent, and have produced a formidable body of new work. Moreover, numerous 'versions' of Wilde himself, and different 'schools of thought' about his life and writings, have been classified, and these classifications are multiplying even as I write this: the 'Gay' Wilde, 'Irish' Wilde, 'Materialist' Wilde, 'Idealist' Wilde, 'Catholic' Wilde.[2] Wilde studies is a dynamic and exciting area in which to work; it can also be a contentious and sometimes treacherous one, and this in part because Wilde is a writer in whom the reading public have a large stake. I vividly remember giving a public lecture in Dublin in 2001 on Wilde's interest in Catholicism, a lecture which turned out to be fraught with tension and almost ended in a shouting match between myself and a spirited member of the audience. Another public lecture (in 2010) was interrupted by an audience member noisily departing, but not before delivering a potentially fatal parting shot, loudly proclaiming that I was talking 'disgusting nonsense'. Lest I give the mistaken impression that my public lectures are riveting and unmissable, I should in honesty record that on another occasion two members of my audience fell fast asleep and snored deafeningly throughout my clearly less-than-scintillating talk. However, it is fair to say that Wilde attracts a great deal of passionate and engaged attention both inside and outside the academy, and that it is therefore understandable that a great many million words have been devoted to him. Academics have certainly not tended towards restraint in their criticism of colleagues in Wilde studies. A now notorious example of this academic acrimony is the war of words that followed the publication of Melissa Knox's psychoanalytic biography of Wilde, *A Long and Lovely Suicide* (1994) – at one stage it looked like accusations of syphilitic infection would spread from Wilde himself to reviewers and critics.[3] If Wilde criticism began in a storm of controversy after the trials, and continued in acrimony in the battles between Robert Ross, Alfred Douglas, Frank Harris and Robert Sherard, contemporary scholars seem eager to continue the fight, and have in the recent past accused each other of everything from plagiarism and ignorance, to political bias and silliness.[4]

Although every contributor to this book (and the editor as well), is involved to some degree or other in the 'Wilde wars', we have genuinely tried to avoid being too divisive in our chapters, and the book as a whole includes as many perspectives across the range of opinion on Wilde as I found possible; at times, however, differences in approach and the ideological fissures between contributors should become obvious. This is as it should be, and to pretend that everyone writing for this collection is in ideological or interpretive agreement would be misleading. The collection tries to cover all aspects of Wilde's work, from his neglected poetry to *The Picture of Dorian Gray* (1890) and the society plays. Each chapter is written by a different scholar and taken as a whole the book represents a (relatively) balanced view of Wilde studies as it is currently comprised. Those involved range from long-established, internationally-renowned expert Wildeans to relatively new voices in the field, and it is hoped that the volume amounts to a cross-generational dialogue, pointing the way forward for future research. The main focus is on the genres in which Wilde wrote, but there are also special chapters on Wilde's life, Wilde as a Victorian (still a neglected topic), and even a (short) chapter covering Wilde on the Web. The aim is to provide a fairly extensive profile in relatively jargon-free prose, that will appeal to academics, students and to the fabled general reader who, given attendances at public lectures dedicated to Wilde, still seems attracted by this most fascinating of Victorian intellectuals.

Despite the range of material covered in the chapters that follow this one, some of Wilde's writings have always proved recalcitrant to any attempt to fit them under a stable generic label such as 'fiction', 'drama', 'criticism' or 'poetry'.[5] Of course, one collection of essays on a writer cannot possibly expect to be definitive, and that many gaps will remain is inevitable. However, it may be instructive to begin a collection such as this one with an examination of at least some of the formally 'awkward' material, and to this end, this chapter will focus on two examples of Wilde's writings which often end up under the heading, 'Miscellaneous', both published towards the end of 1894, both of them collections of aphorisms. 'A Few Maxims for the Instruction of the Over-Educated' appeared anonymously in the *Saturday Review* in November, and 'Phrases and Philosophies for the Use of the Young' was published in the first and only edition of the Oxford undergraduate magazine the *Chameleon* in December (the magazine also contained John Francis Bloxham's 'The Priest and the Acolyte', and the appearance of Wilde's collection in the same edition as this blatantly homoerotic story was to provide the Marquess of Queensberry's defence team with considerable ammunition in the libel trial).

These 'articles' are interesting for a number of reasons, and have been rather sidelined in Wilde studies which is surprising given that they include some of the epigrams for which Wilde is most famous. In many ways, these publications can be seen as 'typical' of Wilde's writing in general. After all, Wilde is best known as epigrammatist, a specialist in witty one liners rather than discursive prose. Wilde's failure to emerge as a major novelist in an age when the form reached what many consider its apotheosis has always attracted some very contentious attention. It has been argued that his dependence on pithy, terse (and generally funny) statements is an indication that Wilde simply lacked the necessary energy required to write Victorian three-volume tomes, and to lack also the seriousness that would have enabled him to take on such a lengthy project with any verve.[6] Examination of Wilde's manuscripts demonstrates that he was not particularly interested in (or, possibly, good at) plot or character, generally working from what Josephine M. Guy and Ian Small call 'rudimentary' plot sketches and basic character types. What he *was* interested in was the individual line or dialogue exchange, concentrating what intellectual energy he had mainly on quips and sharp cracks which he then (sometimes arbitrarily) distributed among his various characters, stories, plays, poems, articles, without any real evidence of consistency. This epigrammatic manner of structuring leads in some cases to extremes of self-plagiarism, and the shifting of lines between characters that would seem inconceivable to a writer interested in character-consistency, such as George Eliot. This technique, basic to his best writing, appears to extend back to Wilde's time in university, as examination of the apparently unsystematic remarks and observations made in his undergraduate note-books demonstrates.[7] Given his dependence on the one liner, Guy and Small believe that 'it is as if Wilde's very creativity itself was manifest via the composition of small, discrete units', and they are at pains to demonstrate the 'modular' nature of Wilde's composition.[8] Indeed, echoing their findings, I think it would not be too much of an exagger-ation to argue that Wilde's career was based on his mastery of the epigram, maxim and aphorism, and if this is the case it is small wonder that the three-volume novel was far beyond his interests (or, as Guy and Small would have it, his ability). On this reading, his only novel *The Picture of Dorian Gray* (1890) is a formal anomaly in his canon, if not an ambiguous failure.

Guy and Small insist that there is little that could be called 'ideological' or 'political' about Wilde's attraction to the aphorism and epigram. For them, Wilde was simply not very good at extended narrative, found plot difficult, character relatively uninteresting, and therefore concentrated on what he was best at, perfecting the pithy. More controversially, they conclude that 'Wilde was a writer who did not have an abundance of either intellectual resources or material', recognizing that this 'may seem to justify some of the judgements of Wilde made by his contemporaries and by critics in the first half of the twentieth century, that he was a writer of relatively slender talents, whose work was derivative'.[9] This is probably a step too far for others. Both Sandra Siegel and Jerusha McCormack (two of the small number of critics who have devoted attention to this issue) stress the ideological rather than the materialist in their analysis of Wilde's aphorisms. Siegel insists that Wilde consciously chose to work with the aphorism because it 'was bound to antagonise [the English reader] to the extent that it represented the eruption and animation of the Celtic self'.[10] McCormack sees his use of the epigram as a kind of 'guerrilla warfare' against the English.[11] I am not all that convinced that the materialist/careerist view of Wilde as a writer who was forced to write epigrams because he wasn't particularly good at writing anything else, is incompatible with the view of Wilde as a political writer who saw the epigram as a weapon in a cultural and colonial battle – could it not be argued that Wilde's formal talents coincided with his ideological sympathies?

Before looking at the aphorisms collected in the two 'articles', it may be useful to point out that Wilde had an opinion about the genre in which he did not excel. It is fairly clear that Wilde was not a great fan of what we now think of as the typical 'Victorian novel', despite the fact that he lived, as Francis O'Gorman has recently put it, in the great 'age of the novel'.[12] One of the funniest lines he ever wrote was given to Miss Prism in The Importance of Being Earnest (first performed 1895, first published 1899), who declares ominously about her own three-volume novel: 'The good ended happily, and the bad unhappily. That is what Fiction means' – or what it means to the kind of novel reader/writer she represents (the kind, probably, who would cry rather than laugh over the death of Charles Dickens' Little Nell, especially since her novel is, as Lady Bracknell indicates, one of 'more than usually revolting sentimentality').[13] A disdain for the realist novel is also evident in Wilde's scathing attack on what he believed to be the imaginative failures involved in an investment in realism. He was a writer, after all, who believed 'superstition' rather than reason to be 'the colour element in thought'.[14] In opposition to the interest of the realists in a discrete and accurate rendering of everyday life, in one review Wilde insists that 'This is the supreme advantage that fiction possesses over fact: it can make things artistically probable, and by force of mere style, compel us to believe. The ordinary novelists, by keeping close to the ordinary incidents of commonplace life, seem to me to abdicate half of their power.'[15] While he admired certain kinds of popular non-realist fiction (such as mesmerist, 'magic picture' and Gothic novels[16]) he recognized that this was not a class of writing accorded much intellectual weight in elite circles compared with that given to the realist novel. Much of the disdain wielded by Vivian in 'The Decay of Lying' (1889) is reserved for realism. Vivian attacks 'the modern novelist' who 'presents us with dull facts under the guise of fiction' for which 'the Blue Book is ... his ideal both for method and manner'.[17] While it is dangerous to simply assume that Wilde is 'speaking through' his character here, Vivian's views certainly echo Wilde's comments elsewhere, and in connecting realism to the 'Blue Books' (reports published by the British parliament) the dialogue implicitly indicts it for political as well as aesthetic reasons. We could, of course, read these comments suspiciously, as the defensive posturing of a writer incapable of meeting the demands of a particular kind of fiction. It seems improbable, however, that Wilde is not genuinely objecting to realism as a literary project and if this is the case, it may be that the aphorism offered a suitable alternative that coincided with his particular talents.

Realism was serious, perhaps even (for Wilde), earnest.[18] Against various kinds of generic fiction — the romance, the sensation novel, Gothic — which played fast and loose with historical reality, realists believed that their audience could be trusted with the truth rather than patronized by petty fictions. The realists were committed to treating 'things as they are and not as the story teller would like them to be for his convenience';[19] in comparison to this, romance was mere wish-fulfilment. The realist novel invested heavily in the empirical, the observable; it tended to associate itself with the methodologies of Victorian science.[20] One reason for the close approximation to the natural sciences was that realism was one response to the cultural unease and anxiety caused by contemporary scientific discoveries — Victorian realism can be read as a quasi-scientific reaction to the 'crisis of faith' which emerged, in part, from the new realities put forward by geology, biology and physics. George Levine has argued that one of the reasons for the importance of the realist experiment was that its Victorian audience was suffering through an extraordinary assault on certainty itself given the discoveries of science about the world in which it lived, a world most had until then been fairly certain of in its lineaments, contours and time-span, that 'the confident moralism of which the great

Victorian writers are frequently accused turns out almost invariably to be an attempt to rediscover moral order after their primary energies have been devoted to disrupting conventions of moral judgement'.[21] For example, the Victorians were the first modern civilization to cope with the impact of an awareness of 'deep time'. Linked particularly to the arguments of Charles Lyell's *Principles of Geology* (1830–33), time and history were expanded to dizzying lengths that proved frightening to the Victorian imagination. According to the geologists, time was virtually immeasurable, and given this, the individual man and woman looked inconsequential and completely unimportant, and this appears to have genuinely terrified the audience who first became aware of it. If 'deep time' was true, individual life appeared pointless. Critics have pointed out that the Victorian realist novel attempted to dispel the fear of time by demonstrating the integration of the individual with temporal structures which could then be seen as ordered and progressive. In the realist novel individual, personal history and the movement of historical time were woven together as seamlessly as possible.[22]

As many literary historians have pointed out, the insistent past-tense narration of the typical Victorian realist novel places the reader and the characters in a distinct relationship to historical processes. In other words, that the events of the novel happened in the past, but are being narrated in the present, demonstrates that each past event is not random or unintelligible, but is rather part of an ordered pattern of reality whereby personality and history accumulate meaning over time (sometimes, immense stretches of time). This kind of narration is reassuring about the future also, because, if each and every event in the past had, at the least, an historical meaning then the future will also surely be a development of and from the present moment.[23] This process of explaining and domesticating time linked the realist novel to the evolutionary approach to history of a popularized Darwin – best exemplified by Herbert Spencer's famous 1852 lecture 'The Development Hypothesis' – which effectively made 'Progress' appear the reason for the systems of 'deep time'. Time is a major factor in both Victorian science and the realist novel, and the realist novel can be seen as in many ways the reconciliation of the individual to the processes of deep time. As Elizabeth Deeds Ermath argues, 'The conception of time as a common medium in which distinctions between past, present, and future are meaningful (i.e. mutually informative) is a conception predicated by realistic narrative as well as confirmed by it.'[24] Since the present can only be understood as that which has emerged from the past, the future of the story is, at least in one sense, guaranteed. Although we cannot be *sure* as to what will happen, a progression, a movement towards some better future is in store.

This often blatant emphasis on 'Progress' – inherent, for example, even in the title of George Eliot's *Middlemarch* (1871–72) – provides the realist novel with a distinct ideological inflection because the integration of the individual with history also simultaneously articulates a version of history as a process of civilization, a movement from savagery to civility. The focus of realist novels on the individual makes sense from this perspective. Realist novels make a point of, as David Lloyd describes, 'repeatedly telling the tale of an individual's passage from singularity or particularity to social integration' whereby 'the anomalous individual learns to be reconciled with society and its projects'. However, the apparent focus of the plot on the development of the individual is really a means to address the more abstract interests of the realist novel which sees 'the individual narrative of self-formation ... subsumed into the larger narrative of the civilising process, the passage from savagery to civility, which is the master narrative of modernity'.[25] Moreover, this movement forward in time from a primitive to a civilized state is linked to the master narrative of secularization, the movement (progress) from a time of superstition to a time of rationalism. According to George Levine, 'the realist novel is predominately a secular form, in which the implicit order of the world ... can only be achieved in worldly terms', and this is a view of the realist novel echoed by many major critics.[26] As Georg Lukács insists, this makes the novel the epic of modernity, and consequently the epic of a world supposedly 'growing out of' God.[27]

Given this history, it may be clearer why Wilde opted for another method for the elucidation of his 'principles' for living: the epigram, the quip, the aphorism. Whereas the realist novel suggests that time should be considered progressive and developmental, compilations of aphorisms offer an alternative sense of history: after all, as collections of 'great sayings', 'great truths' static across time and space, collections of aphorisms effectively refuse to play the game of evolution and progress. An aphorism is an implicit denial of the evolutionary view of history as some kind of magnificent organism that is developing and refining itself throughout time itself. If a collection calls itself *True Sayings For All Time* or *The Wisdom of the Ages*,[28] the insistent trust in historical evolution witnessed in the realist novel is ruled out of court. Aphorisms contradict 'Progress'. Of course, Irish writers often found the Victorian emphasis on 'Progress' oppressive, because this progressive model configured the Celtic fringes as stuck in the infantile phase in the history of mankind waiting to be replaced by the maturity of Anglo-Saxon culture. The distinguished anthropologist E.B. Tylor, wrote in 1871 that, 'To the human intellect in its early childlike state may be assigned the origin and first development of myth ... we may ... claim the savage as a representative of the childhood of the human race'.[29] For many thinkers, this childish savagery persisted in Scotland, Wales and Ireland, as well as in far-off colonies.

In the hands of those who wish to subvert the moral and metaphysical certainties of the Victorian elite, aphorisms could indeed be counter-cultural weapons. Indeed, given that their pithy power sometimes works better when they are spoken rather than written, many aphorisms have an oral gravitation, which would bolster studies of Wilde that see him very much within an oral matrix.[30] That the aphorism is Wilde's basic unit of creativity may, therefore, be very ideologically revealing, *pace* Guy and Small. Given his complaints about the realist novel, which was so associated with the ideological project of modernity, the aphorism could be seen as an ideologically useful – because oppositional – mode in which to work. The aphorism cannot be easily or seamlessly assimilated into the realist novel which, as Lloyd points out does not seek 'passively to reflect, amongst other things, the linguistic habits of a given community', but rather 'entails a regularization and hierarchization of sociolects such that its dominance relegates to marginality forms which depend on an instability of register or on the possibilities offered by linguistic instabilities'.[31] That the aphorism does act as an agent of instability is evident from any reading of how it operates when 'integrated' into Wilde's extended narratives. As Amanda Anderson has argued, the epigrams that can be found everywhere in Wilde's work 'announce their easy exit from the text, their extractability'.[32] This view is also articulated by Gregory Mackie who points out that Wilde appeared to regard 'all of his texts as amenable to extraction and reconstitution in lists of *bon mots*',[33] and it is certainly easy to simply lift the epigrams and aphorisms found everywhere in his work from their 'original' contexts and see them as stand alone statements. Indeed, it is often next to impossible to see them as germane to, intrinsic to, the text of which they form a part.

While the realist novel demonstrates the hero moving through history and integrating with its major narrative movements, aphorisms are isolated sayings stripped of context and chronological arrangement. Also, unlike the realist novel, which sets up strict hierarchies of narrative arrangement – facts versus fiction, reality versus superstition – the sheer narrative starkness of the aphorism collection raises problems of hierarchy and is always in danger of looking formally chaotic if not, indeed, anarchic. As Sandra Siegel has shown, some Victorian compilers of aphorisms attempted to counteract this creative and contextless anarchy by imposing order, and many arranged aphorisms in chronological order or grouped them together thematically,[34] but the two collections of Wilde's aphorisms I am examining here do not appear to have any organizational logic. 'A Few Maxims for the Instruction of the Over-Educated', and 'Phrases and Philosophies for the Use of the Young',[35] are not only collections of the aphorisms of a single writer (in direct opposition to the dominant kind of aphorism collection that existed at this time) but they are also apparently *unorganized* in terms of theme or chronology. The 'chaotic' nature of these two texts gives some justification to the sheer number of collections of Wilde's aphorisms that circulate today, collections in which lines are culled from throughout Wilde's life and writing without any contextualization, or recognition that certain lines are spoken by fictional characters and not by Wilde himself. Wilde himself assisted his wife Constance in putting together one such collection – *Oscarania: Epigrams* (1895) – which took lines haphazardly from throughout Wilde's writings.

Placing these aphorism collections in relation to the realist novel helps to indicate that, while they are structurally 'random' in that there does not seem to be any good reason why one aphorism follows another, there are what we might dare to call 'themes' connecting some of the aphorisms together, and many of these themes confirm an opposition to the ideological implications of realism that I have suggested so far. There is, for example, in opposition to the realist embrace of the here and now, a clear rejection of the contemporary world. Wilde opines against 'nowadays', when there is 'so little useless information', and where 'books are written by the public and read by nobody'. 'To be really modern' is to be devoid of soul, but ironically the modern age has perfected the art of dullness. The 'present moment' is populated by beautiful people occupying 'useful professions'. 'Useless information' is presumably information that is irreducible to the demands of technocrats: it is 'useless' as it is anti-utilitarian. Utilitarianism was the principle philosophy driving the industrial revolution, and the creation of the recognizably modernist economy. Yet industry, Wilde tells us, 'is the root of all ugliness'. He attacks the attributes of the modern age in no uncertain terms here: it is the 'age of seriousness' which will bring not 'enlightenment' only 'dullness'; industry is not the solution to poverty only the 'root of all ugliness'; the moral religion of humanity siphoned by the likes of George Eliot from the ruins of Christianity is not an example of moral progress but the opposite as 'any preoccupation with ideas what is right and what is wrong in conduct shows an arrested intellectual development';[36] good resolutions are not indications of moral superiority but are always made 'too soon'; rationality is not the wisdom of the age as 'one should always be a little improbable'. The rejection of 'useful information' explains the satirical rejection of education, which is declared 'an admirable thing', but against which the reader is urged to be wary. After all, 'it is well to remember that nothing that is worth knowing can ever be taught'.

What can be taught is the useful information, the 'facts', which predominate 'nowadays', facts which allow us theoretically to gain control over the world, to recognize the processes of time and history: it is the kind of knowledge we need to integrate ourselves with modernity, and is linked to the education of the individual, and realized through the narrative processes of the realist novel. In contrast to 'useful information' is that which is 'worth knowing' and which cannot be taught, 'wisdom' not designed for utilitarian purposes, and which abounded 'in the old days', a phrase predictably reminiscent of the language of fairy tales. Wilde privileges the discourse of the fairy tale and of myth over that of the realist novel. If the realist novel tends to 'demythologise', Wilde's aphorisms might be thought of as attempts to 'remythologise' (or to 'demythologise the demythologisers').[37] If the present moment is the age of ugliness, the 'old days' were the days of beauty. These aphorisms explicitly reject the facile dichotomies popular in the writings of Herbert Spencer, Thomas Huxley, John Tyndal and epitomized by John William Draper's *History of the Conflict between Science and Religion* (1874) and Andrew Dickson White's *The Warfare of Science* (1876) and *A History of the Warfare of Science with Theology in Christendom* (1896). These thinkers theorized that science and religion were in a perpetual battle, that science was the motor driving progress and that religion was a historical hangover from an earlier, less civilized age.[38] In Wilde's aphorisms, science is not the alternative to religion; indeed, it is a kind of religion for the unbelieving since 'religions die when they are proved to be true. Science is the record of dead religions.' It is important to recognize that this completely reverses Thomas Huxley's famous view of science as littered with the corpses of decomposing theologians, vanquished when scientists proved that certain religious beliefs were *not* true: 'Extinguished theologians lie about the cradle of every science as the strangled snakes beside that of Hercules; and history records that whenever science and orthodoxy have been fairly opposed, the latter has been forced to retire from the lists, bleeding and crushed if not annihilated; scotched, if not slain.'[39] While the positivists insist that what is fact is also truth, Wilde posits that only 'the English are always degrading truths into facts'.

While the realist novel attempted humanely to alleviate the existential dread caused by the discovery of 'deep time' and evolutionary time, problems with time are entirely bypassed in Wilde's aphorisms. Indeed, time itself is debunked as 'a waste of money' to which only the prurient give attention. To accept that time is progress implies that as we grow older (and as societies and nations 'mature') we become wiser, that as experience is gained the individual re-enacts history's linear story, moving from a superstitious infancy to a mature and rational middle age. In this, realism conformed to the popular view that 'ontogeny recapitulates phylogeny', the individual recapitulates the development of civilization and the evolution of the species. It is a view that is consigned to the dustbin by these aphorisms which contrarily insist that whereas the old 'believe everything', and the middle-aged 'suspect everything', only the young 'know everything'. Wilde is praising not those who are literally youthful, but those who live in perpetual youth, because 'those whom the gods love grow young'. This is an explicit denial of mechanical time and a movement into mythic time.

Fascinatingly, these dichotomies (nowadays/old days, science/religion, age/youth, information/wisdom) are placed within a political context, because these aphorisms indict one particular nationality with the fetishisation of the modern: 'the English are always degrading truths into facts. When a truth becomes a fact it loses all its intellectual value.' 'Nowadays', the days of the useful fact propagated through education – and also through the educational principle of the realist novel where the movement is from confusion to wisdom, ignorance to knowledge, the superstitious past to the rationalist present – is the historical time of the English; the olden days, the non-modern, mythic time of fairy-tales, folk-wisdom (aphorisms are not, after all, unlike folk sayings, 'wise words'), are clearly non-English. It is surely legitimate to suggest that the mythic space shadowing these collections is probably the one Wilde was most familiar with: Ireland. After all, in these aphorisms, Wilde is articulating a version of W.B. Yeats's later attack on the 'filthy modern tide' using the weapons of the sacred mythologies of the Celtic Twilight.

In direct opposition to the profane histories propagated by the scientism of George Eliot, and the microscopic realism of many Victorian writers, Wilde's aphorisms evoke sacred time, a time of myth. 'Nothing that actually occurs is of the smallest importance', the emphasis falling here on the actuality of verifiable reality. If 'the ages live in history through their anachronisms', that is essentially because mythic time is endlessly repeatable and repeated in terms of ritual. Mircea Eliade has shown that the trope of the 'eternal return' is central to the 'mythological mindset',[40] and folkloric and mythological narratives. Through such constant repetition, repetitions which seem anachronistic to the modern mind, the past ages of holy history are re-lived: moreover, they can act as repositories of utopian possibilities that have yet to be, or may never be, realized. As Paul Ricoeur noted, myth is 'a disclosure of unprecedented worlds, an opening on to other *possible* worlds which transcend the limits of our *actual* world'.[41] In Wilde's mythic imagination, history is always doubling back upon itself, dismissing 'nowadays' in favour of anachronism and a revocation of what has apparently past. After all 'those that the gods love grow younger'. Lord Alfred Douglas insisted that 'unless you understand that Oscar is an Irishman through and through, you will never get an idea of what his real nature is. In many ways he is as simple and innocent as a child.'[42] Wilde constantly admitted to being two years younger than he actually was, and this may indicate not merely personal vanity (though certainly that too) but also a cultural pressure that defined the Irish as essentially still caught in the childish mythic imagination and not having matured into the historical presence, and a refusal to submit to the fetishisation of time and history central to his age.

In these aphorisms Wilde takes the Mythos of his own age and destabilizes it with the wisdom of the non-modern. In suppressing the mythic you end in the dangerous – or simply the dull. A myth can be explained, these aphorisms hint, but not explained away. Wilde's movement towards the concept of the cyclical nature of time is one other means of debunking the entire scientific logos: after all, if time is cyclical rather than linear, then everything that is happening now has happened before and will happen again. While the realist novel attempted to make the profane sacred in a religion of humanity, the aphorism functions as an opening onto the profane world by the sacred. Wilde's aphorisms are, then, also hierophanies (manifestations of the sacred). Realism is an attempt to divorce Logos from Mythos, but is a dramatic failure of precisely that project as it merely enunciates a new Mythos – a truly white mythology which designates the non-Western non-rational communities as the past, and the rational modern world as its own and everything else's future, a self-perpetuating belief that would eventually lead intellectuals like Francis Fukuyama to believe that liberal capitalism was the End of History.[43] For the modern English world, the mythic spaces of the Celtic fringe could indeed be translated into the modern age, but only through a process of education, and the educational experiments conducted in these places were ideologically weighted projects inherently problematic to anyone who found the development hypothesis nonsensical.

The link between certain kinds of education and civilization probably motivates Wilde's decision to aim these collections at the young and 'over-educated'. Progress towards an ever more refined civilization was not simply the structuring principle behind education in England and the realist novel, but also informed educational experiments in Ireland in the nineteenth century in which national schools were seen – quite blatantly – as ways to civilize a backward and infantile country. John Coolahan has pointed to the establishment in 1812 of a Board of Commissioners as a key moment in the colonial 'civilizing' of Ireland. This Board was given complete control over the kinds of school books used, teachers engaged, pedagogical practices employed, and a threat of dismissal hung over any teacher deemed to be involved in cultural or political 'subversion'.[44] The textbooks used in national schools were bizarre entities. Although used to teach Irish students, no reference to Irish heritage or history was permitted, though 'England and the empire were glorified and references to Ireland emphasised its place within the imperial scheme of things'.[45] Coolahan quotes Joe Lee who has argued that the National System of Education, established in 1831, was designed to 'perform a massive brain-washing operation, obliterating subversive ancestral influence by inculcating in the pupils a proper reverence for the English connection, and proper deference to their social superiors, defined according to the exquisite English concept of class'.[46] One important idea found in textbooks was a distinction between the 'educated' and the 'uneducated'. School children were informed that 'the people of these islands have one and the same language (at least all who are educated)'.[47] The designation that swept all Gaelic speakers into the uneducated was a smooth move by cultural imperialists who wished to induce colonial subservience through methods of forced cultural allegiance. That many who had given their allegiance to the colonial system considered that education was the antidote to the cultural backwardness represented by folk Catholicism is obvious from the claim of the folklore collector Thomas Crofton Croker that 'when rational education shall be diffused among the misguided peasantry of Ireland, the belief in such supernatural beings (the Shefro, the banshee) must disappear in that country, as it has done in England'.[48]

For Wilde, a believer in folklore and superstition, gleaned from extensive reading of his parents' work (and, indeed, assistance to his mother in the compilation of *Ancient Legends, Mystic Charms and Superstitions of Ireland* [1888], and *Ancient Cures, Charms and Usages of Ireland: Contributions to Irish Lore* [1890]) and long and predominantly happy times spent in the West of Ireland as a child, the absence from the education system of folk wisdom might well have come as something of a shock. Owen Dudley Edwards has surmised that Wilde's education in Portora Royal School in Enniskillen during the years 1864–71, fomented in him a passionate dislike of the education system in general,[49] but he surprisingly did not point to these aphorisms as Wilde's definitive reply to such colonizing attempts. On exploring the examination papers of Portora, Edwards notes that 'Not one mention of Ireland is to be found'.[50] The examination papers reveal the extent to which the educational project revolved around the rationalizing subject. Questions focussed on the fetishisation of the 'fact', and Edwards points to questions on the population of England, requiring a list of English queens, asking for anything known about John of Gaunt.[51] A direct result of such pedantic tediousness is Wilde's aphorism that 'in examinations the foolish ask questions that the wise cannot answer'.

Wilde's Irish identity, which had certainly been formed by the time he arrived in Portora, was simply denied by the school. Also denied was the Catholicism he had imbued from Fr Fox down in Glencree, and the folk religion he encountered in the West of Ireland. Wilde stubbornly refused to give up his 'backward' belief in the Banshee, and evidence of this attachment persisted to the end of his life when he told Vincent O' Sullivan that as a child he had heard the Banshee crying.[52] Wilde reduced his years at Portora from seven to one for reasons he knew best, and sometimes Portora seems to have even disappeared from the map of his past.[53] The irony of Wilde's case is that although educated into a system which counselled its students in ignorance of the country of which they were the ostensible ruling class, he was being simultaneously immersed in Irish history and mythology by his parents, whose naming of him as Oscar Fingal singled him out as a possible contributor to the mythology of the land himself, a name his mother claimed was 'grand, misty, and Ossianic'.[54]

Lady Wilde had always identified mythology as one of the key methods through which the 'shrouded part of humanity' would become available for us to understand,[55] and insisted that mythology revealed the relations of a people 'to a spiritual and invisible world', claiming that in Ireland 'the popular belief became, in time, an amalgam of the pagan myths and the Christian legend'. She raged against the educational spirit which attempted to dissipate 'the belief in the supernatural',[56] a mission she passed on to her son; she echoed the worries of her husband, Sir William Wilde who complained that 'the chief Protestant schools of Ireland do not teach Irish history'.[57] Indeed, Lady Wilde's account of wake orgies and funeral games may be the source of this aphorism: 'The only link between Literature and the Drama left to us in England at the present moment is the bill of play' (my emphasis). The aphorism suggests that there does exist a place somewhere other than England where that link is stronger. Wilde's mother noted that the funeral games in Ireland took the form of elaborate folk plays and she claimed that 'an immense amount of dramatic talent was displayed by the actors of these fantastic and symbolic plays'. She notes that on watching the English plays being performed in London, an Irish peasant was very disappointed: 'I have now seen the great English actors, and heard plays in the English tongue, but poor and dull they seemed to me after the acting of our own people at the wakes and fairs; for it is a truth, the English cannot make us weep and laugh as I have seen the crowds with us when the actors played and the poets recited their stories.'[58] Surprisingly, the writings of Wilde's parents have remained relatively untapped as potential 'source texts' for, or even major influences on, his own work, but given that he valued them so much it is generally easy to pick up the echo of their words. In his prison letter to Lord Alfred Douglas, Wilde regrets the loss of his 'beautifully bound editions' of his parents' works, and also regrets the opprobrium he has brought on the name they bequeathed him, 'a name they had made noble and honoured not merely in Literature, Art, Archaeology and Science, but in the public history of my own country'.[59]

Of course, it is crucial not to calcify these aphorisms by reading them in any simple way as expressing the politically playful soul of the Irish as Wilde and his parents understood it. Siegel rightly insists that these aphorisms 'deny the possibility of arriving at any truth at all, including the truth of the Wildean aphorism'.[60] These aphorisms are never at rest. They may discredit the realist attempt to render the world knowable and certain in the face of the existential anxiety of the 'crisis of faith', but they do not offer easy answers to the theological questions being asked by the Victorians. The science that produced the 'facts' of life and killed the religions which they succeeded in proving is not to be countered through another scientific evaluation of the evidence: that would be to concede the logical and rational principle. Only in paradox, in the renunciation of modernity for a pre-modern or non-modern mythic imagination, could the age of dullness and anxiety be vanquished. Myths of tradition are useful, Richard Kearney argues, because they 'defy the historical logic of non-contradiction (either/or); they lay claim to a supralogical order where something can be both what it is and what it is not – the past can be present, the human divine, and so on'.[61] The Wildean aphorism is an agent of 'paradoxy' where received truth is invoked only to be subverted but a new truth is never put in its place. Paradoxes cannot be resolved into prescriptions for living. These aphorisms must not be seen as another version of the monologic.

In one sense, if any of these aphorisms was to be believed and accepted, Wilde's intellectual project would have failed. When the reader is told that 'a truth ceases to be true when more than one person believes in it', Wilde is not asserting the subjectivity of truth, as playful post-modernists would have it. Rather he is pointing out that the truth will always be a paradox of that which is received wisdom. In 1891 Wilde told Catulle Mendes that the New Testament was the model of the paradox as it was stuffed full of them: 'What greater enormity could there be than "Blessed are the poor"?'[62] The danger lies in trying to make a paradox into a truism. This is why 'religions die when they are proved to be true', because religions should be models of paradoxy. The Protestant reaction to the Higher Critical attack on the veracity of the Bible, and the critical relations between Genesis and geology, was to argue that the contradictions raised by such investigations were illusory: that Genesis and geology were in fact both saying the same thing. This was the application of the realist novelist's technique to theology; to Wilde this was not preserving religion from the modern age, but making it part and parcel of an unimaginative, dull discourse that was ultimately oppressive and dangerous. Religion is true until it is proved when it becomes part of science – proved true in the terms of empirical fetishists. This is the kind of religion that can safely be left to the realists, the 'religion of humanity' so important to George Eliot, so mocked by Nietzsche; the interesting religions are those which cannot be proven, those full of logical contradictions.

Undermining the calcified through a critical dialectic of the unorthodox allows us to break into the truth itself even if we are not able to grasp it fully but realize it only through the rituals of the imagination, best expressed by Wilde in the rituals he encountered in the West of Ireland as a young child, the rituals of folkloric Catholicism. A paradox which becomes a truism is no better than the truism we started out with: the truth must remain in tension with the world it hopes to transfigure,[63] a relationship best expressed through the paradox, the very form of knowledge about which one version of the Enlightenment was in gross denial (virgin births, water becoming wine, men rising from the dead). The Wildean paradox – such as the one about a truth ceasing to be true – operates through the medium of the logical contradiction, asserting that something is true even if it is impossible for it to be true. In this context it makes sense to talk about an 'Irish Wilde', as long as this is not taken as an attempt to simplify or reduce Wilde in any way.

Obviously, I have only tried to deal briefly with one of the most important arguments in Wilde studies at the moment, the argument between those who read Wilde ideologically and those who believe that what mattered to Wilde was audience, money and working within his own range. Given that the aphorism is such a formally provocative response to the realist novel, and given Wilde's own rejection of realism as imaginatively bankrupt, I think it makes sense to see the two collections of aphorisms examined here as contributions to a larger, ideologically significant project. In other words, while I agree completely with Guy and Small that Wilde was a writer who worked best with 'small, discrete units', I am not convinced that this in any way diminishes the political dimension of his work – the aphorism (form) is appropriate to the content.

NOTES

1. E.H. Mikhail, *Oscar Wilde: An Annotated Bibliography of Criticism* (London: Macmillan, 1978); Ian Small, *Oscar Wilde Revalued: An Essay on New Materials and Methods of Research* (Greensboro, NC: ELT Press, 1993); Ian Small, *Oscar Wilde: Recent Research, A Supplement*

to Oscar Wilde Revalued (Greensboro, NC: ELT Press, 2001); Melissa Knox, *Oscar Wilde in the 1990s: The Critic as Creator* (Rochester, NY: Camden House, 2001).

2. I put this last category in as a piece of shameless self promotion.

3. Melissa Knox, *Oscar Wilde: A Long and Lovely Suicide* (New Haven, CT and London: Yale University Press, 1994). Merlin Holland, Wilde's grandson, reviewed the book in *The Times Literary Supplement*, 13 January 1995. This review was attacked by Susan Balée's review of Knox's biography in *Victorian Studies*, 38, 2 (1995), pp.319–21. Merlin Holland posted a response to Balée in *Victorian Studies*, 39: 4 (1996), pp.539–41, to which Balée responded in the same issue, pp.542–3.

4. See the rather startling attack on Neil McKenna's *The Secret Life of Oscar Wilde* (London: Century, 2003), by Josephine Guy and Ian Small in *Studying Oscar Wilde: History, Criticism, Myth* (Greensboro, NC: ELT Press, 2006), 25–9.

5. The 'Poems in Prose' pose a problem of genre, but there are similar problems with 'The Portrait of Mr. W. H.'/*The Portrait of Mr. W. H.*, and *De Profundis*.

6. This, of course, can have either positive or negative implications depending on which side of the postmodernist fence you find yourself sitting.

7. I realize that in saying this, I am disagreeing with the fascinating and carefully argued thesis put forward by Philip E. Smith and Michael S. Helfand in their introduction to *Oscar Wilde's Oxford Notebooks* (New York: Oxford University Press, 1989), where they argue that Wilde's undergraduate notebooks reveal a systematic thinker of enormous intellectual range and penetration.

8. Josephine M. Guy and Ian Small, *Oscar Wilde's Profession: Writing and the Culture Industry in the Late Nineteenth Century* (Oxford: Oxford University Press, 2000), pp.245, 247.

9. Ibid., p.281. Though, in fairness, they do accept that 'he did possess qualities of genius which although not unique are certainly rare'.

10. Sandra Siegel, 'Wilde's Use and Abuse of Aphorisms', *Victorian Studies Association of Western Canada*, 12, 1 (1986), p.25.

11. Jerusha McCormack, 'Wilde's Fiction(s)', in Peter Raby (ed.) *The Cambridge Companion to Oscar Wilde* (Cambridge: Cambridge University Press, 1997), p.99.

12. Francis O'Gorman, 'Introduction', *The Victorian Novel* (Oxford: Blackwell, 2002), p.1.

13. Oscar Wilde, *The Importance of Being Earnest* in Oscar Wilde, *The Importance of Being Earnest and Other Plays*, ed. Peter Raby (Oxford: Clarendon, 1995), II, p.273; III, p.303.

14. Oscar Wilde, letter to William Harnett Blanch, January 1894, in *The Complete Letters of Oscar Wilde*, eds Merlin Holland and Rupert Hart Davis (London: Fourth Estate, 2000), p.581.

15. Oscar Wilde, 'Some Literary Notes II', *Woman's World*, February 1889, p.406.

16. Kerry Powell, 'The Mesmerizing of Dorian Gray', *Victorian Newsletter*, 65 (1984), pp.10–15; Kerry Powell, 'Tom Dick and Dorian Gray: Magic Picture Mania in Late-Victorian Fiction', *Philological Quarterly*, 63, 2 (Spring 1983), pp.147–69.

17. Oscar Wilde, 'The Decay of Lying', in *The Complete Works of Oscar Wilde*, vol.4, Criticism, ed. Josephine Guy (Oxford: Oxford University Press, 2007), pp.75–6.

18. It is impossible to give more than a generalized introduction to the enormous body

of scholarship on Victorian realism in a couple of paragraphs, so the reader will have to forgive simplifications for reason of space and go to the studies mentioned for a more detailed and sophisticated explanation.

19. Northrop Frye, *Fables of Identity: Studies in Poetic Mythology* (New York: Brace and World, 1963), p.27.

20. For the close relationship between Victorian science and realism, see Gillian Beer, *Darwin's Plots: Evolutionary Narrative in Darwin, George Eliot and Nineteenth-Century Fiction* (London: Routledge and Kegan Paul, 1983); George Levine, *Darwin and the Novelists: Patterns of Science in Victorian Fiction* (Cambridge, MA: Harvard University Press, 1988), George Levine, *Dying to Know: Scientific Epistemology and Narrative in Victorian England* (Chicago, IL: University of Chicago Press, 2002); George Levine, *Realism, Ethics and Secularism: Essays on Victorian Literature and Science* (Cambridge: Cambridge University Press, 2008).

21. George Levine, *The Realistic Imagination: English Fiction from Frankenstein to Lady Chatterley* (Chicago, IL and London: The University of Chicago Press, 1981), pp.3–22; quotation from p.20.

22. See Paul Ricoeur, 'Personal Identity and Narrative Identity', *Oneself As Another*, trans. Kathleen Blaney (London: University of Chicago Press, 1992), p.114n; Frederic Jameson, *The Political Unconscious: Narrative as a Socially Symbolic Act* (Ithaca, NY: Cornell University Press, 1981), p.30.

23. I have been trying here to summarize some of the points made by Elizabeth Deeds Ermath in her brilliant *Realism and Consensus in the English Novel: Time, Space and Narrative* (Edinburgh: Edinburgh University Press, 1998, 2nd edn), pp.40–54.

24. Ibid., p.41.

25. David Lloyd, *Anomalous States: Irish Writing and the Post-Colonial Moment* (Dublin: Lilliput, 1993), p.135.

26. Levine, *Realism, Ethics and Secularism*, p.198. There is no room here to cover the very large body of work devoted to explaining that the realist novel is inherently secular.

27. Georg Lukács, *The Theory of the Novel: A Historico-Philosophical Essay on the Forms of Great Epic Literature*, trans. Anne Bostock (London: Merlin Press, 1971), pp.81–3, 88. See also Franco Moretti, *The Way of the World: The Bildungsroman in European Culture* (London: Verso, 1987), pp.15–21.

28. Two late Victorian collections, cited by Siegel, 'Wilde's Use and Abuse of Aphorisms', p.16.

29. E.B. Tylor, *Primitive Culture: Researches into the Development of Mythology, Philosophy, Religion, Language, Art, and Custom* (London: John Murray, 1873 [1871]), Vol.1, p.284. Tylor was actually one the more appreciative analysts of mythic structures at the time.

30. See, for example, Deirdre Toomey, 'The Story Teller at Fault: Oscar Wilde and Irish Orality', in Jerusha McCormack (ed.), *Wilde: The Irishman* (New Haven, CT and London: Yale University Press, 1998), pp.24–36.

31. Lloyd, *Anomalous States*, p.131.

32. Amanda Anderson, *The Powers of Distance: Cosmopolitanism and the Cultivation of Detachment*

(Princeton, NJ: Princeton University Press, 2001), p.148.

33. Gregory Mackie, 'The Function of Decorum at the Present Time: Manners, Moral Language, and Modernity in "an Oscar Wilde Play"', *Modern Drama*, 52, 2 (2009), pp.145–67.

34. Siegel, 'Wilde's Use and Abuse of Aphorisms', pp.18–19.

35. For the purpose of this chapter I will quote from *Collins Complete Works of Oscar Wilde*, ed. Merlin Holland (London: HarperCollins, 1999), pp.1242–45.

36. In rejecting the religion of humanity, Wilde was not alone. Nietzsche famously attacked the post-Christian intelligentsia of Victorian England: 'They are rid of the Christian God and now believe all the more firmly that they must cling to Christian morality. That is an English consistency; we do not wish to hold it against little moral-istic females à la Eliot. In England one must rehabilitate oneself after every little eman-cipation from theology by showing in a veritably awe-inspiring manner what a moral fanatic one is. That is the penance they pay there.' *The Twilight of the Idols* (1888), in *The Portable Nietzsche*, ed. Walter Kaufmann (New York: Penguin, 1954), p.515.

37. For realism and demythologization, see David Carroll, 'Silas Marner: Reversing the Oracles of Religion', in George Eliot, *Silas Marner* (Madison, WI: University of Wisconsin Press, *Literary Monographs*, 1967), pp.165–200; Joseph Wiesenfarth, 'Demythologizing *Silas Marner*', *English Literary History*, 37 (1970), pp.226–44.

38. This kind of thinking is basic to contemporary Victorians such as Richard Dawkins, A.C. Grayling and Christopher Hitchens, who have a similarly distorted under-standing of history.

39. [T.H.H. Huxley], 'The origin of Species', *Westminster Review* 17 (n.s.) (1860), pp.541–70.

40. Mircea Eliade, *The Myth of the Eternal Return, or Cosmos and History*, trans. Willard R. Trask (Princeton, NJ: Princeton University Press, 1954).

41. Paul Ricoeur, *Figuring the Sacred: Religion, Narrative, and the Imagination* (Minneapolis, MN: Fortress Press, 1995), pp.489–90.

42. Quoted in Rupert Croft-Cooke, *Bosie: Lord Alfred Douglas, His Friends and Enemies* (Indianapolis, IN: Bobbs-Merrill, 1963), p.93.

43. See John Gray's polemical *Heresies: Against Progress and Other Illusions* (London: Granta, 2004).

44. John Coolahan, 'Imperialism and the Irish National School System', in J.A. Mangan (ed.), *'Benefits bestowed?' Education and British Imperialism* (Manchester: Manchester University Press, 1988), p.77.

45. Ibid., p.85.

46. Ibid., p.86.

47. *Third Reading Book* (1843 edn), p.159, quoted in ibid., p.85.

48. Thomas Crofton Croker, *Fairy Legends and Traditions of the South of Ireland*, 3 volumes (London: Murray, 1825–28), Vol.1, p.362.

49. Owen Dudley Edwards, 'Impressions of an Irish Sphinx', in McCormack (ed.), *Wilde: The Irishman*, p.66.

50. Ibid., p.64.
51. Ibid., pp.63–4.
52. Vincent O'Sullivan, *Aspects of Wilde* (London: Constable, 1936), p.63.
53. Richard Ellmann, *Oscar Wilde* (Harmondsworth: Penguin, 1988), p.3.
54. Letter by Speranza to an unnamed Scottish correspondent, 22 November 1854. Quoted in Joy Melville, *Mother of Oscar: The Life of Jane Francesca Wilde* (London: John Murray, 1994), p.72.
55. Lady Wilde, *Ancient Legends, Mystic Charms, and Superstitions of Ireland; with Sketches of the Irish Past, to which is appended a chapter on 'the ancient races of Ireland,' by the late Sir William Wilde* (London: Ward and Downey, 1887), p.xi.
56. Ibid, pp.xi–xii.
57. Sir William Wilde, *Lough Corrib* (Dublin: McGlashan & Gill, 1867), p.196.
58. Wilde, *Ancient Legends*, p.122.
59. Oscar Wilde, 'In Carcere et Vinculis', in *The Complete Works of Oscar Wilde*, Vol.2, *De Profundis*, 'Epistola: In Carcere et Vinculis', ed. Ian Small (Oxford: Oxford University Press, 2005).
60. Siegel, 'Wilde's Use and Abuse of Aphorisms', p.22.
61. Richard Kearney, *Myth and Motherland* (Cork: Field Day Publications, 1984), p.63.
62. Quoted in Ellmann, *Oscar Wilde*, p.329.
63. For this point I am indebted to Rolf Breuer, 'Paradox in Oscar Wilde', *Irish University Review*, 23 (1993), pp.224–35.

CHAPTER TWO

Oscar Wilde:
Facts and Fictions of Life

NOREEN DOODY

Oscar Wilde celebrated the imagination as a powerful facet of the intellect, one upon which much of what is commonly regarded as 'reality' depends. In many of his works, he illustrates how events are born in the imagination before passing into reality – his greatest play, *The Importance of Being Earnest* (first performed 1895, first published 1899), for example, is based entirely on this premise. So too in Wilde's own life, many incidents which first presented themselves as fiction turned incontrovertibly to fact. The eponymous Dorian Gray, created by Wilde in 1890, presaged his love affair with and enthrallment to Alfred Douglas, a young man of his protagonist's type of beauty. Wilde's own celebrity, driven by his construction of a personal image of urbane flamboyance and studied elegance, existed long before his work was published and the public came to know of any literary entitlement to acclaim. In proposing the adoption of diverse masks to facilitate the expression of personality, in adopting his own pose and so creating its reality, Wilde gave truth to his insight that 'the energy of life ... is simply the desire for expression',[1] and he deployed that creative energy in the construction of a life lived as art, and a body of work as lasting as the image of the man. As Wilde wrote to one friend,

> To the world I seem, by intention on my part, a dilettante and dandy merely – it is not wise to show one's heart to the world – and as seriousness of manner is the disguise of the fool, folly in its exquisite moods of triviality and indifference and lack of care is the robe of the wise man. In so vulgar an age as this we all need masks.[2]

Oscar Wilde was born into the Victorian age, and if that period was deficient in imagination, his immediate family and wider environment supplied a powerful antidote. His mother was gifted with a poetic imagination and his father was a scholar of science, ancient archaeology, folklore and story. The second son of the eminent Irish surgeon, Sir William Wilde, and the nationalist poet and writer, Jane Elgee, he was born on 16 October 1854 at his family home, 21 Westland Row, Dublin. His brother, Willie, was two years his elder while his sister, Isola, was almost three years his junior. On the year following Oscar's birth, the Wildes moved to the more fashionable address of 1 Merrion Square. It was a larger, more elegant house than that in Westland Row and required more household staff. The children had a governess and were all taught to speak French and German. Their games took place on the upper floor of the nursery looking over the central garden of the square. On fine days the children were brought to play in these gardens, which was private to the inhabitants of the square.

Merrion Square, then as now, was one of the most prestigious locations in Dublin and was populated by members of the liberal professions of medicine and the law. Prior to the Act of Union in 1801 and the dissolution of the Irish parliament the houses on the square had been homes to the aristocracy. However, with the centralization of government in London this class had mostly left for that city, leaving Dublin less politically potent and socially important, though a legislative executive presided over by a Lord Lieutenant remained as representative of British rule. The Wildes were well positioned among the professional classes at the upper level of Irish society. Sir William was a celebrated eye and ear surgeon whose book on aural surgery was the standard textbook in its area on both sides of the Atlantic. John Gamble, an English doctor visiting Ireland, said of Merrion Square in 1811: 'the truth is, a physician here is almost at the pinnacle of greatness: there are few resident nobility or gentry since the Union, and the professors of law and medicine may be said to form the aristocracy of the place'.[3] Oscar Wilde would enter English Society in later years with all of the assurance of his privileged early background.

The Wildes were a Protestant Anglo-Irish family and by the time of Oscar's birth, Ireland had been a colony of Britain's for some 700 years. During this time Catholicism, which was the majority religion of the country, had been suppressed through various statutes; as far back as the seventeenth century Catholics had endured violations and privations levied against them on the grounds of their religion, including the confiscation of lands and their distribution amongst Protestant people. By the nineteenth century the harsher laws pertaining to Catholics had been relaxed, although even then, Anglo-Irish Protestants enjoyed a higher standard of living and had fuller employment and greater legislative authority than their Catholic neighbours. A real sense of difference existed between the denominations due to their inequitable treatment and distinct cultural memories.

Ireland was an extremely poor country in the nineteenth century; the worst years of the Great Famine occurred less than a decade before Wilde's birth. Behind the salubrious Georgian square of the Wildes' home lay some of the worst slums of the city. Sir William and Lady Wilde were socially aware, prominent public figures in Ireland. Sir William had handed over to a Board of Trustees the management of St Mark's Hospital Dublin for the 'use and advantage of the afflicted poor in Dublin'. He had originally bought the hospital with his own funds and set it up as the best eye and ear hospital in the country.[4] Oscar was alert to the demands of natural justice and proud of his father's achievement. He would later confide to a friend that his father had built this hospital when he was a young man of 29 and not at all well off.[5]

The Wildes' was an unorthodox house − its politics straddled the divide between Catholic and Protestant Irelands. Both parents were strong personalities, well educated in the arts and culture of Ireland and England. In the 1840s, Lady Wilde had written under the name of 'Speranza' for The Nation, nationalist Ireland's chief journal, whose readership at the time numbered a quarter of a million. One of her more seditious articles 'Jacta Alea Est' ('The Die is Cast', 1848), had led to the arrest of the editor, Charles Gavan Duffy, and the shutting down of the paper. She was a woman of great passion and intelligence and was highly respected by her countrymen who admired the stance she adopted towards social injustice. Whenever her carriage was recognized in city streets it was met by cheers from the passers-by. The poet W.B. Yeats wrote of her: 'She was a great student, a lover of literature, a woman of the finest culture ... she came out of the tradition of her own class and joined herself to the people of Ireland and became Speranza, that famous woman.'[6] It amused Speranza to be greeted on equal terms with the Lord Lieutenant and his circle in Dublin Castle while holding her extreme nationalist views. As she explained to a friend: 'I went to the last Drawing room at the Castle and Lord Aberdeen smiled very archly as he bent to kiss my cheek, which is the ceremony of presentation. I smiled too and thought of *Jacta Alea Est*.'[7] Oscar grew up with this sense of political and social mischief-making and practical experience in subversion that would find their way into his later artistic works. His mother enjoyed a close and loving relationship with her children that lasted into their adult lives. Her eldest child, Willie, sums up what she meant to them: 'she was the best and truest and most loyal friend'.[8]

Hospitality was a feature of the Wilde's home and Lady Wilde's Saturday salon was renowned for the calibre of its guests and the excellence of the conversation. Wit and repartee were highly prized features of conversation in Dublin at the time and spontaneity in both was *de rigueur*. Often the Wilde children were allowed to sit quietly at the end of the table at their parents' dinner parties where they could listen to and imbibe the skilful flow of the talk as Sir William and Lady Wilde conversed with their guests from Ireland's academic, political and theatrical worlds as well as visiting celebrities and dignitaries from abroad. The Wildes numbered among their friends many figures from the professional classes of Dublin and elsewhere, including Trinity College professors such as classicist John Pentland Mahaffy, novelists like Charles Lever, the mathematician William Rowan Hamilton and the patriot and rebel William Smith O'Brien, a leader of the Young Ireland movement. Wilde recalled in later life how he had sat as a child at the feet of O'Brien, listening enthralled to his stories.

Although Sir William did not share the militant nationalist views of his wife, he was an admirer of Young Ireland and a supporter of Home Rule. Sir William was a man of great learning whose knowledge extended beyond medical science to include the arts, archaeology, topography, folklore and the legends of Ireland. He was knighted in 1864 for his outstanding work as medical advisor (1841) and assistant commissioner for the Irish census (1851). During his summers in the West of Ireland he spent long days with his sons fishing and on digs at ancient archaeological sites. The Wildes' summer home, Moytura House, was built by Sir William on what was supposed to have been the battle grounds of the ancient mythological peoples of Ireland, the Tuatha de Danaan, the Firbolg and Fomorians. Life was lived at a leisurely and relaxed pace in their summer home – Lady Wilde noted: 'You may do as you like in our house, read when you like and take breakfast in bed and be entirely *sans gene*'.[9] It was at another summer location, Glencree, County Wicklow, that Lady Wilde had a priest from the local reformatory, Fr Prideaux Fox, baptise her children into the Catholic Church. They were not brought up as Catholics but Oscar returned to this religion often throughout his life, eventually receiving the last rites of the Catholic Church on his deathbed.

While on holiday, the Wilde children were often joined by their half sisters, Emily and Mary, and brother, Henry Wilson, who were Sir William's natural children, born before his marriage to Lady Wilde. Henry trained in the medical profession and became Sir William's assistant surgeon; Sir William's daughters were the wards of his brother, Ralph and his wife, and were raised by them. Sadly, these two girls died young in a tragic accident and their father's grief at their loss was immense. A similar tragedy had struck the family four years earlier in 1867 when Sir William's and Lady Wilde's youngest child and 'pet of the family', Isola, died. It was a great sadness to all of the family. Her mother never recovered from the loss of her daughter and Oscar mourned his little sister very deeply, carrying an envelope containing a lock of her hair with him into adulthood.

Further trouble assailed the Wildes when in 1874 a female patient of Sir William's, Mary Travers, accused him of having molested her while she was in his surgery, and then sued Lady Wilde for libel when she wrote a letter to Mary's father asking him to prevent his daughter spreading lies about Sir William. The boys were away at boarding school, Portora Royal in Enniskillen, County Fermanagh, while this event played out in court. The scandal was the talk of Dublin and echoes of it most surely spread to the boys' school in Fermanagh. While Mary Travers won her action she was awarded only one farthing in costs. Although the judgment can be seen as a vindication of Sir William, he fell into bad health and spent much of the next few years at his summer home, Moytura House.

On leaving Portora Royal School, Oscar won an entrance scholarship to Trinity College Dublin. He studied Classics at Trinity and showed himself a gifted scholar. He was awarded a foundation scholarship and the prestigious Berkeley Gold medal. His brother, Willie, also attended Trinity College; being the sons of high profile people, news about the two boys often appeared in the national newspapers. One journalist had this to say:

> I was right glad to see carrying off the prize of scholarship young Oscar Wilde, one of the two sons of 'Speranza', to whom she dedicates the volume publication of her exquisite poems, with the significant quotation attached
>
> '———— I made them, indeed,
>
> Speak plain the word Country. I taught them no doubt,
>
> That a Country's a thing men should die for at need.'
>
> The said 'Oscar and Willie' are two as splendid specimens, physically, of young Irishmen as could be seen; five foot ten 'in their vamps' and formed like athletes. It is pleasing to see that intellectually also they are likely to prove worthy of their parents.[10]

Wilde's interest in the Catholic religion grew while he was at Trinity and he looked for spiritual advice from the Jesuit confraternity in Gardiner Street. Wilde's advocacy of the power of the imagination extended to his belief in endless spiritual possibility which is one reason why the Catholic religion and its insistence on transubstantiation suited his mindset more exactly than any less imaginatively demanding religious grouping. When he won a demyship to Oxford in 1874, his father was not only pleased at his son's academic success but also that he would be leaving the country and its Jesuitical influence. During his time at Oxford, Wilde published poetry and translations from Aeschylus and Euripides in *Kottabos*, the Classics magazine of Professor Robert Tyrrell of Trinity College Dublin, and also some poetry in the *Dublin University Magazine* and the *Irish Monthly*, the Jesuit magazine edited by Rev. Matthew Russell S.J., and also in another Irish Catholic magazine, *The Illustrated Monitor*. At Oxford Wilde continued to agonize over his attraction to Catholicism and his inclination towards paganism. He was fascinated by the ideas of Cardinal Manning and John Henry Newman;

Manning's 'socialist' ideals appealed to him and, like Wilde, 'Newman was also devoted to youth and beauty';[11] both men were celebrated converts from Anglicanism to Roman Catholicism. Wilde's spiritual struggle is mirrored in his early poems, and it became symbolized by his difficulty in choosing between a trip to Greece with his former Trinity professor, John Pentland Mahaffy, and an excursion to Rome with fellow student, David Hunter Blair. In the event, Wilde managed to fit in both destinations.

During his four years at Oxford Wilde distinguished himself as an outstanding scholar: he graduated with a double First and carried off the Newdigate prize with his long poem, 'Ravenna' (1878). Wilde also became well known in Oxford for his wit and aesthetic ideals and pose; his name would soon become synonymous with the aesthetic movement in England. This movement owed much to the Oxford don, Walter Pater, who believed that beauty was the highest ideal and life should be lived thoroughly and with intensity in pursuit of this ideal. Wilde admired Pater's theories: he called Pater's book, *Studies in the History of the Renaissance* (1873), 'my golden book'. 'I never travel anywhere without it', he told Yeats and declared it 'the very flower of Decadence'.[12] Aestheticism privileged Art and Beauty over morality and social themes, purporting that art is complete in itself and is in no way related to didacticism or morality. The aesthetic movement, whose popular 'catchphrase' was 'Art for Art's sake', in many ways reflected the Symbolist and Decadent movements of the continent. The appeal to the sensual and pleasurable rather than the moral and edifying and the use of symbol and suggestion are tenets of each movement. Already in Oxford Wilde was renowned for his espousal of an aesthetic creed and he was credited with having voiced an exaggerated regret at his inability to live up to the fragilely beautiful blue china that he kept in his rooms. The sentiment was seized on by *Punch* cartoonist, Georges DuMaurier, who made it a subject of ridicule in one of his drawings, 'The Six-Mark Tea-Pot' (30 October 1880). Indeed, aesthetes were often used as objects of derision by *Punch* cartoonists and mocked as effeminate, foppish, languid young men.

In April 1876, during his second year at Oxford and three months before he was awarded First Class in Classical Moderations, Wilde's father died. Sir William's death naturally occasioned sorrow and grief for his family. It was also discovered when the will was read that the family's financial situation was far worse than any of them had expected. Wilde received his Bachelor of Arts degree at Oxford in 1878 and spent the summer months at the family fishing lodge at Illaunroe, in Connemara, from where he wrote: 'I am resting here in the mountains – great peace and quiet everywhere'.[13] The next year the Wilde family would leave the comparative 'peace and quiet' of their home in Ireland to take up domicile in London. Oscar took rooms early in 1879 in London with Frank Miles, an artist friend, and Lady Wilde and her eldest son, Willie, took up residence at Ovington Square, Chelsea. Wilde, as usual despite 'aesthetic' posturing, was hardworking and productive; he published his play, *Vera*, in 1880 and in 1881 his first edition of *Poems* appeared, edited by David Bogue. The poems caused quite a stir, with charges of plagiarism and accusations of immorality made against them. However, not all reviews were opposed to the collection – John Addington Symonds wrote personally to Wilde to acknowledge his high artistic talent. The diversity of Wilde's poems from a sexual and religious stance gave his adversaries the ammunition to denounce Wilde as morally corrupt. This would not be the last time he would meet with such public animosity, nor that he would be called on to defend his work. Richard Ellmann suggests that Wilde 'knew perfectly well that his ideas were shocking to the English, provincial in their conventionality, piety, and conservatism, as he, an Irishman was not'.[14]

Wilde, believing that it was the duty of each person to invent oneself or adopt a pose, was assiduously assembling an image of impeccable taste and polish – it suited Wilde's image-building project well that he should be thought of as languorous and nonchalant while his everyday self got on with the mundane task of making a living. Wilde was becoming very well known in London circles and was fast becoming a public figure. His name was associated with the famous public beauties Lillie Langtry and Ellen Terry. Wilde escorted Langtry to lectures at King's College, London and gave her tuition in Latin. He became friendly with the artist, James McNeill Whistler, who was a neighbour of his and Frank Miles in Tite Street. Their friendship became famous for its exchange of wit; Whistler's volleys were more snide and cutting than

Wilde's, who was also more willing than the painter to enjoy a laugh at his own expense. To Wilde's admiring response to a witticism of Whistler's, 'I wish I had said that', Whistler is said to have rejoined, 'You will, Oscar, you will'.[15] By 1880 Wilde had succeeded in establishing himself in London as a celebrated personality.

In 1881 Wilde was asked by Richard D'Oyly Carte if he would be willing to tour America as the poet of aestheticism, giving lectures on subjects concerning the movement. D'Oyly Carte had a successful production of Gilbert and Sullivan's *Patience* (first performed 23 April 1881) running in America at the time. The opera lampoons aestheticism and in the character of Bunthorne sends up Wilde, Whistler and their ilk. The purpose of the lectures was to create publicity for the opera and give the American audiences an insight into aestheticism in the person and words of Wilde. Towards the end of 1882 Wilde sailed for North America where he would remain for a full year touring the United States and Canada. Wilde's trip would take him on many miles of train tracks from New York to San Francisco and into Canada. He travelled from the drawing rooms of New York and Boston to the mining town of Leadville, Colorado. He met with social celebrities, the literary set, friends of his mother's including Dion Boucicault and Henry Longfellow and the father of American poetry, Walt Whitman. He lectured on aesthetic themes including interior decoration and the beauty of dress. At first his lecturing style left a lot to be desired, looking at his feet instead of the audience. However, he learnt on the job and even attired himself on occasion in the outfit of an aesthete, velvet knickerbocks and jacket complete with flouncy cravat.

News of Wilde's progress was published in communiqués from the States. The story that he had told the customs officer that he had 'nothing to declare – but his genius' was widely circulated, as was his 'disappointment' with the Atlantic Ocean. Wilde's reception in America was varied: while some reporters admired his words and others hailed him as 'son of Speranza', others lampooned him in racist cartoons. Mild amusement characterized many of the articles and perhaps the greatest respect he enjoyed was from the Irish Americans who attended his lecture on Irish Poets in San Francisco and the miners he impressed with his ability to hold his drink and his view of them as the best dressed men in America. Wilde showed tremendous tenacity and physical and mental endurance in carrying the tour through to completion under what were often difficult conditions and crude personal attacks from the media and general public. He exhibited a dogged persistence and an ability to enjoy the company of people from all walks of life that would stand him in good stead in the years ahead.

Wilde earned a lot of money from the tour and on the strength of his new capital he spent February to May 1883 in Paris. He stayed at the Hotel Voltaire on the left bank and went about with his friend, the journalist Robert Sherard, who introduced him to French literary society and many of the celebrated names of the period including Edmond De Goncourt, Victor Hugo and Paul Verlaine. While there Wilde wrote the play, The Duchess of Padua, for the American actress, Mary Anderson, who disappointed him in deciding against accepting the play once it had been written.

On his return to England, Wilde began a lecture tour there that would last most of the year. He travelled back to Ireland in November 1883 to lecture at the Gaiety Theatre, Dublin. While in Dublin Wilde paid a visit on a family friend, Mrs. Atkinson, who lived at Ely Place, a very short distance from his former home in Merrion Square. Wilde's purpose in calling was to propose to her granddaughter, Constance Lloyd, who was on a visit from London to her grandmother's home. Wilde had first met Constance in London in 1881 and had liked her from their very first meeting, writing some time later to his friend, the sculptor Waldo Storey, that they were 'desperately in love'.[16] Their courtship had been carried on since their first meeting through visits to his mother's home and at her grandfather's, John Lloyd QC, at his home in Lancaster Gate. Constance was the daughter of a prominent Irish barrister who had died when she was 16; she did not get on with her mother and since her mother's remarriage, Constance had been living at her grandfather's home. She was lovely to look at, very intelligent and well educated. 'A grave, slight, violet-eyed little Artemis, with great coils of heavy brown hair', as Wilde described her to Lillie Langtry.[17] Constance accepted his proposal and kept the vow she made to love him all of her life, writing to her brother, Otho: 'I am engaged to Oscar Wilde and perfectly and insanely happy'.[18] Lady Wilde was overjoyed at her son's choice of bride and she and Constance would become strong allies and good friends in the years ahead. The couple were married on 29 May 1884 in London, honeymooned in Paris and took up residence in Tite Street in 1885 in a house designed by E.W. Godwin.

The Wildes had two boys – Cyril, born 5 June 1885, and Vyvyan, who was born 3 November 1886. In 1887 Wilde became editor of *The Woman's World* magazine. It had previously been known as *The Lady's World* but Wilde changed the title in line with a more modern perspective on women and their role. This was the era of the *New Woman* – the feminist ideal of independent woman free of the constraints imposed on her by a patriarchal society. Wilde embraced the notion of equal rights for women in societal and educational terms, as did his mother and his wife. Constance was active in associated organizations, speaking at The Women's Committee of the International Arbitration of Peace Association in 1888 and the Women's Liberal Foundation in 1889. Wilde deals with many feminist related issues in his literary work.

In his plays, he questions the social stigma attached to illegitimacy and the single mother. The young American woman, Hesther, in *A Woman of No Importance* (first production, 1893) voices radically modern views on the unequal position of the 'fallen woman' in English society: Hester's words are echoed in a more humorous mirror image, or perhaps cynical way, in *The Importance of Being Earnest*: 'Why should there be one law for men, and another for women?' Ernest cries, on mistakenly believing that Miss Prism is his unwed mother.[19] *An Ideal Husband* (first production, 1895) and *Lady Windermere's Fan* (first production, 1892) also raise issues of female emancipation from social constraints, while the eponymous heroine of *Salome* (1894) defeats male power and overrides patriarchal values in wresting her desire from and imposing her will upon both the powerful Tetrarch and the saintly Iokanaan.

During these early years of marriage, Wilde not only supported his family through his editorial work but also wrote reviews of books and theatre performances. Merlin Holland suggests that the financial security provided by being editor of *The Woman's World* gave Wilde the literary position and necessary peace of mind to launch his writing career seriously.[20] He certainly was regarded now as an established man of letters and from the start of this period Wilde's creative output begins to grow and expand. 'The Canterville Ghost' and 'Lord Arthur Savile's Crime' both appeared in *The Court and Society Review* in 1887 and 'The Sphinx without a Secret' and 'The Model Millionaire' were published in *The World* in the same year. Wilde was a high profile figure who dominated London society with his conversation, wit and force of personality. Despite his intellectual brilliance, he was not overbearing in company but rather delighted in the reciprocity of conversation. Richard Le Gallienne writes of this time: 'One secret of the charm of Wilde's talk, apart from its wit and his beautiful voice, was the evidently sincere interest he took in his listener and what he also had to say.'[21] He was much sought after by society hostesses and he and Constance were in continuous demand at dinner parties and country house weekends.

In May 1888 Wilde's first volume of fairy tales appeared, *The Happy Prince and Other Tales*. Wilde said of this collection that it was 'meant partly for children, and partly for those who have kept the childlike faculties of wonder and joy'.[22] W.B. Yeats believed these stories were the closest Wilde ever came to reproducing his legendary voice in a written text and suggested that this might be because Wilde had told the stories first to his own children and so wrote with a certain audience in mind, as though he were speaking to them. Wilde enjoyed the fun of playing with his children and Vyvyan Holland recalled in later life how his father used to get down on the floor on all fours to join in their games in the nursery and in the dining room where there 'were more chairs and tables and sideboards to dodge through, and more room to clamber over Papa as well'.[23]

The Wildes' dining room in their home in Tite Street was decorated mostly in white with a splash of red provided by a diamond shaped centrepiece on the table on which stood a terracotta statuette. The furniture, curtains, upholstery and carpet were white and the etchings 'let into' the white walls of the drawing room were done by Whistler.[24] Vyvyan Holland recalls that the children's meals were often eaten in this dining room with its high aesthetic décor because the nursery was inconveniently far away.[25] It seems that the *laissez faire*, relaxed atmosphere of Wilde's childhood home prevailed at Tite Street in these years. Yeats, who was befriended by his countryman and his family, regularly visited the Wildes during the 1880s and believed it to be, despite Wilde's communication to him that he had very little money, the happiest period in the playwright's life.

In June 1890 Wilde published *The Picture of Dorian Gray* in serial form in *Lippincott's Magazine* and later that year *The Critic as Artist* was published as 'The True Function and Value of Criticism' in *The Nineteenth Century*. Wilde's essay was quite well received. Critic and anthropologist, Grant Allen, commented on Wilde's Celtic sensibility and the critical depth of his work, declaring him 'a man of rare insight and strong common-sense'.[26] Wilde's story of Dorian Gray, however, was met with an onslaught of negative criticism. The story was castigated as immoral and its author as depraved. A public battle between Wilde and his critics ensued across the pages of the daily newspapers. The reviewer of the *St James's Gazette* inferred that the book sprang from a 'singularly unpleasant mind'. *The Daily Chronicle* referred to *Dorian Gray* as being comprised of 'dullness and dirt'. The review in the *Scots Observer*, a paper owned by W.E. Henley, a former acquaintance of Wilde's, was the most damaging: 'It is not made sufficiently clear that the writer does not prefer a life of unnatural iniquity to a life of cleanliness, health, and sanity.'[27] Wilde defended the story and his position as artist, pointing out 'the unpardonable crime of trying to confuse the artist with his subject matter'.[28] The responses of his adversaries are notable for the personal venom with which they attack Wilde, as though they feared or hated him. It is remarkable that a man who on the one hand could be considered so malign and detestable, on the other was accorded so many testimonies as to his kindness and generosity. W.B. Yeats found in him the tremendous kindness to which so many of Wilde's friends and acquaintances testified, among them author and critic George Slythe Street who said of him: 'This was a humane man, generous to his friends, placable to his enemies.'[29] The Scottish writer and politician, R.B. Cunninghame Graham, was another of Wilde's associates to endorse this view of him: 'I most remember his great kindliness. It is the greatest quality in man.'[30]

By the time the controversy over *The Picture of Dorian Gray* broke, Wilde had already activated another of his life-roles. In 1887 a young Canadian student, Robbie Ross, came to stay as a paying guest in Tite Street; Ross would become a great lifelong friend of Wilde's and eventually his literary executor. It is also possible that Ross was Wilde's first homosexual partner, although questions had been raised and various assertions made about the nature of Wilde's sexual desire long before his encounter with Ross. Merlin Holland writes of Wilde's early experiences with Ross: 'The discovery in himself of a different sexuality, that he may previously have felt but had been reluctant or unable to indulge, could now be given expression.'[31] In 1891 Wilde met and soon after fell in love with Lord Alfred Douglas, an attraction that would prove to be fatal for Wilde. Lord Alfred, or Bosie, as he was known by his friends, was an undergraduate in Oxford when he was first introduced to Wilde by his cousin, Lionel Johnson. Some time after their first meeting Lord Alfred contacted Wilde asking for his help in dealing with a blackmail attempt over a careless letter he had written. Wilde immediately went to the aid of the young man. Their friendship grew, Wilde becoming infatuated with the slim, handsome young lord and he mesmerized by Wilde's gifted conversation and vital personality. Wilde once wrote, 'A truth in Art is that whose contradictory is also true',[32] an assertion that seems to apply aptly to his personal life. He loved his wife but also Douglas. The physical relationships that Wilde enjoyed with both his wife and with Douglas seem not to have lasted very long but the feelings that he felt for both endured, although, as time progressed, Douglas proved to be an unstable young man, who was the occasion of as much pain as pleasure to their relationship. Wilde's life in many ways seemed to be simulating his art – as he had proposed in his essay, 'The Decay of Lying' (1889), life was the imitator of art. Wilde now guarded a dark secret just as many of the characters in his novel and plays do, while Douglas seemed to be conjured from the image of the beautiful Dorian.

Between 1891 and 1895 Wilde published a prodigious amount of work. In 1891 'The Soul of Man under Socialism' was published in The Fortnightly Review and the Picture of Dorian Gray appeared in book form with additional chapters and a 'Preface'. Also in that year, Wilde published his intellectually sparkling book of literary theory, Intentions, containing 'The Truth of Masks' (1891), 'The Critic as Artist' (1890), 'Pen, Pencil and Poison' (1889) and 'The Decay of Lying'. Lord Arthur Savile's Crime and Other Stories and A House of Pomegranates were also published in book form and Wilde finished the year off in Paris writing his play, Salome. The year 1892 began well for Wilde with the production of his play, Lady

Windermere's Fan, at St James's Theatre. Wilde had completed the writing of *Salome* and was planning to stage it in London with the most celebrated actress of the day, Sarah Bernhardt, playing the lead role. Rehearsals were in progress when Wilde was informed that the censor of plays would not grant *Salome* a permit to be staged – the grounds for refusal were ostensibly its biblical content, since an order banning biblical material from being enacted on the London stage was in place. Wilde was devastated. This was perhaps his most prestigious work yet; he had worked hard on it, writing it in French, consulting with experts in the language and having it performed by Bernhardt's company; all was in place and set to go. He could not believe his ill fortune. A full scale public battle ensued. Wilde gave interviews on the philistine nature of the British mindset to English and French newspapers and vowed that he would take out French citizenship. 'I am not English', he remarked, 'I am Irish which is quite another thing'.[33] Wilde's remonstrations were met with cartoons and jibes from the English Press. The upset and strain of the incident left Wilde feeling physically depleted and he left London for Homburg with Douglas to take the waters.

Wilde did not remain idle long and in the late summer he went to Norfolk to write *A Woman of No Importance*. The following year, 1893, Wilde wrote *An Ideal Husband*. The plot involves the unconditional admiration of a wife for her husband and the dangers inherent in such a stance. It may be that Wilde's own personal relationship with Constance had some bearing on the play. *Lady Windermere's Fan* was published in 1893; *Salome* was published in French to the deafening plaudits of the French literati and Wilde's most celebrated play, *The Importance of Being Earnest*, was written by him at Worthing in 1894. This was the year that the antipathy of Douglas's father, the Marquess of Queensberry, towards Wilde and his son escalated to dangerous proportions. Queensberry was a bad-tempered, mentally unstable, volatile man who had violently mistreated his estranged wife, Douglas's mother, and assiduously ignored Douglas and his brothers. However, under the guise of parental concern he followed Wilde and Douglas about town exhorting his son to give up Wilde's companionship on pain of losing his allowance. Douglas refused. In June 1894 Queensberry, accompanied by a prize fighter, turned up at Wilde's home and threatened to thrash him if ever he appeared again in public with his son. Wilde showed him to the door, and referring to the rules for boxing accredited to Queensberry, told him: 'I don't know what the Queensberry rules are, but the Oscar Wilde rule is to shoot at sight'.[34]

An Ideal Husband had been playing in The Haymarket from 3 January 1895 when *The Importance of Being Earnest* premiered at St James's Theatre on the 14 February. While the play was in progress Queensberry, in a perverted congratulatory gesture, attempted to deliver a bouquet of vegetables to the theatre for Wilde. His plans were foiled, however, as the management had already alerted the police in case of a possible incident. Worse was to follow. On 28 February Wilde visited his club, the Albermarle, and was handed Queensberry's card which he had given to the doorman some days previously. Queensberry had written on it: 'For Oscar Wilde posing somdomite [sic]'. The next day Wilde obtained a warrant for Queensberry's arrest and so began an action that would blight the remaining years of Wilde's life.

Wilde's official complaint against Queensberry had not been registered without some anxiety on Wilde's part. He consulted with Ross on the matter who advised him to let it lie and do nothing. Alfred Douglas, on the other hand, was exultantly outraged and felt that this was a prime opportunity to confront his father in court and expose him as a tyrant and bully. Douglas's venom is easily understood given the immaturity of the young man. But Wilde's indulgence of him and ill-advised action in appointing a solicitor, Charles Humphreys, to prosecute Queensberry, has always been difficult to comprehend and is a major puzzle to Wilde's biographers. Wilde was a man who had two successful plays running in the West End, and was clearly at the height of his dramatic career. It was as though his will had been subsumed by the younger man's or as though he believed that he no longer had a say in his own life, leaving it all, as in some Greek tragedy, to fate and the unfolding of events. He tried at one point to step down on grounds of not having the funds to proceed. Douglas countered by having his mother and brother pledge the costs. Wilde, speaking of this time in *De Profundis*, addresses Douglas: 'Between you both I had lost my head. My judgement forsook me. Terror took its place ... Blindly I staggered as an ox to the shambles. I had made a gigantic psychological error.' In the same letter

Wilde declares that his only shame in relation to the trial was that he had appealed to conventionality and respectability and had spent long, boring hours convincing a balding man, his solicitor, of mundane lies.[35] It may well be that, true to form, Wilde was torn between two contraries: a surrender of events to fate and a reckless bid to counter the insolence of Queensberry.

Two days before the start of the trial it became known to Wilde that Queensberry's detectives had gathered damaging evidence about his homosexual association with various young men. Wilde was in imminent danger; in 1885 the Criminal Law Amendment Act had been passed, under which males taking part in acts of 'gross indecency' with other males were liable to a prison sentence of up to two years of hard labour. Even so, Wilde continued with his action. As if blind to reality, he was playing out a part on some imaginative plane where it was supremely possible for him to have his day in court and triumph over the consummate villain, Queensberry. Edward Carson, an Irishman and one time fellow student of Wilde's from Trinity College Dublin, represented Queensberry. The early stage of the proceedings was characterized by a display of wit by an able Wilde: he defended *Dorian Gray* as a work of art and spoke eloquently about the platonic ideal of love. It was Wilde's ease with words, his sense of play and repartee that provided the turning point in the trial. Wilde was poised on a knife edge at perhaps the most crucial moment of his life but was powerless to silence the riposte as it arose in his throat, since repartee was second nature to him: Carson, speaking of the servant in Douglas's house, asked: 'Did you ever kiss him?' Wilde replied: 'Oh no, never in my life, he was a peculiarly plain boy'. Wilde continued: 'I pitied him for it', and Carson pounced, construing Wilde's response to mean that ugliness had been the only obstacle to his not kissing the boy.[36] The case ended the next day as Wilde, on the advice of his legal team, withdrew. Queensberry sent his files to the Public Prosecutor and Wilde was arrested later that day. He refused to go into hiding or make any attempt to flee the country. Yeats believed that he stayed because being Irish he would not flee in dishonour before the old enemy.

The first trial of Oscar Wilde began on 26 April 1895 and was declared a mistrial as the jury failed to agree. At this point it would have been possible for the whole thing to have been dropped, but despite pleas on his behalf made by friends and even by Carson himself to various people of influence, the trial was re-set for 20 May. On 25 May 1895, Oscar Fingal O'Flahertie Wills Wilde was convicted of 'acts of gross indecencies with other male persons', and sentenced to two years' hard labour. He was initially sent to Pentonville prison and transferred to Wandsworth in July and eventually, on 21 November, to Reading Gaol from where he was released on 19 May 1897.

Wilde's trials were followed closely by the press and caused public outcry and condemnation not only in England but also on the continent. His name was blacked out on the billboards advertising his plays in the West End; these plays were eventually closed down and for some years following the trials, no play of Wilde's was produced on the English stage. Wilde's name which had featured frequently in the Irish press was absented from its pages for almost ten years. Wilde writes in De Profundis: '[My mother] and my father had bequeathed me a name they had made noble and honoured not merely in Literature, Art, Archaeology and Science, but in the public history of my own country in its evolution as a nation. I had disgraced that name eternally.'[37] Wilde's family was devastated by the events. To escape the growing hostility and notoriety, Constance eventually sent her children to Switzerland where she herself followed when the trials had ended. But Wilde's 'infamy' and the hostility it engendered had spread before them and the little family was asked to leave the hotel where they had sought refuge on the grounds of their name. It was at this point that Constance decided to protect her children by changing the name of Wilde by deed poll to one of her family names, Holland.

Prison was a dark experience for Wilde. He spent a large part of his time in solitary confinement. His exclusion from company played heavily on him as did being deprived of books and writing materials. He tried to gain remission on the grounds that he feared he might be going insane but his letter was judged too lucid for its author to be mad. Friends organized a petition for his release but nothing came of it. In 1896 his mother died. Constance, although in pain from a serious back injury, travelled to England to break the news to her husband, knowing how much his mother had meant to him. Wilde was deeply affected by her generosity in performing this act of love and kindness. In

Reading Gaol Wilde received more clemency than had been his lot in previous prisons. He was allowed writing materials and books to be sent to him. It was in Reading Gaol that Wilde wrote his last major prose piece, De Profundis. The piece was written in the form of a letter addressed to his former lover, Alfred Douglas. In it Wilde admonishes Douglas and berates himself. It chronicles Wilde's account of how he came to be in his present situation and the role Douglas played in it. De Profundis is a powerful piece of writing that arrests the emotions, as it catalogues and attempts to explain the relationship between the two lovers. It evidences Wilde's unshakeable belief in the self, charts the journey of a soul through pain and humility and proposes a fresh understanding of Christ. It is a quest for knowledge, to find meaning in one's actions.

In May 1897, Wilde completed his sentence and was released from prison. He was met by his friend, More Adey, and the Rev. Stewart Headlam, and went with them to Headlam's house where friends, including Ada (the 'Sphinx' as Wilde had named her) and Ernest Leverson came to meet him. Wilde, looking thin but well, quipped: 'Sphinx, how marvellous of you to know exactly the right hat to wear at seven o'clock in the morning to meet a friend who has been away! You can't have got up, you must have sat up!'[38] He sent word to the Jesuits at Farm Street that he would like to enter for six months to make a retreat, however word came back that this would not be possible as enough notice of his intent had not been given. Wilde wept at the news and left for France that evening and was met in Dieppe by Robbie Ross and Reggie Turner.

The next three years Wilde spent in Europe. At first he stayed in the little village of Berneval-sur-Mer and later in Paris. Constance settled an annuity on him and had let him know that she would meet with him on condition that he never saw Douglas again. Well meaning friends advised Constance against seeing him, the meeting was delayed and Wilde, unable to bear the isolation of his life, succumbed to temptation and met with Douglas in Rouen in August 1897. All hopes for a reconciliation with Constance were over. Wilde never saw his children or his wife again. On 7 April 1898 Constance Wilde died in Genoa following a spinal operation. Wilde visited her grave in 1899 and wept bitterly.

Apart from his letters to the *Daily Chronicle* on the plight of children in jail and the urgent need for prison reform written some days after his release from prison, Wilde only wrote one piece for a public audience in the years remaining to him after leaving jail, *The Ballad of Reading Gaol* (1898). This poem is unlike his other work in its form, as the ballad is a humble form intended to be easily accessible to all people. In sentiment *The Ballad of Reading Gaol* echoes the call for equality among people in his earlier socialist document, 'The Soul of Man Under Socialism'. There were stories of a play Wilde had written and left in a Paris taxi and a scenario, *Mr. and Mrs. Daventry*, that he sold a few times over to various people, once to his good friend, Frank Harris. This was an action bred of need, as was the necessity he found himself in of borrowing money from friends and strangers which more often than not he was unable to pay back. Generosity had always been a great virtue of Wilde's and even in his straitened circumstances after release from jail, he found some money to send to former inmates to help them turn their backs on crime and make a fresh start. Wilde's ineffable charm, openness and refusal to distinguish people on grounds of class or respectability had gained him friends among the outcast criminal classes as it had formerly given him access to the highest echelons of the British establishment.

Although Wilde had little money during his last few years spent in exile, he had good friends who saw to it that he had enough to survive and gave as much of their money and company as they could afford. There were of course others who, having been pleased to be acquainted with Wilde during affluent times, refused to recognize him in his defeat. He was a man of great intellect and his knowledge of the pain which he had brought on his family was acute. He had no knowledge of where his children were. He had written to their guardian asking that he might write to them but permission was refused.

On 30 November 1900, Oscar Wilde died in the Hotel d'Alsace, Rue des Beaux Arts, Paris from meningitis of the inner ear. Robbie Ross and Reggie Turner who had nursed him in his last days were with him when he died. Wilde received the Last Rites of the Catholic Church from Fr. Cuthbert Dunne, an Irish priest of the Passionist Fathers. A review that appeared in the paper *L'Osservatore Romano* in July 2009 describes Wilde as a man who was 'always looking for the beautiful and the good, but also for a God'.[39] He was buried in a leased grave in a cemetery at Bagneux. His remains were transferred to Père Lachaise cemetery in 1909 and reinterred under the monument designed by Jacob Epstein where he lies today. In 1950 the ashes of his friend, Robbie Ross, were laid to rest beside him at Ross's request. Perhaps Ross wished to make it easier for his friend, Oscar Wilde, to fulfil the words he had spoken to him some days before his death; 'Ah Robbie', Wilde said, 'when we are dead and buried in our porphyry tombs, and the trumpet of the Last Judgement is sounded, I shall turn and whisper to you, "Robbie, Robbie, let us pretend we do not hear it".'[40]

NOTES

1. Oscar Wilde, 'The Decay of Lying' in The Complete Works of Oscar Wilde, Vol.4, Criticism, ed., Josephine M. Guy (Oxford: Oxford University Press, 2007), p.95.

2. Letter to Philip Houghton, ? February 1894, in The Complete Letters of Oscar Wilde, eds Rupert Hart-Davis and Merlin Holland (London: Fourth Estate, 2000), p.586.

3. John Gamble, Sketches of History, Politics and Manners, taken in Dublin and the North of Ireland, in the Autumn of 1810 (London), pp.26–7 quoted in Davis Coakley, Oscar Wilde: the Importance of Being Irish (Dublin: Town House and Country House, 1994), p.34.

4. Coakley, Oscar Wilde, p.20.

5. Oscar Wilde, letter to William Ward, 6? September 1876, in Letters, p.32.

6. W.B. Yeats, '1903 American Lecture'. National Library of Ireland TS. W.B. Yeats Collection, Micro-fiche 30,627.

7. Joy Melville, Mother of Oscar – The Life of Jane Francesca Wilde (London: John Murray, 1994), p.40.

8. Ibid., p.265.

9. Quoted in Noreen Doody, 'Oscar Wilde: Landscape, Memory and Imagined Space', in Jose Fernandez Sanchez and M. Elena Jaime de Pablos (eds), Irish Landscapes (Almeria: University of Almeria Press, 2003), p.179.

10. 'Gossip', The Nation, 14 June 1873, p.7.

11. Jarlath Killeen, The Faiths of Oscar Wilde: Catholicism, Folklore and Ireland (London: Palgrave Macmillan, 2005), p.90.

12. W.B. Yeats, Autobiographies (London: Papermac, 1980), p.130.

13. Oscar Wilde, letter to Rev, Matthew Russell, SJ, ? September 1878, in *Letters*, p.71.

14. Richard Ellmann, *Oscar Wilde* (Harmondsworth: Penguin, 1988), p.142.

15. Ibid., p.128.

16. Oscar Wilde, letter to Waldo Storey, 22 January 1884, in *Letters*, p.225.

17. Oscar Wilde, letter to Lillie Langtry, c. 22 January 1884, in *Letters*, p.224.

18. Constance Lloyd, letter to Otho Holland Lloyd, 26 November 1883, in *Letters*, p.222.

19. Oscar Wilde, *The Importance of Being Earnest* in Oscar Wilde, *The Importance of Being Earnest and Other Plays*, ed. Peter Raby (Oxford: Oxford University Press, 1995), Vol.III, pp.399–400.

20. Merlin Holland, *The Wilde Album* (London: Fourth Estate, 1997), p.125.

21. Richard Le Gallienne, *The Romantic Nineties* (London: Robin Clark, 1993), p.143.

22. Oscar Wilde, letter to G.H. Kersley, 15 June 1888, in *Letters*, p.352.

23. Vyvyan Holland, *Son of Oscar Wilde* (Harmondsworth: Penguin, 1957), pp.44, 45.

24. Yeats, *Autobiographies*, p.134.

25. Holland, *Son of Oscar Wilde*, p.35.

26. Grant Allen, 'The Celt in English Art', *The Fortnightly Review* (February 1891), quoted in *Oscar Wilde's Oxford Notebooks: A Portrait of Mind in the Making*, eds Philip E. Smith II and Michael S. Helfland (New York and Oxford: Oxford University Press, 1989), p.81.

27. Quotes from reviews taken from Oscar Wilde, *The Picture of Dorian Gray – Authoritative Texts, Backgrounds, Reviews, and Reactions, Criticism*, ed. Michael Patrick Gillespie (A Norton Critical Edition. New York: Norton, 2007), pp.355, 362, 366, 367.

28. Oscar Wilde, letter to the Editor of the Scot's Observer, 9 July 1890, in *Letters*, p.439.

29. Yeats, *Autobiographies*, p.285; George Slythe Street, 'Out of the Depths', *Outlook*, 4 March 1905, p.294, quoted in Karl Beckson (ed.), *Oscar Wilde: The Critical Heritage*, (London: Routledge and Kegan Paul, 1970), p.287.

30. R.B. Cunninghame Graham, 'Vox Clamantis', *The Saturday Review*, 4 March 1905, p.266, quoted in Beckson (ed.), *Critical Heritage*, p.289.

31. Holland, *The Wilde Album*, p.126.

32. Oscar Wilde, 'The Truth of Masks', in *The Complete Works of Oscar Wilde*. Vol.4, Criticism, ed. Josephine Guy, p.228.

33. Ellmann, *Oscar Wilde*, p.352.

34. Merlin Holland, *Irish Peacock and Scarlet Marquess: The Real Trial of Oscar Wilde* (London: Fourth Estate Ltd, 2004), p.58.

35. Oscar Wilde, 'Epistola: In Carcere et Vinculis', in *The Complete Works of Oscar Wilde*, vol. 2, *De Profundis*, ed. Ian Small (Oxford: Oxford University Press, 2005), pp.43, 130.

36. Holland, *Irish Peacock*, p.207.

37. Wilde, 'Epistola', p.83.

38. Ellmann, *Oscar Wilde*, p.495.

39. Nick Pisa, 'Vatican does U-turn to Praise Oscar Wilde', *Mail Online*, 17 July 2009. http://www.dailymail.co.uk/news/worldnews/article-1200167/Vatican-does-U-turn-praise-Oscar-Wilde.html#ixzz0XPy2g48J.

40. Ellmann, *Oscar Wilde*, p.545.

CHAPTER THREE

'Mixing Memory and Desire': The Scandal of Oscar Wilde's Neo-Classical Poetry

FLORINA TUFESCU

Oscar Wilde's writing career begins and ends with poetry. It was with a volume of *Poems* that he chose to make his entry on the literary scene in 1881, sending it to admired contemporaries such as Matthew Arnold, Algernon Charles Swinburne, Robert Browning and the prime minister and classical scholar William Gladstone; it was to poetry again that he turned in seeking to remake his reputation after the disgrace of his imprisonment, publishing *The Ballad of Reading Gaol* in 1898. Apart from these two much noticed poetic appearances, Wilde wrote two blank verse tragedies, *The Duchess of Padua* (written in 1883) and *A Florentine Tragedy* (never completed), in continuation of the Romantic and Victorian homage to Elizabethan, and in particular Shakespearean, drama, the verse drama tradition that would briefly gain the public's approval with the plays of T.S. Eliot and Archibald MacLeish before once more losing its appeal. He also wrote a number of short poems that appeared in society magazines; a few tales which he published as 'poems in prose', in tribute to Charles Baudelaire and the French tradition; and, as his ultimate challenge to the emerging Victorian canon, a remarkable poem, *The Sphinx* (1894), which adapts the rhythm and some of the sentiment of *In Memoriam* (1850), the poem that comforted the widowed Queen Victoria and brought Alfred Tennyson the Laureateship, for an elegy of unfulfilled sexual fantasies.[1]

Poetry is never far from the surface of Wilde's prose works, either. The Symbolist drama of *Salome* (1894) was called a 'poem' by Wilde himself.[2] One need not even go beyond the best-known Wildean texts to discover the central role that poetry played in Wilde's imagination. 'The Decay of Lying' (1889) pays the greatest tribute to poets who 'have been really faithful to their high mission, and are universally recognized as being absolutely unreliable'.[3] The plot of The Picture of Dorian Gray (1890) is inspired by Shakespeare's sonnets or rather by Wilde's own previous reading of them in 'The Portrait of Mr. W. H.' (1889). Shakespeare's presence remains clear enough in a text whose protagonist defines himself by means of a quotation from Hamlet and falls out of love with an actress after her unsatisfactory performance as Juliet.[4] Bernard Beatty argues that Wilde's prose and verse share many characteristics and that these derive from James MacPherson's Ossian poems, namely 'elaborated alliteration and assonance', 'metrically paired very short sentences, an abundance of similes' and striking pauses instead of complex sentences. He states that Wilde 'never forgot the Irish cadence, forged and authentic, based on a short repeated unit, of his upbringing'.[5] Yet like the majority of critics, Beatty prefers Wilde's prose to his poetry, describing 'Charmides' (1881) as only a 'prose sequence decked out as verse'.[6]

The importance of poetry to Wilde's work and thinking is clear enough; the question of Wilde's importance to poetry has proved much more controversial. Yet Wilde's concepts of the mask and of artistic authenticity went on to have considerable influence on twentieth-century poets, some of his most prominent successors have been thoroughly dismissive of his poetry while simultaneously being influenced by it. Wilde's own friends, to whom he read the manuscript of Salome, first reacted by laughing, uncertain how to respond to its heightened language. Wilde's poetry was often parodied in the newspapers, not least in Punch by one of his closest friends, the novelist Ada Leverson. Walter Hamilton's Aesthetic Movement (1881), an empathetic study that gives ample space to Wilde, praises his 'undoubted genius' on the strength of his recently published Poems and of his influential lectures on art and design. This did not prevent him from including numerous and often skilful parodies of Wilde in volume 6 of his Parodies of English and American Authors (1889). Interestingly, while Robert Browning object- ed to Walter Hamilton's idea of publishing parodies of his works and sent him an 'ungracious' letter to ensure that they would not be accompanied by any extracts from his work, Wilde did not appear to be perturbed, and he sent Hamilton a characteristically charming letter on the subject: 'Parody, which is the Muse with the tongue in her cheek, has always amused me; but it requires a light touch, ... and, oddly enough, a love of the poet whom it caricatures'.[7]

The slighting of Wilde's poetry continued into the twentieth century. W.H. Auden viewed Wilde's interest in poetry and his passion for Alfred Douglas as equally misguided: 'Of his poems, not one has survived, for he was totally lacking in a poetic voice of his own ... Nor was it, I think, personal infatuation that made him so absurdly overestimate Douglas' versified drivel; he quite honestly thought it was good'.[8] W.B. Yeats described Wilde as a clown and thought only *The Ballad of Reading Gaol* worth republishing – in a drastically trimmed-down version.[9] Jorge Luis Borges paid Wilde the compliment of comparing his poetry to that of great contemporaries such as Tennyson, Swinburne and Dante Gabriel Rossetti, yet felt compelled to state that Wilde 'was not a great poet nor a consummate prose writer', but rather an 'enfant terrible'.[10] Fernando Pessoa was equally critical, protesting against comparisons of his work to that of Wilde and noting that the 'exquisite phrase' of the poets, 'the poetic phrase proper, is a thing in which his works are signally lacking'.[11]

Of course, it would be plausible enough to argue that Wilde's disciples were essentially right. The master's dabbling in a genre for which he had no genuine inclination could be explained, if not ultimately excused, by his upbringing and cultural circumstances. Poetry was a highly prestigious, arguably the most significant, art form for the Victorians. In addition, Wilde was the son of the famous nationalist poet Lady Jane Wilde (Speranza) and spent much of his childhood among the Irish poets, 'trained ... to love and reverence them, as a Catholic child is the Saints of the Calendar', as he would recall in his only lecture on the subject.[12] Poetry came easily to him, far too easily, perhaps. But it would also be plausible to argue that his disciples had personal reasons for disparaging Wilde's poetry, reasons connected to what one might call the 'anxiety of association', not only to Wilde's homosexuality (which was only decriminalized and depathologised as late as the 1960s in the UK and the US), but also to old-fashioned aestheticism. E.C. Stedman's wide-ranging study *Victorian Poets* (1876) for example, acknowledges Wilde's 'cleverness, scholarship ... and native poetic gift', yet includes only the briefest discussion of Wilde's poetry, alongside that of his friend and fellow-Oxonian Rennell Rodd, precisely because he views Wilde as a representative of aestheticism, a minor movement that in his view had reached 'almost perfect development at its start with Keats'.[13]

My purpose in the following pages is not to offer yet another definitive statement on the place (if any) of Wilde's poetry within the canon. The best way of understanding Wilde's or anyone's poems remains, of course, simply to plunge into them, to read them aloud and to allow them to take over the imagination, as Wilde wrote of the effect of Baudelaire's verse: 'let its subtle music steal into your brain and colour your thoughts, and you will become for a moment what he was who wrote it ... read the whole book, suffer it to tell even one of its secrets to your soul, and your soul will grow eager to know more, and will feed upon poisonous honey'.[14] I can offer in the following pages no substitute for the experience of feeding on the poisonous honey of Wilde's poetry, or the poetry of his closest and most brilliant associates such as John Gray and Marcel Schwob, or on the canonical poetry that inspired him and that included the masterpieces of French, English and ancient Greek and Latin literature. What I will attempt is the briefest sketch of three possible ways of approaching the poems: biographical (an approach which remains prominent), aesthetic (emphasizing Wilde's self-reflective approach to the writing of poetry), and as a significant influence on twentieth-century poetry, an influence that has been ignored or underplayed in much criticism. Each of these readings builds on some aspect of Wildean critical theory; none of them can explain the poems away, their beauty, whether it may appear faded, truncated, bizarre or indeed fresh and glorious, and their ultimate strangeness as poems in a world that reads so very few and in which the craft of verse itself has almost been forgotten.

'WHO WERE YOUR LOVERS, WHO WERE THEY WHO WRESTLED FOR YOU IN
THE DUST': BREAKING INTO THE POET'S HEART

Oscar Wilde's volume of *Poems* opens with an acknowledgment of the
loss of artistic discipline:

> To drift with every passion till my soul
> Is a stringed lute on which all winds can play,
> Is it for this that I have given away
> Mine ancient wisdom and austere control?
> ('Hélas!' [1881], ll. 1–4)[15]

It ends with a graceful admission of failure:

> I have made my choice, have lived my poems, and, though
> youth is gone in wasted days
> I have found the lover's crown of myrtle better than the poet's
> crown of bays. ('ΓΛΥΚΥΠΙΡΟΣ · ΕΡΩΣ ·' 'Bittersweet Love'
> [1881], ll. 29–30).[16]

Such poetic apologies – Wilde apologizing for being a more interesting and accomplished lover than poet, and for having allowed his life
to taint, and perhaps weaken, his poetry – continue (perhaps even more
ironically) the more gracious stance which is encapsulated in Wilde's
famous observation to André Gide: 'I have put my genius in my life and
only my talent in my works'.[17] Like his observation to Gide, they simultaneously and contradictorily capitalize on the modern fascination with
biography. Wilde's foregrounding of Love as a key theme offers readers
an easy and almost irresistible entry into the intertextual labyrinth of his
poetry, and suggests (hints even) that the poems can be read best as
commentaries on Wilde's (love) life. The illusion of immediacy is
enhanced by the biographical references scattered throughout the
poems: many are clearly associated with Wilde's travelling and
theatrical experiences and have been frequently read in an unproblem-
atically autobiographical manner, from Arthur Ransome's study of 1912
to the current edition of the *Oxford Complete Works* edited by Ian Small
(2000). For example, the quintessentially decadent Sphinx is set in a
recognizably Oxonian setting where Wilde was a student, while the

early editions of *The Ballad of Reading Gaol* were signed 'C.3.3.' – Wilde's number in prison. In addition, the speakers of the poems are not so different from the dandies and the occasional cads of Wilde's comedies, and arguably not so different from Wilde's own public persona, as perceived by his contemporaries. Yet Wilde, like Shakespeare, is careful to maintain the tension between the *potentially* and the *unquestionably* auto-biographical: although some of the poems are dedicated to well-known actresses, the vast majority of poetic speakers and lovers remain nameless and completely unidentified, just as Shakespeare's sonnets promise immortality to the beloved and paradoxically refuse even to name him.

Of course, the autobiographical reading of the poems was dramatically intensified by the trial and its aftermath, far beyond the poet's calculations. His impassioned speech in defence of the 'Love that dare not speak its name' made his poems – even more than his other works – appear far more autobiographical than they need otherwise have been to disciples who shared his erotic or aesthetic inclinations.

Interestingly, before the trial, Wilde had toyed with the fantasy of an elite audience for his poetry, similar to Shakespeare's sonnets, which in the view of most contemporary scholars had not been intended for publication, but only for circulation among Shakespeare's friends. Following the mixed reception of his debut volume of *Poems*, Wilde prevented the reviewing of the re-issued 1891 edition, writing to Grant Richards, who had requested a review copy, that the book was meant 'merely for lovers of poetry, a small and quite unimportant sect of perfect people' and that attention 'would annoy it, books being delicate and most sensitive things, and if they are books worth reading, having a strong dislike of the public'.[18] The 1892 *Poems* and *The Sphinx* were both published as limited editions, exclusive aesthetic objects rather than romantic effusions for the public. Yet the poetry which he had designed as aesthetic and exclusive came to resemble J.O. Halliwell-Phillips's descrip-tion of Shakespeare's sonnets as a 'delinquent's confessions'.[19] Wilde's post-prison publisher was Leonard Smithers, whom he fondly described as 'the most learned erotomaniac in Europe' and 'a delightful companion'. Following Smithers's bankruptcy and loss of copyright in Wilde's titles, his works were frequently pirated by Smithers himself and by Charles Carrington (the pseudonym for Paul Fernando), who also specialized in erotica. This meant that Wildean titles, including the poetry, were published alongside sensational biographies and reports of the trials and that Wilde's works were outside of the realm of reputable publishing until Robert Ross's publication of the *Collected Works* (1908).[20] It was, therefore, unavoidable that the poetry should acquire greater biographical significance.

This biographical impulse even infected those who were Wilde's poetic respondents. J.S. Young's 'Impromptu-Suggested by S.M.' (the initials standing for Wilde's post-prison alias Sebastian Melmoth) in his *Out of Hours* (1909) poetry collection 'homosexualises' the romance of Wilde's 'Panthea' (1881) in the manner that justifies Wilde's observation that 'all bad poetry springs from genuine feeling'.[21] Likewise, Fernando Pessoa's *Antinous* (1918) is filled with covert reflections on Wilde's writing and his love affair with Alfred Douglas. While the poem is ostensibly about the emperor Hadrian's mourning over his beloved slave Antinous, an episode that is also briefly invoked by Wilde in *The Sphinx's* pageant of sexual fantasies, it is impossible not to think of Wilde's sensuous 'fleshly' poetry and of the global significance of the trial in reading lines such as these:

> The end of days, when Jove is born again,
> And Ganymede again pour at his feast,
> Shall see our dual soul from death released
> And recreated unto love, joy, pain,
> Life – all the beauty and the vice and lust,
> All the diviner side of flesh, flesh-staged.[22]

Alfred Douglas's wife, Olive Custance, seems also to have been fascinated by Wilde. Custance's poems 'The White Statue' (1897) and 'Antinous' (1902) play with Wildean representations of androgyny, while 'Saint Sebastian' (1905), 'Hyacinthus' (1905) and 'Peacocks: A Mood' (1905) can be read as comments on Wilde's love-affair with Alfred Douglas.[23] Hart Crane's first published poem was 'C. 3. 3.' (1916), his identification with the dead poet suggested by the signature in the second line:

> He has woven rose-vines
> About the empty heart of night,
> And vented his long mellowed wines

Of dreaming on the desert white
With searing sophistry...[24]

This is a deliberately elusive, thirteen-line poem, an 'almost sonnet that almost makes sense', an ambiguous 'love poem' whose subject is either Oscar Wilde or Materna, forbidden 'homoerotic or oedipal love', or indeed both.[25] Such poems echo Wilde's poetic imagery and ideas in an attempt to recapture his personal voice, as in Alfred Douglas's moving sonnet 'The Dead Poet' (1907). So does Thomas Wright in his recent play, *Death in Genoa* (2009) which imagines Wilde visiting his wife Constance's grave. The only words Wright's Wilde can turn to in order to minimize despair are his own, lines from his poems 'The Grave of Keats' (1877) and from 'Requiescat' (1881).[26]

These rather unproblematized biographical readings of the poetry are, perhaps, understandable in writers influenced by Wilde, and especially those who knew him personally. However, they reappear even in the best academic criticism. Wilde's significance to queer poets as to queer artists in general is briefly discussed by Donald E. Hall, in the 'introductory dialogue' that inaugurates a special issue of *Victorian Poetry* on 'Queer Ethics' (2000), where the poetry is read as an expression of the author's own political and ethical views and as a 'useful entrée ... into a dynamic of rebellion and remorse' that is still relevant for sexuality studies today, with 'Hélas', the opening poem of the 1881 collection seen as a reflection of Wilde's 'deep ambivalence over the consequences of his own [sexual] nonconformity'. While the ethical criteria have changed, they still seem to work against Wilde: Hall tells us that Wilde is a poet 'for whom I really don't care very much', the reason being that his poetry and his art in general are not queer enough.[27]

Even for John Simon who dedicates an entire chapter of his book *Dreamers of Dreams* to 'Wilde the Poet', placing him next to influential figures such as Paul Celan, John Ashberry or Philip Larkin, the value of the poetry is largely or ultimately biographical, as 'an important training ground for the incomparable comedies'.[28] The poems themselves are 'like his life ... a mixed bag'.[29] Other biographical readings are more elaborate, combining the longing for intimacy with creative interpretations. Patricia Behrendt offers an in-depth and often illuminating reading of Wilde's poetry which is perhaps overly focussed on unveiling Wilde's homosexual inclinations.[30] Melissa Knox's *A Long and Lovely Suicide* is a psychoanalytical reading of the entire Wildean oeuvre, including the poems, in which she uncovers 'obsessive erotic fantasies' of Wilde's sister Isola, who died at the age of 8.[31] I could add to these my own reading of 'The Harlot's House' (1885), the poem for which the biographical source may have been the death of Wilde's half-sisters, Sir William Wilde's daughters by an unnamed woman: waltzing past the fireplace during one of the last dances at Drummaconor House, Mary Wilde's crinoline caught fire as did that of her sister Emily (Emma) who attempted to save her; both died from severe burns, respectively nine and twenty-one days after the ball.[32] Dawn's frightened appearance at the end of 'The Harlot's House' corresponds to the time of the tragedy, the unusual verb 'crept' perhaps suggesting their prolonged suffering before death. The condemnation of the 'ghostly dancers' and their presentation as 'phantom puppets' could reflect Wilde's anger at the passivity of the other guests at the dance and their inability to save his sisters. The unforgettable and seemingly unavoidable correlations that he makes in this poem between lust and innocence, dancing and death, and the constant disruption of hedonism and decadent excess by Christian repentance, could perhaps be linked to this family tragedy and to Wilde's ambivalent feelings about his father and his half-sisters' mother – possibly the 'harlot' of the poem's title, the fallen woman that he would spend much of his drama attempting to understand and re-invent. The initial manuscript designation of 'the prince's house' is equally revealing, for it alludes to Edgar Allan Poe's 'The Masque of the Red Death' (1842) and to the prince's ultimately futile attempt to isolate himself from the contagion of death and vulgarity – just as Sir William Wilde strove to keep this tragedy from becoming public, writing to the coroner to request that there should be no inquest on the deaths and possibly, as Theo McMahon suggests,[33] ensuring that the girls' names were misspelt in the official report.[34]

Biographical readings of Wilde's poetry can be interesting and illuminating, provided that they remain speculative. Wilde's theory of Shakespeare's sonnets, as articulated in 'The Portrait of Mr. W. H.', built on close reading and half-forged, half-unacknowledged scholarly quotations, is that they were inspired by Willie Hughes, a boy-actor in

Shakespeare's company. Wilde's biographical imagining far surpasses in its boldness and imaginativeness previous impersonal readings of the sonnets, which sought to explain away the passion of the sonnets by attributing them to sonnet conventions and Renaissance conventions of artistic patronage; yet it is in its turn surpassed by what might be called a trans-personal, trans-individualist reading. Shakespeare's heart is whisked away, to heaven, perhaps, like that of the Happy Prince, or simply whisked out of sight – changed by the magic of language into something else. After horrifying the more conventional among his readers with the suggestion that the dedicatee of the sonnets was a previously unheard of boy-actor, the 'original' of female heroines such as Juliet and Rosalind, and that the homosexual taint of the poetry expands to the entire Shakespearean canon, the Narrator then acknowledges that whether or not Shakespeare wished to unlock his heart in the sonnets he was, like all artists, ulti-mately powerless to do so. All emotions change into something 'new and strange' when they pass into the realm of art. After all, according to 'Roses and Rue' (1885), poets' hearts 'break in music' (l. 55)[35] or perhaps into shimmering crystal fragments (according to 'Sonnet on the Sale by Auction of Keats' Love Letters' [1886], l. 7),[36] but even ordinary hearts break into roses and scent, as in The Ballad of Reading Gaol (ll. 481–2, ll. 607–12).[37] This metamorphosis is the price of admission, with 'poor human life' as one of the sources of art, at once annihilated and perfected into permanence. 'They are the elect to whom beautiful things mean only Beauty.'[38] Whatever the ostensible subject of a work of art, whatever its source, the ultimate subject – for the critic as artist – is always Beauty.

'SPIRIT OF BEAUTY, TARRY YET AWHILE' AND WHY ONE SHOULDN'T EAT MUFFINS IN AN AGITATED MANNER

Biography has its charm, but it must ultimately yield to what Wilde sees as the ultimate goal of poetry itself, Beauty. The critical move should be from biography, strictly speaking, to 'Beauty'. Wilde's poetry, like his critical prose, is after all filled with invocations of Beauty: 'Beauty is the symbol of symbols'; 'Beauty has as many meanings as man has moods.'[39] Or, to quote from the even more extravagant language of one of his poems:

Ay! though the gorgèd asp of passion feed
On my boy's heart, yet have I burst the bars,
Stood face to face with Beauty, known indeed
The Love which moves the Sun and all the stars!'
('Apologia' [1881], ll. 33–6)[40]

As readers of his poetry, we should take heed of the first aphorism in the Preface to the *Picture of Dorian Gray* which defines the artist as 'the creator of beautiful things'.

This definition appeared obsolete at the time it was published – few of Wilde's contemporaries would have thought of 'Beauty' as art's defining quality or agreed with Edgar Allan Poe's definition of poetry as 'the rhythmical creation of beauty',[41] which even the Wildean disciple Stuart-Young tries to render more reassuringly intellectual: 'poetry is the flowering of the mind into rhythmic utterance'.[42] Yet as Wilde understands and practices it, the worship of Beauty could have radical implications, warning in 'The Critic as Artist' (1890) that:

> There are two ways of disliking art ... One is to dislike it. The other, to like it rationally ... If one loves Art at all, one must love it beyond all other things in the world, and against such love, the reason, if one listened to it, would cry out. There is nothing sane about the worship of beauty.[43]

Wilde's privileging of Beauty as Art's essential quality means that his verse is always technically accomplished and frequently modelled on that of previous poets, and that the representation is always graceful, regardless of the subject or the emotional content. When he writes a 'Sonnet on the Massacre of the Christians in Bulgaria' (1881), he does so through the prism of John Milton's 'On the Late Massacre in Piedmont' (1655). When he decides to write a ballad on the hanging of a fellow-prisoner at Reading, he aestheticizes the circumstances of the murder and turns to Samuel Taylor Coleridge's *Rime of the Ancient Mariner* (1798) and to his own 'The Harlot's House' to render the drab world of prison nightmarish. His beautifully designed and gorgeously printed poetry appears liberating and inspiring to some, callous and perhaps immoral to others whose approach to art is primarily emotional or intellectual. Wilde's observation that 'no artist has ethical sympathies'[44] can be understood by analogy to classical painting, in which a representation of the Crucifixion is as carefully composed as a still life or a country scene. To some modern sensibilities, this appears wrong, yet it is not clear why we should think that broken-down, elliptical language possesses greater artistic authenticity than Wilde's mellifluous language, with its brilliant sprinkling of quotations from fellow-poets, some of them long dead. This is really a matter of changing artistic conventions and of different audience expectations. Should the letters of heart-broken lovers be badly spelt to signify emotion, as Cecily suggests in The Importance of Being Earnest? Richard Ellmann is perhaps thinking of the widely held belief in the connection between 'authentic' emotion and inartistic expression when he suggests of 'Roses and Rue' (1885) that one of the rhymes is so bad ('You had poets enough on the shelf/I gave you myself') as to indicate that the 'sentiment is genuine'.[45]

Is there a genuine emotion behind a poem such as 'My Voice' (1881)? Or 'Quia Multum Amavi' (1881)? Is this even a question we should be asking of poetry? The Wildean critic at his most paradoxical would argue that the source, real or fictitious, of the work of art is unimportant since love 'is the child, not the parent of language':[46] all that happens in 'real life' is at best a raw material that Art can accept and transform or reject altogether, while Art itself constantly expands our perception of Life and thereby constantly improves upon it: 'one does not see a thing until one sees its beauty. Then, and then only, does it come into existence.'[47]

While the aesthete can only admit emotion into the realm of Art under some more or less convincing, yet always decorous, guise, for the readers who cling to the 'natural' pose, and to the idea that poetry should be the 'spontaneous overflow of emotion',[48] the prominence of the disguise, the sheer visibility of the mask as mask in Wilde's poetry is enough to devalue it since it invests so clearly in such theatricality. In their Studying Poetry, Stephen Matterson and Darryl Jones despair that far too many appear to think that all poetry should be Romantic, that is, modelled on the Romantic theory of poetry, a view that would help explain why Wilde's poetry is not only alien but alienating to some contemporary readers.[49] At the level of technique, Wilde's smoothly polished verses can appear old-fashioned alongside Walt Whitman's effusive language, Stéphane Mallarmé's postponement of meaning or Robert Browning's fascinating experiments that 'turned language into ignoble clay', yet 'made from it men and women that live'.[50] The perceived failure or tameness of Wilde's poetry has been attributed by critics to a young writer's lack of confidence (Murray, Frankel) or undiscriminating enthusiasm (Ransome), anxiety of influence (Bloom) or even to opportunism, shortage of ideas (Small) and unscrupulous plagiarism (Gardner).[51] Yet Wilde was no dilettante when it came to poetry. As Leslie White has demonstrated in a recent article, Wilde's critical remarks on Browning anticipate the most interesting scholarship of the last twenty years.[52] He was also an early admirer of Walt Whitman, though his appreciation seems to centre on the American poet's personality rather than on his artistic accomplishment: 'Walt Whitman if not a poet is a man who sounds a strong note. He writes neither prose nor poetry but something of his own that is unique.'[53] Wilde's interactions with Mallarmé and other avant-garde poets deserve more attention than they have so far received. In Paris, Wilde was, if not perhaps 'the prince of poets', as the Romanian symbolist Dimitrie Anghel described him, certainly an influential and admired figure who paid tribute to Mallarmé as the only 'maître' of French contemporary poetry and was in his turn admired by Mallarmé for The Picture of Dorian Gray: 'un des seuls [livres] qui puissent émouvoir, vu que d'une rêverie essentielle et des parfums d'âmes les plus étranges s'est fait son orage. Redevenir poignant a travers l'inouï raffinement d'intellect, et humain, et une pareille perverse atmosphère de beauté, est un miracle que vous accomplissez'.[54] Wilde's Sphinx is dedicated to the young French poet and scholar Marcel Schwob whose Livre de Monelle, published in the same year (1894), is an equally decadent elegy of a prostitute, written in highly unusual free verse with echoes of the Psalms.

Moreover, Wilde's reviews of contemporary poetry for the journals, not least his 'Literary Notes' as editor of Woman's World, reveal the breadth of his interests and his critical discrimination, ranging as they do from William Morris' translation of The Odyssey (1887) (which Wilde is able to compare with previous translations from the Greek) to Joseph Skipsey's Carols from the Coal Fields (1886), from Yeats' Wanderings of Oisin (1889) to Edward Carpenter's edition of Chants of Labour: A Song Book of the

People (1888), from the verse tragedies of Michael Field to Constance Naden's *A Modern Apostle and Other Poems* (1887). Wilde's decision to write in slightly antiquated beautiful language cannot plausibly be attributed to a lack of understanding of contemporary trends and possibilities. It might instead be linked to his sense that unlike Victorian drama, a commercial genre that he helped to turn once again into an art form, Victorian poetry was in fact highly accomplished and varied – it was the public that needed to be reinvented and taught to appreciate beauty of form and design, as Wilde undertook to do through his poetry and his lectures. Wilde's choices are more fully explained in his review of William Henley's poetry where he asserts: 'If English Poetry is in danger ... what she has to fear is not the fascination of dainty metre or delicate form, but the predominance of the intellectual spirit over the spirit of beauty'.[55] What Wilde calls here 'the intellectual spirit' is related to the 'unimaginative realism' that threatens art in 'The Decay of Lying', to the 'brute reason ... hitting below the intellect' and to the 'creeping common sense' that kills most people, which he condemns in *The Picture of Dorian Gray*.[56] Or, as he put it in one of his poems: 'the crimson flower of our life is eaten by the cankerworm of truth, / And no hand can gather up the fallen withered petals of the rose of youth'; mere rationality without artistic empathy makes the appreciation and writing of poetry (almost) impossible ('ΓΛΥΚΥΠΙΡΟΣ · ΕΡΩΣ ·' 'Bittersweet Love', ll. 19–20).[57] He also insists that poets should not give up formal verse:

> Rhyme gives architecture as well as melody to verse; it gives that delightful sense of limitation which in all the arts is so pleasurable, and is, indeed, one of the secrets of perfection; it will whisper, as a French critic has said, 'things unexpected and charming, things with strange and remote relations to each other', and bind them together in indissoluble bonds of beauty.[58]

By privileging craft rather than self-expression and trusting aesthetic instinct above time- and place-bound ethics, the poet could hope to become possessed by 'the ancient gods of Grecian poesy' ('The Burden of Itys' [1881]), inspired in the pre-Romantic sense of the word in which genius was not individual, but a gift from the gods.[59] Long before the Oulipo group, who realized that artistic creativity can be released by collaborative play and by linguistic constraints, Wilde agreed to Goethe's observation that 'it is in working within limits that the master reveals himself'.[60] By concentrating on Beauty and the perfection of verse, one can avoid falling into discursive habits and free the mind from all too obvious associations and biases. It then becomes possible to move beyond the expression of one's own intellectual and ethical views and tap into the collective imagination. Imagination is 'simply concentrated race experience' and might be stimulated by the practice of traditional verse.[61]

Within the space of one of Wilde's aesthetic poems, it is possible to be free from our everyday personalities, emotions, prejudices and know-ledge, and even to free ourselves from what one might call the tendency towards useless and ultimately self-destructive emotional involvement. Wilde is capable of writing a poem that is a sheer celebration of movement and colour such as 'Fantaisies Décoratives II: Les Ballons' (1887); or else he can write poems such as 'Symphony in Yellow' (1889) or 'Impression du Matin' (1881) in which human subjects appear as minor elements of the overall design. Even those poems that feature a famous human subject quickly move towards vague reverie. A glimpse of the beautiful actress Lily Langtry, whom Wilde called 'Helen of Troy, now of London' is enough to inspire verses such as these:

> Where hast thou been since round the walls of Troy
> The sons of God fought in that great emprise?
> Why dost thou walk our common earth again?
> Hast thou forgotten that impassioned boy,
> His purple galley, and his Tyrian men
> And treacherous Aphrodite's mocking eyes?
> For surely it was thou, who, like a star
> Hung in the silver silence of the night,
> Didst lure the Old World's chivalry and might
> Into the clamorous crimson waves of war! ('The New Helen'
> [1879], ll. 1–10)

What perhaps begins as an extravagant compliment to a living beauty turns into a dream of the beautiful past, the poem's living subject replaced by an apparition of Helen, as re-imagined in Goethe's *Faust*:

> Alas, alas, thou wilt not tarry here,

But, like that bird, the servant of the sun,
Who flies before the northwind and the night,
So wilt thou fly our evil land and drear,
Back to the tower of thine old delight,
And the red lips of young Euphorion. (ll. 61–6)

Yet the ultimate revelation of this poem which provocatively fuses the image of Christ and that of the mythical Helen, is only the flimsiest of images:

Lily of love, pure and inviolate!
Tower of ivory! red rose of fire!
Thou hast come down our darkness to illume:
For we, close-caught in the wide nets of Fate,
Wearied with waiting for the World's Desire,
Aimlessly wandered in the House of gloom,
Aimlessly sought some slumberous anodyne
For wasted lives, for lingering wretchedness,
Till we beheld thy re-arisen shrine,
And the white glory of thy loveliness (ll. 91–100).[62]

The subjects of Wildean poems are often so slight as to make them an easy target for parody. This is Wilde's 'Impression: II La Fuite de la Lune' (1877):

To outer senses there is peace,
A dreamy peace on either hand,
Deep silence in the shadowy land,
Deep silence where the shadows cease.

Save for a cry that echoes shrill
From some lone bird disconsolate;
A corncrake calling to its mate;

The answer from the misty hill.

And suddenly the moon withdraws
Her sickle from the lightening skies,
And to her sombre cavern flies,
Wrapped in a veil of yellow gauze.[63]

In a parody, 'La Fuite des Oies' in the 28 May 1881 edition of Punch magazine, this becomes:

> To outer senses they are geese,
> Dull drowsing by a weedy pool;
> But try the impression trick, Cool! Cool!
> Snow-slumbering sentinels of Peace!
>
> Deep silence on the shadowy flood
> Save rare sharp stridence (that means 'quack')
> Low amber light in Ariel track
> Athwart the dun (that means the mud).
>
> And suddenly subsides the sun,
> Bulks mystic, ghostly, thrid the gloom
> (That means the white geese waddling home),
> And darkness reigns! (see how it's done?)[64]

What the parodists may have failed to realize is that for Wilde, in the words of his 'successor' T.S. Eliot, 'poetry is not a turning loose of emotion, but an escape from emotion; it is not the expression of personality, but an escape from personality. But, of course, only those who have personality and emotions know what it means to want to escape from these things'.[65] When Wilde worked on a poem he generally attempted to remove emotion, particularly of the biographical kind. In the original version of 'Impression: II La Fuite de la Lune', published as 'Lotus Leaves' in The Irish Monthly in 1877, the cool impression had actually started from a Tennysonian elegy on the death of Sir William Wilde, in which the final stanza read:

> And, herald of my love to Him
> Who, waiting for the dawn, doth lie,
> The orbéd maiden leaves the sky,
> And the white firs grow more dim.[66]

Wilde takes his father's body out of the poem and fragments it to create a series of aesthetic, virtually subjectless stanzas.

Robert L. Peters writes that Wilde tends to use primary colours in his impressionist poems, in contrast to Arthur Symons's more

Whistlerian, 'subtler blendings of color'.[67] It seems to me that Wilde's use of pictorial and musical titles and references is meant to mark the poems' remoteness from ordinary life and emotions, by emphasizing links and connections to other art forms. The protagonists are only 'leaves whirling in the wind', 'ghostly dancers' or – like the children glimpsed in 'Le Jardin des Tuileries' (1885) – only 'little things of dancing gold' (l. 4).[68] The protagonists of the Wildean poems are, perhaps, unfree because 'when man acts, he is a puppet', but we become free in contemplating them, as in contemplating any event recreated for us by art.

'YOUR LOVERS ARE NOT DEAD, I KNOW, / THEY WILL ARISE AND HEAR YOUR VOICE / AND CLASH THEIR CYMBALS AND REJOICE', OR WHY INFLUENCE IS ALWAYS A VERY DANGEROUS THING

I think it extremely likely that Wilde's influence on poetry and poets has so far been underestimated.[69] The impact of his critical theory, in particular of his theories of the mask and of artistic authenticity as necessitating a multiplicity of selves, has been documented in relation to the works of W.B. Yeats, T.S. Eliot and Fernando Pessoa. T.S. Eliot's early poetry is haunted by the 'tired Sphinx of the physical' and by marionettes. His remarkable 'The Love Song of St Sebastian' (written 1914) combines the story of the favourite Uranian saint with Wilde's *Salome* and with the leitmotif of *The Ballad*. 'The Love Song of J. Alfred Prufrock' (1915) is perhaps equally Wildean. This is a poem with a Speaker who wishes 'to have squeezed the universe into a ball', a line which distinctly echoes the words of Wilde's Ernest in 'The Critic as Artist' when he accuses Gilbert of treating 'the world as if it were a crystal ball'.[70] Prufrock even presents his own head on a platter. Even the *Four Quartets* (1936–42) cannot help echoing Wilde and aestheticism. 'Burnt Norton' emphasizes the uncanny potential of Wilde's 'Jardin de Tuileries' and uses the Wildean trick of making the artist's sense of alienation and unreality seem universal.

> Go, said the bird, for the leaves were full of children,
> Hidden excitedly, containing laughter.
> Go, go, go, said the bird: human kind
> Cannot bear very much reality. (ll. 42–5)[71]

T.S. Eliot's juxtapositions of past and present, most notably in the collage of *The Waste Land* owe a great deal to Wilde's theories of the critic as artist who should go to previous art for his raw material and who should make the past live in his work, make the past part of the critical present. W.B. Yeats's poetry is close to Wilde's in its devotion to Beauty and Love, those ancient ideals that make one feel as 'hollow as the moon' ('Adam's Curse' [1903]). Yeats' *A Full Moon in March* (1935) is, of course, largely inspired by Wilde's *Salome* and indeed the very continuation of verse drama by both Yeats and Eliot is probably sustained by Wilde's belief in verse and in verse drama. When it comes to W.H. Auden, a poem such as 'As I Walked Out One Evening' (1937), with its dancing clichés, its thrilling proximity to the absurd and its ultimate hollowness, is not unlike Wilde's *Sphinx* combined with Wilde's love poems such as 'Her Voice' (1881). Auden was very dismissive of Wilde's poetry, but he acknowledged *The Importance of Being Earnest* as 'the only pure verbal opera in English'.[72] Fernando Pessoa owned and heavily annotated a copy of Wilde's poems in addition to many works by Wilde and his friends, even translating seventeen lines of *The Ballad* and writing a poem, in English, on Antinous. Over thirty of his manuscripts entries are about Wilde and many of his aphorisms are clearly inspired by Wilde. Hart Crane's first published poem was dedicated to C.3.3., Wilde's number while in prison. Olive Custance's poetry, like that of her husband, includes invocations of Wilde and of his poetry. Althea Gyles, the remarkable illustrator of many of Yeats's volumes of poetry and of Wilde's own 'Harlot's House', never saw her own poetic work published because she insisted on the dedication of her volume 'to the beautiful memory of Oscar Wilde'.[73]

All this is very suggestive of Wilde's elusive presence within twentieth-century poetry. Yet to argue that the value of Wilde's poems lies in paving the way for modernism (or anything else) is ultimately to argue beyond them or at least against Wilde's aesthetic intentions. It is not my intention to suggest that Wilde was a powerful poetic precursor, but simply that he was an enabling and inspiring presence in the lives of many artists, including major poets. Space here does not allow for a discussion of more than a few of Wilde's poems. As he wrote in defence of one of Douglas's sonnets, a poem should not be regarded as 'a corpse for a callous dissecting table, but as a flower to gild one grey moment'.[74] To analyze some of Wilde's poems might be to unravel their charm, which perhaps explains why it has so seldom been attempted. It is enough that they can blossom for us as flowers, unremarkable perhaps in their beauty, more precious for having been handled by Wilde, for having retained their youthfulness and joy.

Many of them have certainly blossomed in the electronic environment, such as in an animated version with the soundtrack of Henry Mancini's 'Love Theme from Romeo and Juliet' (1968) which is so like Wilde's 'Silentium Amoris' (1881). Wilde's poetry has been performed as rock music by musicians such as Gavin Friday in his Ballad of Reading Gaol (1989), or (surprisingly) as country music, as in Colin Rudd's versions of various poems including 'The Harlot's House' (2008), and even as classical music as in Elaine Fine's version of 'In The Gold Room' (2009) for flute, mezzo-soprano and piano and her 'Dances from The Harlot's House' (2008) for a string quartet.[75] A poem-well-read can almost materialize, as Oscar Wilde suggested in 'To My Wife: With A Copy of My Poems' (1893). The sustained attention to Wilde's poems, to their imagery and musicality, without attempting to form a theory about them or to explain them away with the help of biographical, intertextual or any other clues is the closest we can come perhaps to the artist's frame of mind. That is the sense of Wilde's observation that 'creation imitates', that the appreciative reader can only recreate the text in her mind. Yet the reading will only be of interest to the extent that it is different from the author's, to the extent that it becomes a new text, 'that need not bear any obvious resemblance to the thing it criticises. The one characteristic of a beautiful form is that one can put into it whatever one wishes, and see in it whatever one chooses to see.'[76]

I fear that the scholarly criticism of Wilde's poems (my own included) has not yet reached this level of creativity and remains too close to the various clues, sources and the 'textual evidence' – it seldom reaches the level of independence and independent value from its artistic source that Wilde envisaged for it. This may have something to do with the transformation of English literature into an academic subject around the time that Wilde's poetry was published and to the expectations of objectivity and pseudo-scientific jargon that have crippled literary criticism since. Instead of academic criticism being contaminated by the boldness and imaginativeness of art, many contemporary poets have become full-time academics, in the US especially, which boasts over 800 university level courses in creative writing. But that is the subject of a different article...

NOTES

1. Wilde's 'poems in prose' started as tales he invented for empathetic audiences. The vast majority of these was never written down or published by himself. Guillot de Saix's *Contes parlés d' Oscar Wilde* (Paris: Mercure de France, 1942) is the most extensive collection of reconstructed versions based on interviews with Wilde's contemporaries; the stories lack Wilde's textual authority and have been largely ignored by scholarship. The fullest English collection of Wilde's oral tales is *Table Talk* edited by Thomas Wright (London: Cassell, 2000). For an account of modern verse drama in English, see Denis Donoghue, *The Third Voice: Modern British and American Verse Drama* (Princeton, NJ: Princeton University Press, 1959).

2. Oscar Wilde, letter to the Editor of *The Times*, c. 1 March 1893, in *The Complete Letters of Oscar Wilde*, eds Merlin Holland and Rupert Hart-Davis (London: Fourth Estate, 2000), p.559.

3. Oscar Wilde, 'The Decay of Lying', in *The Complete Works of Oscar Wilde*, vol.4, Criticism, ed. Josephine Guy (Oxford: Oxford University Press, 2007), pp.86–7.

4. Horst Breuer, 'Oscar Wilde's Dorian Gray and Shakespeare's Sonnets', *English Language Notes*, 42, 2 (December 2004), pp.59–68.

5. Bernard Beatty, 'The Form of Oscar: Wilde's Art of Substitution', *Irish Studies Review*, 11, 1 (2003), p.33.

6. Ibid., pp.41, 43, 35.

7. Oscar Wilde, letter to Walter Hamilton, 29 January 1889, in *Letters*, p.390.

8. W.H. Auden, 'An Improbable Life', *New Yorker*, 39, 3 (9 March 1963). Reprinted in Richard Ellmann (ed.), *Oscar Wilde: A Collection of Critical Essays* (Englewood Cliffs, NJ: Prentice, 1969), p.118.

9. William Butler Yeats (ed.), 'Introduction', *The Oxford Book of Modern Verse: 1892–1935* (Oxford: Clarendon, 1936).

10. Jorge Luis Borges, 'A Poem by Oscar Wilde' (1925), trans. Suzanne Jill Levine. http://www.themodernword.com/borges/borges_wilde.html.

11. Fernando Pessoa, 'Concerning Oscar Wilde', manuscript fragment first published in *Selected Prose of Fernando Pessoa*, ed. and trans. Richard Zenith (New York: Grove Press, 2001), p.219.

12. Michael J. O'Neill, 'Irish Poets of the Nineteenth Century: Unpublished Lecture Notes of Oscar Wilde', *Irish University Review*, 1, 4 (Spring 1955), p.30.

13. Clarence Stedman, *Victorian Poets* (Boston, MA and New York: Houghton & Mifflin, 1901 [1876]), p.476.

14. Oscar Wilde, 'The Critic as Artist', in Guy (ed.), *The Complete Works of Oscar Wilde*, vol.4, *Criticism*, p.172.

15. All quotations from the poems are taken from *The Complete Works of Oscar Wilde*, Vol.1, *Poems and Poems in Prose*, eds Bobby Fong and Karl Beckson (Oxford: Oxford University Press, 2000). 'Helas', p.156.

16. ΓΛΥΚΥΠΙΡΟΣ · ΕΡΩΣ ·' 'Bittersweet Love', in *Poems*, p.127.

17. André Gide, *Pretexts; Reflections on Literature and Morality*, selected, edited and introduced by Justin O'Brien, trans. Angelo P. Bertocci and others (London: Secker & Warburg, 1959), p.126.

18. Oscar Wilde, letter to Grant Richards, June 1892, in *Letters*, pp.526–7.

19. J.O. Halliwell-Phillipps, *Outlines of the Life of Shakespeare* (London, 1881), p.110.

20. Oscar Wilde, letter to Reginald Turner, 10 August 1897, in *Letters*, p.924; Gregory Mackie, 'Publishing Notoriety: Piracy, Pornography and Oscar Wilde', *University of Toronto Quarterly*, 73, 4 (Fall 2004), pp.980–90.

21. J.M. Stuart-Young, *Out of Hours: Poems, Lyrics and Sonnets* (London: Stockwell, 1909). A few other poems in this collection that focuses on Uranian love are dedicated to Oscar Wilde such as 'In Memory of S.M.' and 'A Dead Poet'; Wilde, 'The Critic as Artist, Part II', p.195.

22. Fernando Pessoa, *Antinous* (Lisbon: Monteiro, 1918), www.gutenberg.org/etext/24262.

23. See Patricia Pulham, 'Tinted and Tainted Love: The Sculptural Body in Olive Custance's Poetry', *Yearbook of English Studies*, 37, 1 (2007), p.174.

24. Hart Crane, 'C. 3. 3.' (1916), in Langdon Hammer (ed.), *Complete Poems and Selected Letters* (New York: Library of America, 2006), p.61.

25. Brian Reed, *Hart Crane: After His Lights* (Tuscaloosa, AL: University of Alabama Press, 2006), p.45.

26. Thomas Wright, *Death in Genoa*, audio play, *The Independent*, 4 December 2009, www.independent.co.uk.

27. Donald E. Hall, 'An Introductory Dialogue: "Is there a Queer Ethics?"', *Victorian Poetry*, 38, 4 (Winter 2000), p.467.

28. John Simon, 'Wilde the Poet', in *Dreamers of Dreams: Essays on Poets and Poetry* (London: Ivan R. Dee, 2001), p.66.

29. Ibid., p.65.

30. Patricia Flanagan Behrendt, *Oscar Wilde: Eros and Aesthetics* (New York: St Martin's Press, 1991).

31. Melissa Knox, *A Long and Lovely Suicide* (New Haven, CT and London: Yale University Press, 1994).

32. Theo McMahon, 'The Tragic Deaths in 1871 in County Monaghan of Emily and Mary Wilde – Half-Sisters of Oscar Wilde', *Clogher Record*, 18, 1 (2003), pp.129–45.

33. Ibid.

34. Manuscript versions of poems are published in Bobby Fong, 'The Poetry of Oscar Wilde: A Critical Edition' (unpublished Ph.D. thesis, University of California, Los Angeles, 1978, UMI).

35. 'Roses and Rue', *Poems*, p.121.

36. 'Sonnet on the Sale by Auction of Keats' Love Letters', *Poems*, p.166.

37. *The Ballad of Reading Gaol*, *Poems*, pp.210, 215.

38. *The Picture of Dorian Gray* (1891), in *The Complete Works of Oscar Wilde*, vol. 3, ed. Joseph Bristow (Oxford: Oxford University Press, 2005), p.167.

39. Wilde, 'The Critic as Artist: Part I', p.158.

40. 'Apologia', *Poems*, p.123.

41. E.A. Poe, Review of Henry Wadsworth Longfellow's *Ballads and Other Poems*, in *Graham's Lady's and Gentleman's Magazine*, 20 (1842), p.249.

42. Stuart-Young, *Out of Hours*, p.vi.

43. Wilde, 'The Critic as Artist: Part II', p.188.

44. Wilde, *The Picture of Dorian Gray*, p.167.

45. Richard Ellmann, *Oscar Wilde* (Harmondsworth: Penguin, 1988), p.108.

46. Wilde, 'The Critic as Artist: Part I', p.147.

47. Wilde, 'The Decay of Lying', p.95.

48. William Wordsworth, 'Preface', in William Wordsworth and Samuel Taylor Coleridge, *Lyrical Ballads*, ed. R.L. Brett and Alun R. Jones (London: Routledge, 1991), p.266.

49. Stephen Matterson and Darryl Jones, *Studying Poetry* (London: Arnold, 2000), pp.53–6.

50. Wilde, 'The Critic as Artist: Part II', p.130.

51. Arthur Ransome, *Oscar Wilde: A Critical Study* (London: Secker, 1912); Nicholas Frankel, '"Ave Imperatrix": Oscar Wilde and the Poetry of Englishness', *Victorian Poetry*, 35, 2 (1997), pp.117–37; Ian Small, 'Introduction', *The Complete Works of Oscar Wilde*, volume 1, *Poems and Poems in Prose*, pp.ix–xxvi; Isobel Murray, 'Introduction', *Oscar Wilde: Complete Poetry*, ed. Isobel Murray (Oxford: Oxford World's Classics, 1998), pp.ix–xvi; Averil Gardner, '"Literary Petty Larceny": Plagiarism in Oscar Wilde's Early Poetry', *English Studies in Canada*, 8, 1 (1982), pp.49–61.

52. Leslie White, 'Wilde, Browning and the "New Obscurity"', *English Literature in Transition*, 42 (1999), pp.4–22.

53. Oscar Wilde, 'The Apostle of Beauty in Nova Scotia', *Halifax Morning Herald*, 10 October 1882, p.2, quoted in 'Walt Whitman and Oscar Wilde: A Biographical Note', *Walt Whitman Quarterly Review*, 25 (Winter 2008), p.116.

54. Dimitrie Anghel, 'Oscar Wilde', in *Versuri si proza* (Albatros: Bucuresti, 1989), p.104; Oscar Wilde, letter to Stéphane Mallarmé, November 1891, in *Letters*, p.492; Stéphane Mallarmé, letter to Oscar Wilde, 10 November 1891, in *Letters*, p.492.

55. Oscar Wilde, 'A Note on Some Modern Poets', *Woman's World* (December 1888), in *Oscar Wilde: Selected Journalism*, ed. Anya Clayworth (Oxford: Oxford World's Classics, 2004), p.146.

56. Wilde, 'The Decay of Lying', p.81; Wilde, *The Picture of Dorian Gray*, p.204.

57. ΓΛΥΚΥΠΙΡΟΣ · ΕΡΩΣ ·' 'Bittersweet Love', *Poems*, p.127.

58. Wilde, 'A Note on Some Modern Poets', p.141.

59. 'The Burden of Itys', *Poems*, p.61.

60. Wilde, 'The Decay of Lying', p.85.

61. Wilde, 'The Critic as Artist: Part II', p.178.

62. 'The New Helen', Poems, pp.106–9.

63. 'Impression: II La Fuite de la Lune', Poems, p.155.

64. Quoted in full in Stuart Mason, Bibliography of Oscar Wilde (London: T. Werner Laurie, 1914), p.83.

65. T. S. Eliot, 'Tradition and the Individual Talent', in The Sacred Wood: Essays on Poetry and Criticism (London: Methuen, 1920), p.54.

66. Oscar Wilde, 'Lotus Leaves', The Irish Monthly, 5 (1877), p.134.

67. Robert L. Peters, 'Whistler and the English Poets of the 1890s', Modern Language Quarterly, 18 (1957), pp.251–61 (p.253).

68. 'Le Jardin des Tuileries', Poems, p.159.

69. See Richard Ellmann, Yeats: The Man and the Masks (New York: Macmillan, 1948) and Mariana de Castro, 'Oscar Wilde, Fernando Pessoa and the Art of Lying', Portuguese Studies, 22, 2 (2006), pp.219–49. For Wilde's influence on T.S. Eliot's poetry and critical theory, see Ronald Bush, 'In Pursuit of Wilde Possum', Modernism/Modernity, 11, 3 (September 2004), pp.469–85 and T. S. Eliot, Inventions of The March Hare: Poems 1909–1917, ed. Christopher Ricks (London: Faber, 1996).

70. Wilde, 'The Critic as Artist: Part I', p.147.

71. T.S. Eliot, 'Burnt Norton', in Collected Poems 1909–1962 (London: Faber and Faber, 1963), p.190.

72. Auden, 'An Improbable Life', p.136.

73. Quoted in Karl Beckson, 'Introduction', Oscar Wilde: The Critical Heritage (London: Routledge, 1970), p.18.

74. Oscar Wilde, letter to Stanley V. Makower, 14 October 1897, in Letters, p.960.

75. Gavin Friday, Each Man Kills the Thing He Loves (Island Records, 1989), Elaine Fine's Thematic Catalog http://thematiccatalog.blogspot.com/; for the other interpretations of Wilde's poetry, see www.youtube.com.

76. Wilde, 'The Critic as Artist: Part I', p.159.

CHAPTER FOUR

Oscar Wilde's Short Fiction: The Hermeneutics of Storytelling

ANNE MARKEY

Oscar Wilde's short fiction, consisting of the thirteen stories contained in The Happy Prince and Other Tales (1888), Lord Arthur Savile's Crime
and Other Stories (1891), A House of Pomegranates (1891), as well as 'The
Portrait of Mr. W.H.' (1889), has until recently received less critical consideration than other elements of his literary output.[1] Since the 1990s,
however, there has been a noticeable upsurge of interest in these texts,
as critics have argued for their importance both in their own right and for
the insights they provide into Wilde's other works. A survey of existing
criticism shows that it usually supports a more general argument or
particular biographical approach to Wilde's life or work, such as his
sexuality, spirituality or the importance of his Irish background to an
appreciation of his writing. So, for example, John-Charles Duffy
explored 'Gay-Related Themes in the Fairy Tales of Oscar Wilde' while
Elizabeth Goodenough placed the same stories within the context of
widespread Victorian speculation about the divinity of Christ.[2] Maureen
O'Connor, by contrast, arguing for 'recognition of a particular strain of
subversive Anglo-Irish literature reaching from Edgeworth to Wilde',
claimed that Wilde's recourse to the form of the fairy tale 'carried a
considerable political and cultural charge'.[3] In addition to attracting a
range of varying interpretations, Wilde's short fiction has also been
explored in relation to his other work; Josephine Guy and Ian Small
compared the three collections of stories to The Picture of Dorian Gray
(1890), while Lawrence Danson considered 'The Portrait of Mr. W.H.' in

relation to Wilde's critical writings. By providing valuable, sometimes complementary, sometimes conflicting, readings of the short fiction, existing criticism points to the complexity of what constitutes a significant aspect of Wilde's literary legacy. This critical diversity also suggests that interpretation, an issue central to Wilde's own developing aesthetic, is an equally significant concept in relation to the production and reception of his stories. Indeed, the short fiction can be regarded as a coherent body of work in which Wilde explored his ongoing artistic and personal preoccupations through a prismatic emphasis on the hermeneutics of storytelling.

Wilde's short fiction was published during the period between 1887 and 1891, when the author was establishing a reputation as a provocative critical thinker but before he achieved popular success as a playwright. As his stories investigate apparent oppositions – such as illusion and reality, honesty and deceit, love and desire – that resurface in his other work, Wilde's manipulation of familiar modes of writing within his short fiction provides early evidence of his continuing thematic preoccupations and innovative approach to form. So, in his hands, the fairy tale variously becomes a vehicle for the valorisation of childhood vision or the vindication of decadent desire, while the protean form of the short story, still an emergent genre at the end of the nineteenth century, lends itself to creative mimicry of literary criticism in 'The Portrait of Mr. W.H.', and parodic use as social satire in Lord Arthur Savile's Crime and Other Stories.[4] As he draws on, parodies and transforms narrative structures as diverse as the oral folktale, the French conte, and Victorian ghost and detective stories, Wilde's short fiction illustrates an inventive approach to literary genre, influence and interpretation. Simultaneously, it reveals that the muddle, misery and mystery of human existence cannot be reduced to neat abstractions or made to fit conventional formulas. Illuminating his highly individual concern with the relationship between art and life, Wilde's stories consistently probe and collapse other oppositions, including surface and depth, selflessness and selfishness, sin and redemption, to show that one element always reflects and depends on the other. Although each individual story provokes contemplation of at least some of these complex relationships, taken as a whole Wilde's short fiction celebrates the indubitable power of storytelling but draws attention to the unpredictable nature of interpretation.

By concentrating on the stories themselves, rather than on their documented and indisputable similarities to his other work, the ensuing discussion of the contents of the three collections, and of the version of 'The Portrait of Mr. W.H.' that appeared during Wilde's lifetime, will show that claim to be justified. Even the order in which these fictions were published testifies to their complementary complexity. That order might seem straightforward, given that May 1888 witnessed the publication of The Happy Prince and Other Tales, with 'The Portrait of Mr. W.H.' appearing in the July 1889 edition of Blackwood's Magazine, while Lord Arthur Savile's Crime and Other Stories was published two years later in July 1891, and A House of Pomegranates appeared four months later in November 1891. On the basis of these dates, Wilde apparently began composing literary fairy tales, before progressing through experimentation with critical fiction to social satire, finally reverting to the fairy tale again – a circular, experimental journey of which the origin proved to be the terminus. Closer inspection, though, reveals the situation to be more complicated than might first appear, as these dates neither reflect the sequence in which Wilde composed his stories nor the order in which they first became available to the reading public.

Periodical publication during the first six months of 1887 of the four narratives that would later make up Lord Arthur Savile's Crime and Other Stories (1891) preceded the appearance of The Happy Prince and Other Tales (1888): 'The Canterville Ghost' appeared in the February-March 1887 editions of The Court and Society Review; 'The Sphinx without a Secret' (under its original title of 'Lady Alroy') was published in The World in May 1887; 'Lord Arthur Savile's Crime' also appeared in May 1887 in The Court and Society Review, while 'The Model Millionaire' was published in The World in June 1887. Richard Ellmann reports that Wilde first told 'The Happy Prince' in November 1885 to a group of Cambridge students whose enthusiastic response prompted him to write it down.[5] He promptly submitted a written version of the story for publication in the English Illustrated Magazine, but later reported that it had 'languished in the magazine chest' for eighteen months before being finally returned in time to become the title story of Wilde's first collection of short fiction, published in 1888.[6] Having commenced work in October 1887 on a story 'connected with Shakespeare's Sonnets', Wilde rehearsed it on friends and acquaintances, including the artists Charles Ricketts and Charles Shannon and the politicians Arthur Balfour and Herbert Asquith, before submitting it for publication in Blackwood's Magazine in April 1889.[7] Published in the July edition, 'The Portrait of Mr. W.H.' was also scheduled for inclusion in a proposed new series of Tales from Blackwood's, a suggestion to which Wilde initially agreed before withdrawing his assent, proposing instead that William Blackwood 'bring it out in a special volume of essays and studies by me'.[8] Although Blackwood declared himself very happy to consider this proposal, the volume never appeared. Wilde went on to publish Intentions (1891), a collection of previously published critical essays, while he set about revising and expanding 'The Portrait of Mr. W.H.', transforming what had originally been conceived and published as a short story into a much longer text, which was announced for publication by Elkin Mathews and John Lane at the end of 1893.[9] Meanwhile, Wilde undertook minor revisions of the previously published stories that appeared in Lord Arthur Savile's Crime and Other Stories and A House of Pomegranates (1891). 'The Young King', the opening story in Wilde's second collection of fairy tales, had been published in the December issue of The Lady's Pictorial in 1888, while 'The Birthday of the Infanta', the third story in the collection, first appeared as 'The Birthday of the Little Princess' and 'La Naissance de la petite Princesse' in both the French- and English-language editions of Paris Illustré on 30 March 1889. That year too, Wilde was working on 'The Fisherman and his Soul', as he offered it for publication in Lippincott's Magazine to J.M. Stoddart in August 1889, although it did not appear in printed form until its appearance in A House of Pomegranates over two years later.[10]

Convoluted as this outline of the gestation and publication history of the short fiction may appear, close attention to detail amply repays the effort involved, as it reveals that between 1885, when he first delivered an oral version of 'The Happy Prince', and 1891, the year which marked the publication of two very different collections of his stories, Wilde was involved in continual, eclectic experimentation with various forms of short fiction. As early as 1948, Robert Merle drew attention to the significance of the disparity between the sequence of the original publication of Wilde's short fiction and its appearance in volume form.[11] In Merle's view, though, that significance lay in how the symbolism of the pessimistic stories in *A House of Pomegranates* reflected their author's ashamed awareness of his increasingly transgressive sexuality.[12] While aspects of Wilde's experience indubitably informed his literary output, resisting the temptation to read the work through the prism of the life more fruitfully focuses attention on the texts themselves. That Wilde was conscious of, albeit ambivalent about, the importance of chronology to the interpretation of literary works is evinced by the central role played by precise dating in the exposition of Cyril Graham's theory concerning the identification of the dedicatee of Shakespeare's sonnets in 'The Portrait of Mr W.H.'. There, Cyril refers to the historical record to argue convincingly that as the sonnets were written in the years immediately preceding Shakespeare's acquaintanceship with William Herbert, the third Earl of Pembroke could not have been the young man by whom the poems were inspired and to whom they were addressed. Although the story proceeds to satirize a type of literary analysis that relies on external evidence, the insistence on rejecting anachronistic conclusions is never debunked. In relation to Wilde's fiction, careful attention to chronology reveals that during the years in question, far from embarking on a circular journey that began and ended with the apparently simple form of the fairy tale, Wilde consciously and consistently adapted and transformed familiar narrative templates for his own artistic purposes.

The differences between the tone and complexity of the stories contained in *The Happy Prince and Other Tales* and *A House of Pomegranates* testify to the contrasting ways in which he approached the form of the fairy tale, imbuing it with unexpected resonances while suffusing it with surprising interpretative possibilities. His ongoing critical engagement with the fairy tale and his concurrent commitment to the manipulation of other forms of short fiction provided Wilde with a variety of approaches to themes that resurface in disparate guises in his work. So, for example, while the influence of fate on the actions of the individual is handled in humorous fashion in 'Lord Arthur Savile's Crime', a parody of the popular genre of the detective story in which Wilde subverts the Victorian notion of duty, that same theme is treated in more sombre vein in 'The Young King', where heredity and destiny shape the protagonist's maturation from callow youth to majestic ruler. Both 'The Selfish Giant' and 'The Canterville Ghost' deal with the redemptive potential of an innocent child, albeit with varying emphases and with different results. Perhaps most tellingly of all, both 'The Devoted Friend' and 'The Portrait of Mr W. H.' engage with the theme of interpretation, with the fairy tale suggesting that the relationship between art and life is arbitrary while the critical story recounts the tragic effects of confusing the two. Overall, then, Wilde's short fiction testifies to an appreciation of the power of storytelling of all types and so can be read as a vindication of the imaginative, rather than mimetic, function of art.

Given that the four stories that would later be included in *Lord Arthur Savile's Crime and Other Stories* appeared in periodical form before the publication of *The Happy Prince and Other Tales*, the two volumes may have more in common than has generally been recognized. Contemporary reaction to Wilde's first collection of fairy tales, which was muted but generally favourable, emphasized the distinctiveness of the author's approach to form, while nonetheless detecting similarities between the contents of the volume and other popular examples of the genre. Early reviewers did not consider thematic similarities between Wilde's fairy tales and the author's previously published fiction, most probably because short fiction, which appeared in popular periodicals, seldom attracted much critical attention.[13] Having identified a superficial similarity between Wilde's style and that of Hans Christian Andersen, the Danish writer whose acclaimed fairy tales were first translated into English in 1846, one commentator remarked on 'a piquant touch of contemporary satire which differentiates Mr Wilde from the teller of pure fairy tales'.[14] Another critic claimed that the collection would not appeal to a child reader: 'Children do not care for satire, and the dominant spirit of these stories is satire – a bitter satire differing widely from that of Hans Andersen'.[15] Early critics, then, liked the volume, but were aware that its contents were not easily reconciled with contemporary perceptions of the fairy tale as a genre suited to the Victorian nursery.

Although Regina Gagnier claimed that Wilde's fairy tales 'reek of middle-class virtue and sentimentality', many recent critics agree with the contemporary identification of satire as a characteristic of the contents of *The Happy Prince and Other Tales*, concurring with Jack Zipes's categorization of the stories as subversive texts that cast a caustic eye on Victorian moral complacencies.[16] Critical opinion, though, is more divided on the related issues of the reasons behind Wilde's choice of the fairy tale form and the question of intended audience. As Wilde himself was ambivalent about his ideal reader, originally stating that the collection was 'really meant for children', and later claiming that it was 'meant partly for children, and partly for those who have kept the childlike faculties of wonder and joy', the lack of contemporary and later critical consensus on this question is relatively unsurprising.[17] Wilde is drawing his understanding of the 'childlike', at least in part, from George MacDonald, who claimed that he did 'not write for children, but for the childlike, whether of five, or fifty, or seventy five'.[18] Nevertheless, the link between the child reader and the fairy tale remained tenacious, despite the fact that many Victorian examples of the genre, including Charles Kingsley's *The Water Babies* (1863), and William Thackeray's *The Rose and the Ring* (1855), addressed a dual audience.

Recent critics also differ on the reasons behind Wilde's choice of literary form. Jack Zipes identified several factors 'that led Wilde to turn his attention to the writing of fairy tales', amongst them Wilde's recent experience of fatherhood and acknowledgement 'of his homosexual inclinations', as well as a general renaissance of English interest in the genre during the closing decades of the nineteenth century.[19] Drawing attention to Sir William and Lady Wilde's mutual interest in Irish folk-lore, Jerusha McCormack, in turn, suggested that Wilde, 'in publishing his tales, [was] associating himself with such Protestant nationalists as his parents, Lady Gregory, William Butler Yeats and John Synge' but claimed that 'the stories were not so much composed for children – as for Wilde himself ... not as Irishman, not as father, but as a lover of other men'.[20] In similar vein, John-Charles Duffy, acknowledging that the stories explore other themes, argued that the general perception of the fairy tale as an innocuous and irreproachable literary form facilitated covert 'meditations on Wilde's first homosexual experiences'.[21] Other critics have drawn on post-colonial theory to echo McCormack's linkage of Wilde's Irish background and choice of literary form. Maureen O'Connor, for instance, claimed that Wilde 'paradoxically counter[s] and invert[s] the infantilization of the Irish by wilfully inhabiting and deploying it through genre, suggesting the possibility of subverting and transforming repressive authority from "below"'.[22] Clearly, *The Happy*

Prince and Other Tales raises interesting questions about the significance of the relationship between form, content and meaning.

Nevertheless, critics generally agree about the collection's central focus on the related and variously presented themes of selfishness and selflessness, sin and redemption, sacrifice and self-aggrandisement. In the title story, sacrifice is divinely rewarded when God decrees that 'in my garden of Paradise this little bird will sing for evermore, and in my city of gold, the Happy Prince shall praise me'.[23] In 'The Nightingale and the Rose', by contrast, sacrifice is linked not to redemption but to artistic creation as the Christ-like bird, inspired by her belief in a love 'more precious than emeralds', dies while creating a beautiful red rose.[24] As Christ, in the form of a little boy, repays the once selfish giant's generosity with the promise of paradise, Wilde contrasts selfish sinfulness with divinely rewarded selflessness. Undercutting this apparently conventional moral, the two final stories explore the advantages of egotism. In 'The Devoted Friend', the Miller thrives on the exploitation of his hapless neighbour, so never rejects his selfish ways. The remarkable rocket, for his part, blithely ignoring all evidence of his lack of importance in the greater scheme of things, expires convinced that he has made a great sensation. Overall, then, while the stories suggest that sacrifice is preferable to self-aggrandisement, selfishness is ultimately shown to bring its own, solipsistic rewards.

Storytelling, too, is shown to produce unexpected effects, as the contents of *The Happy Prince and Other Tales* reveal a pervasive fascination with narrative authority. The prolific and persistent invocation of other texts within the five stories testifies to the power of influence on literary creation. In addition to the obvious allusion to Andersen in the person of the little match girl who features in 'The Happy Prince', the figure of the weary seamstress in that story recalls her suffering predecessor in Thomas Hood's 'The Song of the Shirt' (1843). The Charity Children, meanwhile, resemble their counterparts in William Blake's 'Holy Thursday' (1789), where their innocent radiance contrasts with the pitiless wisdom of their ancient guardians. Echoing the opening lines of Percy Bysshe Shelley's *Queen Mab* (1813), the swallow's description of death as the brother of sleep invokes an intertext that criticizes corrupt, tyrannical political systems. His accounts of the marvels of Egypt reflect the widespread European fascination with the oriental birthplace of *The Arabian Nights* and a more particular knowledge of Théophile Gautier's poem, 'Ce que disent les hirondelles' (1852), thus introducing an exotic, decadent note into a story whose primary concern seems to be with the vindication of Christian ethics. 'The Nightingale and the Rose', in turn, not only evokes the Greek myth of Philomela, but also simultaneously engages with John Keats's investigation of life, death and art in 'Ode to a Nightingale' (1819). These varied intertextual allusions, interwoven with the fabric of Wilde's fairy tales, greatly add to their aesthetic complexity, thus complicating their interpretation.

These evocative allusions to other texts are enhanced, in turn, by an insistent exploration of the nature, function and effects of storytelling. In 'The Happy Prince', for example, the swallow's tales of the wonders of Egypt are initially juxtaposed with the Prince's accounts of the suffering of the inhabitants of the city, so that storytelling sets up an opposition between the allure of the exotic and the misery of the mundane. Later, that opposition is collapsed when the swallow decides to stay with the Prince but continues to regale him with descriptions 'of what he had seen in strange lands', so that storytelling now provides comfort and distraction from harsh reality.[25] The relationship between storytelling and life is further investigated in 'The Devoted Friend', where hermeneutic speculation, flagged by the title, suffuses both the framing narrative and the embedded moral tale. Who is the devoted friend: Hans, who acts the part, or the Miller, who claims the title for himself? If language can support more than one fixed meaning, then interpretation, too, must remain indeterminate. Wilde's ironic treatment of the exploitative Miller, whose noble ideas are at odds with his actual behaviour, highlights the gaps between language and action, theory and praxis. When the linnet learns that a tale told for ethical effect may not achieve its expected result, the narrator agrees that telling a story with a moral is 'always a very dangerous thing to do'.[26] In playfully stressing the disparity between authorial intention and biased interpretation, Wilde transforms a fairy tale about selflessness into a self-reflexive allegory on narrative function and effect. Throughout the collection as a whole, storytelling is shown to be a complex form of interaction whose outcome is impossible to predict because interpretation is invariably subjective.

Storytelling and the related issue of interpretation are central to the plot of 'The Portrait of Mr. W.H.' in both its original and expanded forms.[27] As Lawrence Danson observed, 'most of Wilde's readers then and now think they know exactly what it says: that Shakespeare, like Oscar Wilde, loved boys and acted on that love'.[28] As Danson astutely implies, both versions of the story defy such simplistic explication.[29] Indeed, as Horst Schroeder has demonstrated, the vast majority of contemporary reviews did not discuss the piece 'from the point of view of morality, or rather immorality, but in the first place from the point of view of Shakespearean criticism'.[30] The story revolves around a theory devised by Cyril Graham, recounted by his friend Erskine, and developed by the unnamed narrator, that Shakespeare's sonnets were inspired by, and addressed to, an Elizabethan boy-actor named Willie Hughes. Combining the known facts of Shakespeare's life and milieu with a careful reading of the sonnets themselves, Cyril becomes convinced that he has discovered 'the true meaning of the poems'.[31] That true meaning lies in the story they tell of the relationship between the poet and the putative boy actor. Encouraged by Erskine to find independent evidence that would place the existence of Willie Hughes beyond doubt, Cyril resorts to fraud, committing suicide when the deception is discovered. Like the nightingale who was prepared to die for the sake of love, 'Cyril Graham sacrificed his life to a great idea', and the narrator is determined that his martyrdom and faith should be remembered and vindicated.[32] As Erskine relates the sad account of Cyril's short life and of his own affection for the beautiful young man to the sensitive narrator, who becomes haunted by the memory of the dead youth and convinced of the veracity of his theory, stories merge. Willie Hughes becomes 'as real a person as Shakespeare', and the presence of this Elizabethan spirit not only invades Erskine's Victorian library but also takes possession of the narrator's mind.[33]

Combing Shakespeare's poetry for proof of the existence of the boy-actor, he frustratingly finds himself 'always on the brink of absolute verification', but ultimately decides that Willie Hughes is nothing more that 'a mere myth, an idle dream, the boyish fancy of a young man'.[34] Erskine, though, influenced by the narrator's passion, just as he was previously swayed by his dead friend's enthusiasm, comes to believe 'that Willie Hughes is an absolute reality'.[35] When he, in turn, fails to verify the Willie Hughes theory, Erskine writes to the narrator, telling him of his intention to kill himself for the sake of the truth of what he now sees as a heroic cause. This proposed act of martyrdom turns out to be another fraud when his death, which takes place shortly afterwards, is revealed to be the result of consumption rather than suicide. By interlinking the story of Erskine and his friends with a literary theory on the significance of Shakespeare's sonnets, 'The Portrait of Mr. W.H.' presents interpretation as both an ethically dubious aesthetic practice and a potentially fatal obsession. The narrator's concluding reflection that 'there is really a great deal to be said for the Willie Hughes theory' underlines the impossibility of ever discrediting or proving any particular textual exegesis.[36]

Interpretation of situations, as well the hermeneutics of storytelling, informs *Lord Arthur Savile's Crime and Other Stories*. Initial critical response to the volume was divided, with the *Graphic's* anonymous reviewer announcing that all four stories were excellent, while William Sharp opened his *Academy* review by observing that '*Lord Arthur Savile's* Crime, and its three companion stories, will not add to their author's reputation'. The *Graphic* critic singled out the title story for particular praise but Sharp found 'A Model Millionaire' to be 'much the best of the series'. W.B. Yeats, for his part, declared himself a little disappointed with the volume, noting: '"The Sphinx without a Secret" has a quaint if rather meagre charm; but "The Canterville Ghost" with its supernatural horseplay, and "The Model Millionaire", with its conventional motive, are unworthy of more than a passing interest.'[37] Yeats's and Sharp's low opinion of the volume has been reflected in recent criticism, which has tended to concentrate on individual stories, usually 'Lord Arthur Savile's Crime' and 'The Canterville Ghost', rather than on the collection as a coherent entity.[38] While this criticism usefully addresses issues as varied as Wilde's formulation of a theory of performance, reference to a widespread contemporary interest in spiritualism, engagement with social debates, recourse to parody, and manipulation of genre, it neglects the importance of the persistent emphasis on interpretation that provides a unifying theme within the collection as a whole.

'Lord Arthur Savile's Crime', subtitled 'A Study of Duty' for volume publication, explores the relationship between fate and individual responsibility by recounting the story of a young man whose life is changed by a chance encounter with a fortune-teller who foretells that he will commit murder before he marries the lovely Sybil Merton. The stories that Mr Podgers, a cheiromantist with dubious credentials, finds etched on the palms of his privileged clients cause a frisson in Lady Windermere's crowded, fashionable salon: 'when he told poor Lady Fermor, right out before every one, that she did not care a bit for music, but was extremely fond of musicians, it was generally felt that cheiromancy was a most dangerous science'.[39] Just as telling a story with a moral is always a dangerous thing to do, because the listener's response can never be accurately predicted, foretelling the future is a 'mad and monstrous' practice wrought with uncertainty because of its paradoxically unforeseen consequences.[40] When Mr Podgers recoils in horror from what he sees written on Lord Arthur's hand and provides the expectant audience with an abridged and censored account of what has been revealed to him, the young aristocrat is filled with desire to know the full story. On learning that murder 'is what the cheiromantist had seen there', Lord Arthur suffers the combined turmoil of mental confusion and moral hesitation until he interprets the unwelcome revelation as a call to duty.[41] Exegesis provides relief and impels him to action. Once he decides that it is his duty to murder someone, in line with the narrative and biological imperatives revealed by his hand, conventional ethical considerations mean nothing to Lord Arthur: 'The only question that seemed to trouble him was, whom to make away with; for he was not blind to the fact that murder, like the religions of the Pagan world, requires a victim as well as a priest.'[42] Convinced that his interpretation of Mr Podger's prediction is the correct one, he becomes increasingly frustrated when his various attempts at murder come to nothing, until he unexpectedly encounters the palm reader on a dark summer's night and throws him into the Thames, thereby leaving Lord Arthur free to live happily ever after. Although Mr Podgers is revealed, years later, to have been a dreadful impostor, Lord Arthur continues to credit cheiromancy for all the good things that life has brought him. While this unexpected twist calls the veracity of the fateful prophesy into question, the conclusion of 'Lord Arthur Savile's Crime' underlines the enduring power of interpretation, regardless of the reliability of the basis on which rest subjective readings of subsequent events. By suggesting that apparently inscrutable fate is little more than a dubious fiction, Wilde implies that individual volition, which depends upon personal exegesis, ultimately determines destiny.

In the 'The Sphinx without A Secret', interpretation is linked to an exploration of identity based on readings of characters and events that reflect cultural ideals and myths rather than actual circumstances. Employing the age-old, fictional device of the embedded narrative, a structuring device also found in 'The Portrait of Mr. W.H.' and 'The Devoted Friend', Wilde relates the story of Lord Gerald Murchison's obsession with the mysterious Lady Alroy, whom he first sees, then meets, then pursues with increasingly ardent devotion, driven ever onwards by his misinformed understanding of her motives and actions. Placing this enigmatic tale within the broad cultural context of Protestant suspicions of Catholicism, Jarlath Killeen describes Lady Alroy as 'the personification of the Scarlet Woman who wishes to seduce the Protestant gentleman into the clutches of Rome'.[43] By contrast, Nils Clausen's biographical approach to interpretation leads him to deduce that the narrator was leading the same type of double life as the author was pursuing at the time of the story's composition and that Lady Alroy's secret may well lie in an undisclosed intimate and loving relationship with another woman.[44] Both ingenious readings attest to the veracity of Bruce Bashford's claim that 'the story turns out to be more artful than it may appear'.[45]

Various cultural allusions add considerably to the complexity of this brief narrative and complicate its interpretation. The title invokes the mythical, Graeco-Egyptian figure of the enigmatic sphinx who sets a riddle and destroys everything around her until a solution is found. In this case, the solution is prosaic as Lady Alroy is finally decreed to be 'merely a Sphinx without a secret'.[46] Before that, though, she has been called 'the Gioconda in sables', an evocative description that refers to Leonardo da Vinci's famous portrait of the Mona Lisa, renowned for its depiction of a beautiful woman's mysterious half-smile.[47] Here, in a story subtitled 'An Etching', Wilde invokes a resonant visual image, lyrically described for a Victorian readership by Walter Pater in The Renaissance (1875), to suggest the disparity between an imaginative ideal and disappointing reality. Lady Alroy sees herself as a romantic heroine and devotes her energies to performing that role; the narrator, who plays the role of detached dandy and talks of the Sphinx and the Gioconda, suggests that life is shaped by images borrowed from art. As the artificial appearance of mystery is apparently stripped away, the story implies that construction of character is guided by conventional images so that the possibility of fixed, individual identity becomes nothing more than an elusive chimera. Echoing the conclusion of 'The Portrait of Mr. W. H.', Murchison's final comment, 'I wonder?', reasserts the mysterious power of suggestion by underlining the inconclusive nature of interpretation.

The two remaining tales in *Lord Arthur Savile's Crime and Other Stories* engage with the interplay between expectation, imaginative empathy and interpretation. Hughie Erskine discovers that the man posing for his artist friend is not the beggar man he took him to be when he gave him his last sovereign. Instead, the he turns out to be the model millionaire of the title who acts like a fairy godfather by giving Hughie a cheque for £10,000, thus enabling the relatively impoverished young man to marry his beloved Laura Merton. Here, imaginative empathy, guided by a conventional reading of a situation, results in a very fortuitous and unforeseen outcome. In 'The Canterville Ghost', conventional expectation is pitted against imaginative empathy so that interpretation becomes even more crucial to its outcome. Hiram B. Otis, the American Minister, a phlegmatic product of his New World upbringing, attaches no credence to ghost stories, and so initially dismisses reports that his recently acquired English country house is haunted. As the story progresses, he comes to recognize that his culturally conditioned expect-ations have been misleading. Faced with an accumulation of evidence, including mysterious red stains which magically reappear each evening on the floor, the sound of clanking metal in the corridor at night, and the appearance 'in the wan moonlight' of 'an old man of terrible aspect', Mr Otis, along with his wife and three sons, is left with little option but to interpret these signs as indisputable proof of the existence of the Canterville ghost.[48] This volte face, though, makes little difference to their pragmatic approach to life and the afterlife, as these members of the Otis family not only refuse to be frightened by the phantom but also belittle and terrify him, placidly cleaning the floor with Pinkerton's Champion Stain Remover, providing Tammany Rising Sun Lubricator for his creaking chains, and even dressing up as ghosts themselves. For his part, the increasingly dispirited ghost is forced to acknowledge that his understanding of the Otis family, based on his reading of Longfellow, has been misleading, as they show no 'respect for their national poet ... over whose graceful and attractive poetry he had himself whiled away many a weary hour'.[49] In order to gain a proper imaginative grasp of the new situation, he withdraws to a quiet room, where young Virginia Otis unexpectedly comes upon him. Judging his actions by conventional standards, she points out that killing one's wife is a terrible crime and initially feels little sympathy for the forlorn figure who is indeed an uxoricide, condemned to remain on earth until a little girl redeems him with her tears. When the ghost describes his suffering and tells Virginia of his desire to enter the beautiful garden of death, she is so moved by his account that she forgets her former, unforgiving interpretation of his actions and does all that she can to help him. Imaginative empathy casts a new light on his character, thus forcing a reappraisal of his situation and his story that changes both their lives forever.

Transformation lies at the heart of *A House of Pomegranates*, Wilde's second collection of fairy tales, echoing and complicating its predecessor's central concern with selfishness, selflessness, sin and redemption. As with the earlier volume, the nuanced investigation of these issues is accompanied by a celebration of the power of storytelling and a probing of the dangers of interpretation. With illustrations by Charles Ricketts and Charles Shannon,[50] the book was designed for a connoisseur adult reader but production problems resulted in a poor quality finish, to which early reviewers drew disapproving attention, and the volume was not a commercial success. Critics were equally disparaging about the stories, variously wondering if they were written as 'a deliberate provocation to the *bourgeois au front glabre* [the middle class man with the smooth forehead; i.e. an unthinking philistine]', criticizing what they called the '"fleshly" style of Mr Wilde's writing', and asking: 'Is *A House of Pomegranates* intended for a child's book?'[51] In response, Wilde claimed that 'in building this *House of Pomegranates* I had about as much intention of pleasing the British child as I had of pleasing the British public'. In his defence of the collection, Wilde invoked the shadow of Shakespeare, just as he did in the exposition of Cyril Graham's interpretative theory of the sonnets, this time alluding to *The Winter's Tale* to justify his personal theory of art: 'Mamilius is as entirely delightful as Caliban is entirely detestable, but neither the standard of Mamilius nor the standard of Caliban is my standard. No artist recognises any standard of beauty but that which is suggested by his own temperament.'[52] Artistic creation, Wilde claims, is not directed by external standards, however delightful or detestable they may be, but by the individual temperament of the artist.[53] Accordingly, all four stories explore the many facets of temperament, showing how it reflects experience, controls action and influences response.

On his arrival in court, the young king's temperament is influenced by heredity, through the commingling in his veins of royal and common blood, by his upbringing as a noble savage reared by a lowly peasant and his wife, and by the unexpected change of fortune that follows the dying king's acknowledgement of the handsome goatherd as heir to the throne. Filled with 'that strange passion for beauty that was destined to have so great an influence over his life', the youth revels in the beautiful fittings and lush furnishings of the palace, taking particular pleasure from the jewelled paraphernalia assembled for his forthcoming coronation.[54] Three dreams shatter his composure by laying bare the misery of those who toil to make his clothes, who drown while diving for pearls, and who sicken and die while searching for rubies. Each dream is both an embedded narrative and a story with a moral. Their cumulative power is demonstrated by the transformation they effect on the young King's temperament and by the way in which they redirect the framing narrative. Interpreting his dreams as cautionary tales, the young king renounces hedonism, embraces asceticism, and becomes a Christ-like figure by the end of the story.

The temperament of the Infanta is similarly shaped by heredity and upbringing. The neglected but indulged daughter of a father who prefers the company of his dead wife to that of his living child, the Infanta 'had all the Queen's pretty petulance of manner'.[55] This inherited predilection for selfishness is exacerbated by the little princess's immersion in the heartless values of the venal Spanish court. Into this corrupt but superficially charmed world stumbles the unlikely figure of the little dwarf, an ingénue who seems to have stepped from one of Voltaire's philosophical *contes* into the pages of Wilde's perverse fairy tale. When the princess throws him a white rose, 'partly for a jest and partly to tease him', the naive interloper misinterprets her motives and believes that she loves him.[56] On seeing his reflection for the first time, the realization of his ugliness leads to despair. Unlike the ugly duckling who discovers that he is really a swan, and unlike the Beast who regains his human form when kissed by Beauty, the little dwarf dies unloved, unchanged and unlamented. As he expires at her feet, the Infanta misinterprets the situation, believing that he is acting a part for her amusement. When the Chamberlain explains that the funny little dwarf will never dance again because his heart is broken, the Infanta cedes to this more convincing interpretation of the situation but responds disdainfully: '"For the future let those who come to play with me have no hearts", she cried, and she ran out into the garden.'[57] Just as the Miller construes the death of little Hans as an unfortunate occurrence because it prevents him from disposing of a useless wheelbarrow, the death of the dwarf merely discommodes the Infanta and confirms her heartless selfishness.

Throughout the volume as a whole, a fascination with the fallible process of interpretation is counterbalanced with an exploration of the power of storytelling. As the mermaid sings at the fisherman's command, the stories she weaves of the wonderful life of the sea-folk seduce her human listener. The captive so enchants her captor that he cuts loose his soul and joins her beneath the waves. Each year, the soul comes back to tempt him with marvellous accounts of his adventures on dry land. Eventually, the fisherman succumbs to this temptation, unable to resist the lure of the image of a dancing girl whom the soul has described in exotic, decadent terms. Abandoning the mermaid, he searches in vain for the elusive dancer and falls prey to the evil urgings of his malevolent soul. Later repenting his betrayal of his beloved, the fisherman returns to the sea only to find her dead body on the shore. Now storytelling becomes redemptive: 'And to the dead thing he made confession. Into the shells of its ears he poured the harsh wine of his tale.'[58] When his drowned corpse is found clasping the body of the little mermaid, the two are buried in unhallowed ground of the Fullers' Field. Three years later, the strange and beautiful flowers that blossom there are used to adorn the altar of God. In 'The Star-Child', storytelling is less integral to the construction of plot than to the evocation of atmosphere. The opening account of the woodland animals transports the reader into the type of forest landscape associated with familiar folktales such as 'Hansel and Gretel'. The account of the protagonist's transformation draws on the conventions of hagiography as it echoes details of the life of St Francis of Assisi, of whom Wilde wrote: 'He understood Christ, and so he became like him'.[59] Allusions to Gustave Flaubert's version of the medieval legend of St Julian, 'La Légende de St Julien l'Hospitalier' (1877), combine with biblical echoes to imbue Wilde's story with resonant spirituality. When the Star-child dies, worn out by suffering, 'he who came after ruled evilly'.[60] This final sentence in Wilde's last published collection of short fiction punctures any hope of a magical happy ending, so that the relationship between storytelling and life is shown to be reciprocally unsettling.

Wilde's short fiction, in all its variety, testifies to the eclecticism of its author's approach to storytelling and reveals the complex, composite character of his thought and temperament. Given that seven of the four-teen stories first appeared in the periodical press and that Wilde's letters, reviews and critical writings provide evidence only of his views on the aesthetic potential of the fairy tale, rather than short fiction in general, Ian Small's conclusion that the transition to writing such fiction represented a desire to establish a literary career 'attuned to the twin imperatives of creative and commercial success' seems justified.[61] While commercial imperatives may have influenced Wilde's decision to write fairy tales and short stories, his manipulation of narrative form ensured that his creativity was not overshadowed by literary convention. The emphasis on temperament in his defence of A House of Pomegranates is significant because it suggests that the various forms of short fiction allowed him to explore several facets of his own artistic personality. He tried out different voices, all of them his own but all of them containing echoes of other voices, in his short fiction. As a result, allusions to other texts and narrative traditions imbue his stories with subliminal echoes that complicate interpretation, while an ongoing exploration of the power of storytelling confirms Wilde's attachment to that process. His short fiction can be seen as a form of dialogue, wherein control of meaning passes between author and reader, producing varied and valid interpretations that are nonetheless always subject to review and revision. Although this claim could equally be made of Wilde's other writings and those of other authors, the pervasive emphasis on storytelling and interpretation that connects the individual stories reveals the short fiction to be a coherent, if not distinctive, body of work that provides its own valuable insights into the multidimensional character of Wilde's creative genius.

APPENDIX – CHRONOLOGY OF WILDE'S SHORT FICTION

1885

November: Wilde tells an early version of 'The Happy Prince' to a group of students in Cambridge, after which he unsuccessfully offers it for publication in the *English Illustrated Magazine*.

1887

February/March: 'The Canterville Ghost' is published in *The Court and Society Review*.

May: 'Lady Alroy' (later 'The Sphinx without a Secret') is published in *The World*.
'Lord Arthur Savile's Crime' appears in *The Court and Society Review*.

June: 'The Model Millionaire' is published in *The World*.

October: Wilde starts work on a story connected with Shakespeare's Sonnets that will become 'The Portrait of Mr. W. H.'.

1888

May: *The Happy Prince and other Tales* (containing 'The Happy Prince', 'The Nightingale and the Rose', 'The Selfish Giant', 'The Devoted Friend', and 'The Remarkable Rocket') is published.

December: 'The Yong King' appears in *The Lady's Pictorial*.

1889

March: 'The Birthday of the Little Princess' (later 'The Birthday of the Infanta') is published in *Paris Illustré*.

July: 'The Portrait of Mr. W. H.' appears in *Blackwood's Magazine*.

August: Wilde offers 'The Fisherman and his Soul' for publication in *Lippincott's Magazine*.

1891

July: *Lord Arthur Savile's Crime and Other Stories* (in addition to the title story containing 'The Sphinx without a Secret', 'The Canterville Ghost', and 'The Model Millionaire') is published.

November: *A House of Pomegranates* ('The Young King', 'The Birthday of the Infanta', 'The Fisherman and his Soul', and 'The Star-Child') is published.

NOTES

1. *The Happy Prince and Other Tales* (1888), contained five stories – 'The Happy Prince', 'The Nightingale and the Rose', 'The Selfish Giant', 'The Devoted Friend' and 'The Remarkable Rocket'; *Lord Arthur Savile's Crime and Other Stories* (1891) contained four stories – 'Lord Arthur Savile's Crime', 'The Sphinx without a Secret', 'The Canterville Ghost' and 'The Model Millionaire'; *A House of Pomegranates* (1891) also contained four stories – 'The Young King', 'The Birthday of the Infanta', 'The Fisherman and his Soul', and 'The Star Child'.

2. John Charles Duffy, 'Gay-Related Themes in the Fairy Tales of Oscar Wilde', *Victorian Literature and Culture*, 29, 2 (2001) pp.327–49; Elizabeth Goodenough, 'Oscar Wilde, Victorian Fairy Tales, and the Meaning of Atonement', *The Lion and the Unicorn*, 23, 3 (1999), pp.336–54.

3. Maureen O'Connor, 'Maria Edgeworth's Fostering Art and the Fairy Tales of Oscar Wilde', *Women's Studies: An Interdisciplinary Journal*, 31, 3 (2002), pp.399, 413.

4. See Heather Ingman, *A History of the Irish Short Story* (Cambridge: Cambridge University Press, 2009), for a brilliant study of the short form in Ireland.

5. Richard Ellmann, *Oscar Wilde* (Harmondsworth: Penguin, 1988), p.253.

6. Josephine M. Guy and Ian Small, *Oscar Wilde's Profession: Writing and the Culture Industry in the late Nineteenth Century* (Oxford: Oxford University Press, 2000), p.6; Oscar Wilde, letter to George Macmillan, January 1889, in *The Complete Letters of Oscar Wilde*, eds Merlin Holland and Rupert Hart-Davis (London: Fourth Estate, 2000), p.385.

7. Oscar Wilde, Letter to an Unidentified Correspondent, October 1887, in *Letters*, p.325; Ellmann, *Oscar Wilde*, p.279. Following Frank Harris's own claim, various critics report that Wilde first submitted 'The Portrait of Mr W. H.' for publication in the *Fortnightly Review*, then edited by Harris, but that it was turned down by Harris's disapproving deputy. However, there is no evidence in Wilde's correspondence to support that claim: see Ellmann, *Oscar Wilde*, p.282; Marshall Brown (ed.), *The Uses of*

Literary History (Durham, NC and London: Duke University Press, 1995), p.140; Jonathan Fryer, Wilde (London: Haus, 2005), p.61.

8. Oscar Wilde, Letter to an Unidentified Correspondent, October 1887. Letters, p.325; Oscar Wilde, letter to William Blackwood, 30 May 1889, Letters, p.401; Oscar Wilde, letter to William Blackwood, 7 July 1889, Letters, p. 405.

9. In fact, the expanded text of 'The Portrait of Mr. W. H.' did not appear in print until 1921 due to a combination of the effects of termination of the Mathews-Lane partnership in 1894, concerns over its content, and the loss of Wilde's manuscript; see Letters, p.606n; Oscar Wilde, letter to Elkin Mathews and John Lane, circa 8 September 1894, Letters, pp.608–9.

10. Oscar Wilde, letter to J.M. Stoddart, 30 September 1889, Letters, p.413; Oscar Wilde, letter to J.M. Stoddart, 17 December 1889, Letters, p.416; Oscar Wilde, letter to Arthur Conan Doyle, ? April 1891, Letters, p.478.

11. Robert Merle, Oscar Wilde (Paris: Hachette, 1948), p.266.

12. Ibid., p.273.

13. 'The Portrait of Mr W. H.' was an exception; see Horst Schroeder, Oscar Wilde, The Portrait of Mr W.H. – Its Composition, Publication, and Reception (Braunschweig: Technische Universtät Carolo-Wilhelmina zu Braunschweig, 1984), pp.14–21.

14. Reprinted in Karl Beckson (ed.), Oscar Wilde: The Critical Heritage (London: Routledge & Kegan Paul, 1970), p.60.

15. Ibid., p.61.

16. Regenia Gagnier, Idylls of the Market Place: Oscar Wilde and the Victorian Public (Aldershot: Scolar Press, 1986), p.63; Jack Zipes, Fairy Tales and the Art of Subversion (London: Heinemann, 1983), p.114. For a study which claims that the tales are both conservative and subversive, see Jarlath Killeen, The Fairy Tales of Oscar Wilde (London: Ashgate, 2007).

17. Oscar Wilde, letters to W.E. Gladston (June 1888) and G.H. Kersley (15 June 1888), in Letters, pp.350, 352. For opposing views on Wilde's intended audience, see Guy and Small, Oscar Wilde's Profession, p.231, who argue that publishing choices and decisions suggest the collection was intended for young readers; Michelle Ruggaber, 'Wilde's The Happy Prince and A House of Pomegranates: Bedtime Stories for Grown-Ups', English Literature in Transition, 46, 2 (2003), pp.141–53, who claims that Wilde's stylistic choices reveal that it was clearly aimed at children; Sarah Marsh, 'Twice Upon a Time: The Importance of Rereading "The Devoted Friend"', Children's Literature, 36 (2008), p.73, who suggests that 'it might simultaneously appeal to adults and to children'.

18. George MacDonald, 'The Fantastic Imagination', in The Gifts of the Christ Child: Fairy Tales and Stories for Children, 2 vols. (London and Oxford: A.R. Mowbray, 1973), Vol.1, pp.23–8 (p.25).

19. Jack Zipes, When Dreams Came True: Classical Fairy Tales and Their Traditions (London: Routledge, 1999), pp.135, 137.

20. Jerusha McCormack, 'Wilde's fiction(s)', in The Cambridge Companion to Oscar Wilde, ed. Peter Raby (Cambridge: Cambridge University Press, 1997), pp.102, 105, 106.

21. Duffy, 'Gay-Related Themes', p.329.

22. O'Connor, 'Maria Edgeworth's Fostering Art', pp.414–15. Setting the stories in an Irish context is central to Killeen's *Fairy Tales*.

23. Robert Ross (ed.), *The Collected Works of Oscar Wilde*, 15 vols (London: Routledge, 1993), Vol.10, p.188.

24. Ibid., p.188.

25. Ibid., p.179.

26. Ibid., p.231.

27. Amongst recent critics who agree, at least to some extent, on the importance of the theme of interpretation in this story are Gagnier, *Idylls of the Marketplace*, pp.39–46; Bruce Bashford, 'Hermeneutics in Oscar Wilde's "The Portrait of Mr. W.H."', *Papers on Language and Literature*, 24, 4 (1998), pp.412–22; *Oscar Wilde's Oxford Notebooks: a Portrait of the Mind in the Making*, eds Philip E. Smith II and Michael Helfland (New York: Oxford University Press, 1989), pp.87–96; Suzy Anger, *Victorian Interpretation* (Ithaca, NY: Cornell University Press, 2005), pp.155–60.

28. Lawrence Danson, *Wilde's Intentions: The Artist in his Criticism* (Oxford: Clarendon Press, 1997), p.105; Gagnier, *Idylls of the Marketplace*, p.42 argues for the central role of homoeroticism in the story, claiming that 'Wilde was practically concerned with what the narrator calls "the ambiguity of the sexes"'.

29. For an informed and nuanced discussion of same-sex desire in 'The Portrait of Mr. W. H.', see Richard Halpern, *Shakespeare's Perfume: Sodomy and Sublimity in the Sonnets, Wilde, Freud, and Lacan* (Philadelphia, PA: University of Pennsylvania Press, 2002), pp.32–58.

30. Schroeder, *Oscar Wilde, The Portrait of Mr W. H.*, p.15.

31. Ross, *Collected Works*, Vol.7, p.161.

32. Ibid., p.171.

33. Ibid., p.162.

34. Ibid., pp.187, 192.

35. Ibid., p.194.

36. Ibid., p.199.

37. Beckson (ed.), *Oscar Wilde: The Critical Heritage*, pp.107, 108, 110.

38. See, for example, Lydia Reineck Wilburn, 'Oscar Wilde's "The Canterville Ghost": The Power of an Audience', *Papers on Language and Literature* 23, 1 (Winter 1987), pp.41–55; Josephine M. Guy, 'An Allusion in Oscar Wilde's "The Canterville Ghost"', *Notes and Queries*, 243 (N.S. 45), 2 (1998), pp.224–6; Andreas Höfele, 'Oscar Wilde, or, the Prehistory of Postmodern Parody', *European Journal of English Studies*, 3, 2 (1999), pp.138–66; Caroline Lesjack, 'Utopia, Use, and the Everyday: Oscar Wilde and a New Economy of Pleasure', *English Literary History*, 67 (2000), pp.179–204; Linda Dryden, *The Modern Gothic and Literary Doubles: Stevenson, Wilde and Wells* (London: Palgrave Macmillan, 2003), pp.110–14; Maureen O'Connor, 'The Spectre of Genre in "The Canterville Ghost"', *Irish Studies Review*, 12, 3 (2004), pp.329–38.

39. Ross, *Collected Works*, Vol.7, p.11.

40. Ibid., p.16.

41. Ibid., p.20.

42. Ibid., p.29.

43. Jarlath Killeen, *The Faiths of Oscar Wilde* (London: Palgrave Macmillan, 2005), p.40.

44. Nils Clausen, 'Lady Alroy's Secret: Surface and Symbol in Wilde's "The Sphinx Without a Secret"', *The Wildean*, 28 (2006), pp.24–32.

45. Bruce Bashford, 'Thinking in Stories: Oscar Wilde's "The Sphinx Without a Secret"', *The Oscholars*, 42 (October/November 2007) at http://www.oscholarship.com/TO/Archive/Forty-two/And_I/AND%20I.htm#_%E2%80%98Thinking_in_Stories%E2%80%99: accessed 20 October 2009.

46. Ross, *Collected Works*, Vol.7, p.132.

47. Ibid., p.125.

48. Ibid., p.75.

49. Ibid., p.82.

50. For a discussion of the significance of illustration and binding to the production and reception of Wilde's work, see Nicholas Frankel, *Oscar Wilde's Decorated Books* (Ann Arbor, MI: University of Michigan Press, 2002).

51. Beckson (ed.), *Oscar Wilde: The Critical Heritage*, p.113.

52. Oscar Wilde, letter to the Editor of the *Pall Mall Gazette*, early December 1891, in *Letters*, p.503.

53. For more on Wilde's view of artistic temperament, see the essay by Bruce Bashford in this volume.

54. Ross, *Collected Works*, Vol.10, p.5.

55. Ibid., p.37.

56. Ibid., p.46.

57. Ibid., p.64.

58. Ibid., p.124.

59. Oscar Wilde, 'Epistola: In Carcere et Vinculis', in *The Complete Works of Oscar Wilde*, Vol.2, *De Profundis*, ed. Ian Small (Oxford: Oxford University Press, 2005), p.123.

60. Ross, *Collected Works*, Vol.10, p.161.

61. Ian Small, 'Introduction', in *Oscar Wilde: Complete Short Fiction*, ed. Ian Small (London: Penguin, 2003), pp.x–xxxi (p.xix).

CHAPTER FIVE

From Romanticism to Fascism: The Will to Power in *The Picture of Dorian Gray*

MICHAEL PATRICK GILLESPIE

In 1993, the Princess Grace Irish Library hosted a conference in Monaco to examine the works of Oscar Wilde from a variety of perspectives.[1] During the sessions, all of which were plenary, a number of participants – from well-known critics to scholars just beginning their careers – offered papers. At one point, a young woman developed the argument that within the dialogue of Wilde's play, *Salome* (1894), lies a confession of sexual intimacy between a 12-year-old Oscar and his 9-year-old sister Isola. This thesis clearly shocked a great many people in the auditorium, and for a few moments after the paper's conclusion the hall remained deadly silent. Then, Merlin Holland, Wilde's grandson, got up, and in a booming voice declared to the assembly that 'Sigmund Freud has a great deal to answer for'.

This anecdote may seem an extreme example of the consequences of biographical speculations derived from Wilde's canon. In fact, it stands as the logical extension of a pattern – begun by writers close to Wilde or his circle – of using the author's art to illuminate his life.[2] Given the drama that punctuated so much of that extraordinary public career, culminating in Wilde's 1895 trials, one can hardly be surprised by the inclination of many readers, continuing through contemporary critics, to collapse the boundaries between life and art.[3]

One certainly can understand the temptation to tease fact from fiction, for a great many details – from date of birth to final words – had been occluded by Wilde throughout his life and obscured by others ever since. Unfortunately, even the most rigorous biographical research often can produce little definitive critical insight.[4] A good recent example of this appears in a study of Oscar Wilde's role in the efforts to overturn the miscarriage of justice in 1894 when Captain Alfred Dreyfus, a French artillery officer, was unjustly convicted of treason and imprisoned on Devil's Island. An article by J. Robert Maguire details Wilde's association with the Dreyfus affair by drawing on unpublished material both from Wilde's correspondence and from the papers of Carlos Blacker, who had been one of Wilde's 'oldest and closest friends',[5] to lay out Wilde's involvement in events in Paris leading up to the public revelation of the injustice of Dreyfus's imprisonment.[6] However, even Maguire's scrupulous research leads only to dubious conclusions – particularly his characterization of Wilde as an anti-Semite – without offering any real insight into Wilde's nature during the final years of his life, and certainly the essay adds nothing to one's ability to interpret the canon, written well before these events occurred.

A more effective critical approach to understanding the forces shaping Wilde's writing comes from linking it to examinations of the imaginative and cultural environments from which it emerged. The last four decades in particular have produced abundant examples of efforts to do just that, a series of sociologically oriented studies that attempt to integrate intra- and extra-textual concerns for an amalgamated view of the writer and the writings.[7] To this end, they acknowledge the impact of the Victorian world, but they also take more direct cognizance of Wilde's works than did their biographically oriented predecessors.[8]

Once pioneering studies in this category had established a conjunction between fundamental critical concerns and the broad cultural features surrounding Wilde's life, subsequent approaches narrowed their appraisals to sharply delineated contexts. Not surprisingly, many explored the impact of sexual orientation on Wilde's writing, and the best examined the interpretive potential of the author's complex representations of gender and sexuality, elaborating on how recognitions of such gestures inform broader understandings. Unfortunately, some critics went a step further and fell into the flawed pattern of many early readers, using this approach not to engage textual cruxes but rather to proselytize personal beliefs. All too often, in these instances, inferences within texts are stripped of their ambiguities, transposed into Wilde's life, and presented as biographical certainties. While the essays referenced show pronounced skill at close readings, their inclinations to use these readings to foster ideological agendas sharply limits one's perspective of Wilde.[9] Of course, criticism that draws on extra-textual material can have an illuminating effect upon one's understanding of the text. Reading James Joyce's fiction with an awareness of the way Catholic dogma, liturgy and history shapes his narrative enhances one's sense of his work. At the same time, labelling Joyce a Catholic writer circumscribes it. The same holds true for Wilde and his sexuality.

The inclination not simply to situate extra-textual elements in interpretive hypostasis but to give them polemical force in assessing the man behind the work stands as particularly prevalent in examinations of The Picture of Dorian Gray. Its critical history began with acerbic reviewers focussing attention on the world surrounding Wilde's fiction, charging that the narrative's central concerns glorified unhealthy, depraved impulses that threatened the moral equilibrium of anyone exposed to it. Although the idea of The Picture of Dorian Gray as a work of prurient interest may now seem quaint, the implicit point of these initial critiques, that the novel's narrative functions in a didactic fashion, has become a popular view among a number of Wilde's readers.[10] While interpretive methods and assumptions have changed over the years, certain constants remain. In particular, early critics examining Wilde's writing introduced a tendency toward Manichean readings, fuelled by subjective attention to Wilde's biography, that continues to be a staple approach to this novel.[11] This view can highlight exciting interpretive possibilities, but under its influence even the most innovative approaches tend to foreground interpretations of Wilde over those of his text and to limit themselves to readings based upon the either/or dichotomies that characterize didactic writing. As a consequence, the very specificity that gives such analyses originality in turn sharply limits the scope of any interpretations, but, as David Rose has demonstrated, this same epistemology can produce far more efficacious results when one sees cultural context as part of the imaginative milieu from which Wilde's writing emerged and not as its sole source.[12]

The pages that follow take up a singular aspect within The Picture of Dorian Gray – gratification – and show how careful and deliberate attentiveness to extra-textuality greatly enhances one's ability to engage Wilde's novel without inevitably leading to prescriptive assumptions about the text or its author's life. In pursuing this line, I have followed a more focussed approach than the tradition of contextualization that I have already outlined, exploring specific extra-textual representations that demonstrate Wilde's creative interests throughout his process of composition. Let me clarify what I mean by reviewing the events surrounding the revision and expansion of *The Picture of Dorian Gray* from novella to novel.

Over the summer of 1890, following *Lippincott's Magazine* publication of the novella–length version of Wilde's story, a series of hostile reviews, each condemning a narrative celebrating immorality, appeared in a number of English papers. Wilde, always quick to engage public criticism, countered with assertions defending his imaginative representations. He went on to reject the validity of the reviewers' implicit assumptions that art pursues polemic ends, though he did not dispute art's inclination to examine complex ideas or explore controversial points of view.[13] Initially Wilde made his case by simply dismissing the central suppositions that served as the foundation for attacks: that *The Picture of Dorian Gray* offended moral tenets which his critics frequently invoked though never identified. He also endeavoured to focus discussion on a consideration of the novel's worth based on its artistic merits. Over the course of his epistolary exchanges with reviewers and editors, however, Wilde's responses made it increasingly clear that he understood the danger that moral judgments, however inaccurate and irrelevant they might be, would distort public perceptions of his narrative's central artistic concerns.[14]

After the uproar died down, Wilde turned to revising *The Picture of Dorian Gray* for publication as a novel, and a number of commentators have subsequently concerned themselves with what effect public controversy had on the evolution of the novella into a novel. Perhaps the most assiduous has been Donald Lawler, who has spent much of his professional life examining the draft texts of *The Picture of Dorian Gray*.[15] In his most detailed study, after a careful account of the process shaping the manuscript's expansion, Lawler asserts that the driving force behind the changes that Wilde made in his text was a desire to respond to reviewers' charges by eliminating any material that might provide a basis for interpretations founded on issues of morality, particularly regarding the

novel's conclusion.[16] Certainly, no one would doubt that Wilde's disposition and inclinations profoundly affected the final construction of The
Picture of Dorian Gray, and the attacks on his novella could hardly have
failed to make an impression on him. However, assuming that his
changes were introduced to forestall additional criticism presumes a kind
of timidity on Wilde's part that his public response to his adversaries does
not support. Throughout these exchanges Wilde vigorously reiterated the
view that reading a moral into a novel imposes a simplistic interpretation
that runs contrary to creative efforts, and the material in his Preface demonstrated his willingness to continue the fight of the previous summer. It
seems an intuitive leap unsupported by the evidence at hand to claim a
reversal of this view influenced his process of revision.

Clearly, Wilde felt the need to respond to charges of immorality, but
his letters to editors show that he did so not because he wished to avoid
contentiousness but because these claims distracted attention from the
novel's most controversial idea: power, not the self-indulgence that so
outraged English reviewers, is the drive dominating characters in The Picture
of Dorian Gray. Tracing that impulse in his final version allows readers to see
a far richer and more complex world than his reviewers imagined. Let
me be clear that I do not for a moment question the scholarship that
went into Lawler's investigation of the revision process. In fact, I feel he has
provided students of Wilde with a valuable scholarly resource chronicling
the painstaking process of revision. At the same time, extrapolating
motives behind particular revisions, and by extension the decision not to
make other changes, can often amount to nothing more than educated
guessing. I agree that it is useful to have some idea about Wilde's
concerns while he was revising, but I feel that a more accurate measure
can be taken by pointing to extra-textual material, in this case various
writings, to show the issues engaging Wilde's attention while he was
revising his novella into a novel.

It is important to remember that in both the novella and the novel, the
fundamental supposition of New Hedonism, for instance, the doctrine
Lord Henry so glibly propounds to Dorian on their first meeting, rests on
the view that sensuality is only one manifestation of the real concern.
Pursuing self-gratification is one way to demonstrate one's ability to
behave without restraint, although Harry acknowledges the prevalence

of a conventional timidity within the populace that causes most to shrink from this effort. '[T]he bravest man amongst us is afraid of himself. The mutilation of the savage has its tragic survival in the self-denial that mars our lives. We are punished for our refusals. Every impulse that we strive to strangle broods in the mind, and poisons us.'[17] Lord Henry goes on to declare what he sees as the proper approach to life: 'Be afraid of nothing ... A New Hedonism – that is what our century wants' (23).[18]

The narrative of *The Picture of Dorian Gray* shows that Wilde remains truer to these sentiments than the man who propounds them in the novel, for the author does not hesitate to face directly a range of desires and the consequences of pursing them. Harry, as late as chapter nineteen, deflects Dorian's attempt to show that complete power includes the willingness to commit any crime, even murder, for Lord Henry, like those whom he has disparaged earlier, proves to be 'afraid of himself' (175–6).[19] Wilde's narrative disdains such self-delusion, and forces readers to confront what many of his characters assiduously avoid. Any impression of the nobility of Harry's philosophy can last no further than the realization of the consequences of Dorian's first self-indulgence, the suicide of Sibyl Vane. Even before that dramatic moment, however, Wilde's writings have subtly acknowledged that the celebration of the individual through the impulse of Romanticism always holds the danger of moving to the degradation of the majority by the tyranny of Fascism.[20]

Others have seen signs of this interest in power in Wilde's novel, though they have not come to the same conclusions as to its significance. Mary C. King, for example, explores Darwinian links to the atmosphere of *The Picture of Dorian Gray*.[21] In the process, she notes highly charged modifications of Darwin's views by others that would have had particular resonance with the basic ideas of Wilde's discourse: 'Darwin's painstaking work on the origin of species was rapidly appropriated and distorted to underwrite those master-race theories promoted in England by Herbert Spencer and later by Darwin's cousin, Francis Galton' (views that were appropriated by fascist thinkers in the 1930s to support the idea of racial superiorities).[22] King goes on to assert that the work of Irish thinkers and Irish writers in general and of Wilde in particular undermined these views of a master-race. Unfortunately, King's argument suffers from too many generalizations about Wilde and Darwin, and it lacks sufficient evidence to support them. Nonetheless, I do feel that she raises important issues regarding the struggle for identity and the definition of self in the novel. I want to examine here Dorian's proto-fascist impulse manifest in the sense of his right to use society as a means to attain whatever gratification he seeks.

I realize that both Romanticism and Fascism are complex conditions, particularly when applied to large-scale movements, but when considered as impulses governing personal behaviour a fairly simple link obtains. The common feature of both is power. What distinguishes the two is how power is applied. Romanticism privileges the unique individual by setting him or her free of the restraints of society (a view akin to the philosopher Friedrich Nietzsche's ubermensch). A fascist disposition privileges the unique individual by legitimizing the impulse to subordinate the mass of society to his or her desires. (This may be evinced through the overt control of others as in Dorian's domination of Alan Campbell, pp. 140–5,[23] or through a lack of concern for the consequences of one's behaviour on others as delineated by Basil Hallward's account of the ruin of a series of Dorian's acquaintances, pp. 126–8).[24] Other critics have already explored the larger philosophical implications of the links between politics and art, offering rigorous critiques of these attitudes as they apply to larger social networks in developmental and completed form.[25] Isaiah Berlin, for example, has offered a powerful, book-length exploration of the evolution of such attitudes adumbrated in the following paragraph of his introduction:

> These [approaches] invariably begin by liberating people from error, from confusion, from some kind of unintelligible world which they seek to explain to themselves by means of a model; but they almost invariably end by enslaving those very same people, by failing to explain the whole of experience. They begin as liberators and end in some sort of despotism.[26]

Berlin's views offer a powerful critique of the dynamic that unfolds when ideals evolve through human interaction, but that topic, with all its implications, goes well beyond the scope of this essay.[27] My aim is to examine inchoate manifestations, those that appear within the individual.

I have not always taken the position that seeing the expansion of the text of The Picture of Dorian Gray as an exercise in self-censorship missed the central issue evident from the work's first appearance. A decade ago, I followed more closely Lawler's approach, taking the view that Wilde was succumbing, albeit subtly, to public pressure and making the homo-eroticism of the narrative less direct.[28] I have now come to see that response as too narrow, for like other critics I placed more emphasis on events surrounding the first appearance of *The Picture of Dorian Gray* than upon the text of the novel that grew out of it. In fact, close readings discover abundant evidence that the inclinations that so offended the early reviewers, like the homoeroticism in nearly every scene involving Dorian and Basil, still exist. They take on significance beyond what early critics had imagined, however, when one realizes that the impulse toward gratification suggested in these exchanges does not function as an end but highlights one of a variety of ways of exerting control explored in the novel. I understand that this aim is not always immediately apparent and that manifestations of power can distract attention from the impulse itself. For example, the aspects of self-gratification that readers generally associate with New Hedonism may seem to explain fully the actions of Dorian and Lord Henry throughout the novel. That connection, however, confuses consequences with motivations. In fact, neither Dorian Gray nor Lord Henry Wotton confines himself simply to seeking pleasure. Rather each advocates complete personal freedom (for himself if not universally), and thus seeks full control in any and every situation. As a consequence, a Nietzsche-like will to power stands as their dominant motive, and its recognition gives rise to a broader sense of why Dorian behaves as he does.

This is an important point too easily obscured by the extravagant prose Wilde uses to describe pleasure. In fact, New Hedonism is not about self-indulgence, at least not in a limited material way. Rather it is about striving for the power to behave without restraint. Dorian Gray, like most characters featured in Wilde's writings, succeeds to the degree that he achieves freedom of action. This means that, unlike the masses that the narrative implicitly scorns, Dorian is unfettered by the rules, laws or morals of society. In the narrative, power affirms individuality, denying any meliorating impulse towards the common good. Thus, the more Dorian exercises power, the more tyrannical and ruthless his attitude toward society inevitably becomes.

Wilde's writings always showed an interest in the power that individuals wield, but material that appeared immediately before the novel's publication demonstrates just how much it preoccupied him while he was revising The Picture of Dorian Gray.[29] In the February 1891 issue of Fortnightly Review Wilde published an essay entitled 'The Soul of Man under Socialism'. Though ostensibly about political ideology, its argument provides ample evidence that the kind of individualism that would be privileged in the evolving nature of Dorian Gray would go well beyond mere sensual gratification. 'The Soul of Man under Socialism' paradoxically reveals its concern for the power of the individual, and more specifically for the power of the artist, through an idiosyncratic approach to an ideology that stresses communal welfare. Other critics have noted this, though not all see it so iconoclastically. For example, Isobel Murray, through a very detailed explication, puts Wilde's writing squarely within the context of contemporaneous political thought and links it to Ralph Waldo Emerson's views on self-reliance.[30] Lawrence Danson follows a similar approach in neatly contrasting Wilde's assertions with those of William Morris.[31] Others take a more sceptical perspective of his attitudes. Josephine M. Guy challenges Murray's connection of Wilde with the ideas of Emerson and believes instead that the presence in 'The Soul of Man under Socialism' of 'significant figures in political philosophy is simply Wilde's version of name dropping'.[32] Jarlath Killeen critiques Guy's dismissal of Wilde's sincerity as 'problematic',[33] and he goes on to temper her remarks by offering his own political gloss. Killeen explores the impact on Wilde of the Irish politician Charles Stewart Parnell's political troubles, seeing 'The Soul of Man under Socialism' to be more situational than Murray or Danson supposes and more sincere than Guy allows, characterizing the essay as 'Wilde's reaction, written in sarcastic white heat, to the events of the day [i.e., the fall of Parnell, leader of the Irish Home Rule Party, after being pilloried by the British press]'.[34]

Each of these critics makes useful hermeneutic observations, and my point is not to challenge any. Rather, while acknowledging the value of reading 'The Soul of Man under Socialism' for its own sake, I wish to look at it in relation to The Picture of Dorian Gray.[35] For me Wilde's essay contributes to a pattern of interpretive realignment. It moves from

102

lauding a political movement (socialism) to highlighting the individual to privileging the artist, and it signals to readers Wilde's growing interest not in efforts to maximize pleasure but in the consequences of broad endeavours to accumulate power (a year earlier, Wilde performed a similar rhetorical manoeuvre, though one done more blatantly, in his essay 'The Critic as Artist' [1890]).

Although standard conceptions would not immediately recognize the similarity, Killeen touches on the point I wish to make about the idiosyncrasy of Wilde's views. Killeen notes: 'Wilde is not here declaiming his socialist leanings, but indicating that such leanings need to be read in a wider frame, that frame being anarchism.'[36] Killeen's introduction of that term as the essay's true subject comes close to the point I wish to make: Anarchism privileges the individual over social institutions, giving the individual the responsibilities usually relegated to those institutions. At the start of 'The Soul of Man under Socialism', Wilde's prose veers between a straightforward commentary on the fundamental value of communal welfare and an insistent argument for privileging individuality. 'Socialism would relieve us from that sordid necessity of living for others which, in the present condition of things, presses so hard upon almost everybody.'[37] By the mid-point of the essay, Wilde openly emphasizes his central concern – the welfare of the artist. As his exposition moves toward a conclusion, his purpose becomes increasingly evident, celebration of the unique character of the artist and the assertion of the need to allow that individual full license.

Although a graceful style covers the blatant insistence of the argument, Wilde's primary interest can hardly be ignored. Under the cover of a broad concern for the human condition, he advocates privileging the artist. By the essay's end, Wilde is celebrating not ideology but artistic individualism, and in *The Picture of Dorian Gray* he will extend that view to make the definition of artist even more flexible than that offered in 'The Critic as Artist' – at one point Harry tells Dorian 'Life has been your art' (179)[38] – and to illustrate, through Dorian's unrestrained self-expression, the brutal consequences of allowing an individual to impose his will on others with no restraint.

Wilde continues his exploration of power and intellectual freedom in a series of aphorisms first published in March of 1891 in *The Fortnightly Review* and then included as a Preface when the novel-length version of *The*

Picture of Dorian Gray appeared the next month. The piece clearly replies to much of the early criticism. Nonetheless, it serves as more than a simple rebuttal of misconceived and distorted interpretive views. In an abridged fashion, the Preface offers a blueprint for reading the novel that would avoid the reductive, linear assumptions made by those who attacked the novella. On the one hand, it presents a broad aesthetic outline for under-standing creativity reminiscent of Gustave Flaubert and prescient of James Joyce: 'The artist is the creator of beautiful things. To reveal art and conceal the artist is art's aim.' At the same time, the Preface expands its scope to privilege the critic in a reiteration of the sentiments of Wilde's earlier essay, 'The Critic as Artist': 'The critic is he who can translate into another manner or a new material his impression of beautiful things.' It also singles out that portion of the audience showing concern for individuality over vocation: 'They are the elect to whom beautiful things mean only Beauty' (3).[39] These and other statements highlight the individual who is distinguished from others by superior abilities. It is this individual and the consequences of possessing unique traits that become the central concern of the text that follows.

While the letters, essay and preface I have referenced all clarify the narrative direction of Wilde's novel, they do not delineate a new creative approach for *The Picture of Dorian Gray*, for the fundamental attitudes that I highlight existed in the novella as well – power is the true seductive force for Dorian. The ability to control others while resisting any effort to circumscribe his own behaviour presents the real impetus driving his character. The interim works I have cited clarify Wilde's profound interest in individualism and the consequences of its unfettered pursuit. This, in turn, suggests the most productive interpretive approach for readers to take with the novel: a view of Dorian as more closely resembling a fascist than a sensualist.

The first examples of support for this appear in Lord Henry's early disquisition on New Hedonism, a doctrine that Dorian comes to adopt wholeheartedly. While Lord Henry advocates complete self-indulgence, he disdains the limits that concentration merely on sexual or even sensual pleasure would impose on the project: 'It has been said that the great events of the world take place in the brain. It is in the brain, and the brain only, that the great sins of the world take place also' (20).[40]

When Lord Henry goes on to talk of human Beauty (22–3),[41] he presents it implicitly as a means to an end: organic Beauty produces pleasure and when such Beauty fades so also does the pleasure that one derives from it. In fact, as its transitory condition suggests, this form of Beauty serves as a limited agent, enabling the acquisition of certain kinds of gratification. In contrast, power offers the ability to gratify oneself far more broadly:

> Live the wonderful life that is in you! Let nothing be lost upon you. Be always searching for new sensations. Be afraid of nothing .... A new Hedonism – that is what our century wants. You might be its visible symbol. With your personality there is nothing you could not do. The world belongs to you for a season.... (23, Wilde's ellipses)[42]

Though the point remains understated in Lord Henry's introduction to this alternative mode of living, linking the exceptional individual with the power to control gradually emerges over the course of the narrative as the primary concern of Wilde's work.

Even before Dorian appears, the initial interaction between Basil Hallward and Lord Henry calls attention to this ability to exercise control. As Basil elaborates on the power Dorian exerts over him (9–13),[43] he introduces images of the dominance and submission that will characterize interactions for the rest of the narrative. In the next chapter Lord Henry signals the inherently paradoxical elements of a personal fascination with power, and in the process he gives a sense of the impulse toward fascism to which I have referred: He asserts that control over another is wrong – '[a]ll influence is immoral' (19)[44] – yet in fact by his actions he shows that he believes this subtle display of authority exerted over another is wrong only if he is the subject of such assertions. Harry not only continually strives for control over others; he takes great pleasure in the practice. As he states when musing over his impact on Dorian: 'He had merely shot an arrow into the air. Had it hit the mark? How fascinating the lad was' (20).[45] Indeed, throughout the narrative one finds evidence of Lord Henry's detached yet relentless interest, as when he learns of Dorian's love for Sybil Vane:

> Certainly few people had ever interested him so much as Dorian Gray, and yet the lad's mad adoration of someone else caused him not the slightest pang of annoyance or jealousy. He was pleased by

it. It made him a more interesting study. He had always been enthralled by the methods of natural science, but the ordinary subject-matter of that science had seemed to him trivial and of no import. And so he had begun by vivisecting himself, as he had ended by vivisecting others. Human life – that appeared to him the one thing worth investigating ... It was clear to him that the experimental method was the only method by which one could arrive at any scientific analysis of the passions; and certainly, Dorian Gray was a subject made to his hand ... (51)[46]

From the first chapter onward, one finds the subtle insinuation of power and control, almost always exercised at the expense of another, as the defining features of the narrative. Initially, the discourse devotes a great deal of space to Basil's seeming ingenuous homoerotic attraction to Dorian that asserts itself as an obsessive dependence. 'I couldn't be happy if I did not see him every day. He is absolutely necessary to me' (12).[47] Basil's fixation on Dorian in turn can make it appear logical to pursue the applications of queer theory that have become popular approaches to the novel. In fact, following only that course produces a limited understanding of the narrative dynamics. Much of what Basil says about their relationship and all that he does rests on the power that Dorian exerts over him. 'Dorian's whims are laws to everybody, except himself' (18).[48]

Interactions throughout the rest of the narrative remind readers of the primacy of concern for the force of the will. Anything else is merely the consequence of that drive. For instance, despite the assumption of many readers that images of physical gratification predominate in the narrative, not even a kiss (other than a chaste one between Sibyl and Mrs Vane, p.57,[49] another between Sibyl and her brother, James, p.61,[50] and a third between James and Mrs Vane, p.62[51]) is directly depicted. In contrast, a more overt manifestation of power, violence or at least the threat of violence, recurs with great frequency and is graphically represented.

In whatever form it takes, power remains the dominant concern. After the diverting homoerotic arabesques in chapter one, the first interaction between Lord Henry and Dorian in the next episode clearly underscores control. It begins with Dorian compelling Basil to implore Lord Henry to remain with them (18),[52] and it ends with Dorian fawning after Harry: 'I have promised Lord Henry Wotton to go with him' (29).[53]

While the locus of power will shift over the discourse, its pre-eminence in the narrative is never in doubt. After his introduction to the systematic approach to self-absorption of New Hedonism, Dorian begins to develop himself beyond Basil and Harry. While it may seem initially that he simply gratifies his senses, in fact his actions all revolve around efforts at control. His relations with Sybil are based on the power she exerts through her acting and on the effect that his interest has on her. 'She is all the great heroines of the world in one. She is more than an individual. You laugh, but I tell you she has genius. I love her, and I must make her love me' (49).[54] Sybil's death may teach Dorian about the limitations of controlling others, but, once he has listened to Lord Henry's seductive assessment of how one should react to such tragedies, it does not diminish his taste for power (83–7).[55]

Dorian's subsequent relations all focus on control. In the confrontation over the rumours of his scandalous life (126–8),[56] every incident that Basil recounts deals with Dorian's power to lead others into reprehensible behaviour. He subsequently uses blackmail to compel Alan Campbell to dispose of Basil's remains (140–3).[57] Finally, when in the penultimate chapter Dorian tells Lord Henry of a moral transformation, Harry characterizes Dorian's decision not to seduce Hetty Merton as simply a variation on conventional modes of the exercise of power (173–4).[58] In the end Dorian dies while attacking his picture in an effort, arguably misplaced or even unnecessary in this case, to affirm control. At the same time, a great many readers seemed then and continue to seem impervious to these suggestions. Remarks made as early as 1891 by Walter Pater in a review in *The Book-Man* embody this. '[Wilde's] story is also a vivid, though carefully considered, exposure of the corruption of a soul, with a very plain moral pushed home, to the effect that vice and crime make people coarse and ugly.'[59] Writing one hundred years later, Sheldon W. Liebman takes a similar tack arguing that '[a]s a victim of this psychological double bind, [Dorian] is not merely a hedonist paying for his sins, but a kind of Everyman, whose dilemma is a product of his human endowment'.[60] As the passages above demonstrate, reading Dorian as giving in to social pressure or feeling guilt based on society can produce a sophisticated but narrow sense of the character. The novel is not about Dorian Gray's failure to overcome the pull of his conscience but about the human limitations, in this case a lack of emotional control, that circumscribe the will to power.

The ambiguity of the novel is charged with greater force when the concept of power is recognized. One can project from it to the consequences of twentieth-century fascism. At the same time, there is not an aura of inevitability. Even the death of Dorian does not force us to see a single point of view. The Picture of Dorian Gray is an open-ended work because it returns us to the most fundamental of human drives. From there we can draw our own conclusions, make our own interpretations. Seeing echoes of Romanticism and avatars of Fascism is not inherently prescriptive. One can find those impulses in Chaucer, Shakespeare, Milton or almost any prolific writer. Recognizing these possibilities delineates broad boundaries for the novel without imposing great restrictions on reading.

Wilde's life and motivations are important to the same degree that any author's are. They shape the creative context. Even if one could identify them precisely, that would not prescribe the interpretation. However, thinking about what they might be provides a guide to understanding. The narrative and its history of revisions clearly indicate that power is one of Wilde's central concerns and that we miss a crucial aspect of the narrative if we ignore its presence.

NOTES

1. The proceedings of this conference have been published in Rediscovering Oscar Wilde, ed. C. George Sandulescu (Gerrards Cross: Colin Smythe, 1994).
2. For some examples, see Lord Alfred Douglas, Oscar Wilde: A Summing Up (London: Duckworth, 1940); André Gide, Oscar Wilde: In Memoriam (Reminiscences) de Profundis, trans. Bernard Frechtman (New York: Philological Library, 1949); Arthur Ransome, Oscar Wilde: A Critical Study (New York: M. Kennedy, 1913); Charles Ricketts, Recollections of Oscar Wilde (London: Peter Davis, 1932); Lloyd Lewis and Henry Justin Smith, Oscar Wilde Discovers America (New York: Harcourt, 1936); Vincent O'Sullivan, Aspects of Wilde (London: Constable & Co., 1936); Hesketh Pearson, Oscar Wilde: His Life and Wit (New York: Harper and Brothers, 1946); H. Montgomery Hyde, Oscar Wilde: The Aftermath (London: Methuen, 1963).
3. One finds a very welcome exception to this in the work of Ian Small who has rigorously opposed the tendency in biographical criticism to overstate what is known about Wilde and how this material affects his writings. See in particular his Oscar Wilde Revalued: an Essay on New Materials and Methods of Research (Greensboro, NC: ELT Press, 1993);

Oscar Wilde's Profession: Writing and the Culture Industry in the Late Nineteenth Century, co-authored with Josephine Guy (Oxford: Oxford University Press, 2000); *Studying Oscar Wilde: History, Criticism, and Myth*, with Josephine Guy (Greensboro, NC: ELT Press, 2006).

4. For a good example of work done to correct some of the numerous errors in Richard Ellmann's popular biography of Wilde, see Horst Schroeder's *Additions and Corrections to Richard Ellmann's* Oscar Wilde, second edition, revised and enlarged (Braunschweig: Privately Printed, 2002).

5. J. Robert Maguire, 'Oscar Wilde and the Dreyfus Affair', *Victorian Studies*, 41, 1 (Autumn 1997), p.2.

6. Ibid., pp.1-30. For a contrasting account, see Richard Ellmann, *Oscar Wilde* (New York: Knopf, 1988), pp.563-564, though Ellmann himself used the works of James Joyce to fill in gaps in the author's biography.

7. See, for example, Samuel Hynes, *The Edwardian Turn of Mind* (Princeton, NJ: Princeton University Press, 1968); Jerome H. Buckley, *The Victorian Temper: A Study in Literary Culture* (Cambridge, MA: Harvard University Press, 1969); J.E. Chamberlin, *Ripe Was the Drowsy Hour: The Age of Oscar Wilde* (New York: Seabury, 1977); Regenia Gagnier, *Idylls of the Marketplace: Oscar Wilde and the Victorian Public* (Aldershot: Scalar Press, 1986); Richard Ellmann, *Oscar Wilde* (Harmondsworth: Penguin, 1988).

8. Of course, other approaches to the canon obtained as well. These efforts first concentrated on producing traditional close readings anchored by thematic orientations. Often they emphasized moral choices made in the narrative or confronted the reader with ethical anomalies to resolve. See, for example, Epifanio San Juan, Jr, *The Art of Oscar Wilde* (Princeton, NJ: Princeton University Press, 1967); Donald H. Ericksen, *Oscar Wilde* (Twayne's English Authors Series, no. 211) (Boston, MA: G.K. Hall, 1977); Philip K. Cohen, *The Moral Vision of Oscar Wilde* (London: Associated University Press, 1978).

9. Camille A. Paglia, 'Oscar Wilde and the English Epicene', *Raritan*, 4 (Winter 1985), pp.85–109; Ed Cohen, 'Writing Gone Wilde: Homoerotic Desire in the Closet of Repression', *PMLA*, 102 (October 1987), pp.801–13; Jonathan Dollimore, 'Different Desires: Subjectivity and Transgression in Wilde and Gide', *Genders*, 2 (Summer 1988), pp.24–41; Richard Dellamora, *Masculine Desire: The Sexual Politics of Victorian Aestheticism* (Chapel Hill, NC: University of North Carolina Press, 1990); Christopher Craft, *Another Kind of Love: Male Homosexual Desire in English Discourse, 1850–1920* (Berkeley, CA: University of California Press, 1994); Simon Joyce, 'Sexual Politics and the Aesthetics of Crime: Oscar Wilde in the Nineties', *English Literary History*, 69, 2 (2002), pp.501–23; Yvonne Ivory, 'Wilde's Renaissance: Poison, Passion, and Personality', *Victorian Literature and Culture*, 35, 2 (September 2007), pp.517–37.

10. For examples of both contemporaneous reviewers' attitudes and Wilde's responses, see my Norton Critical Edition of *The Picture of Dorian Gray* (New York and London: W.W. Norton, 2007), pp.345–75. See it also for a sampling of contemporary approaches to the work, pp.385–510.

11. I take this up in greater detail in *Oscar Wilde and the Poetics of Ambiguity* (Gainesville, FL: University Press of Florida, 1996), pp.36–56. One finds an example of a variant form of this dichotomous view in Virginia Brackett's application of Northrop Frye's archetypal views. 'Oscar Wilde's *The Picture of Dorian Gray* as Secular Scripture', *Wildean*, 32 (2008), pp.43–56.

12. See in particular David C. Rose, 'Oscar Wilde: Socialite or Socialist', in Uwe Böker, Richard Corballis and Julie Hibbard (eds), *The Importance of Reinventing Oscar: Versions of Wilde during the Last 100 Years* (Amsterdam and New York: Rodopi, 2002), pp.35–55.

13. As previously noted, selections of this exchange appear in the Norton Critical Edition of *The Picture of Dorian Gray*. For a fuller record of Wilde's reactions, see *The Complete Letters of Oscar Wilde*, eds Merlin Holland and Rupert Hart-Davis (London: Fourth Estate, 2000).

14. See Gillespie, *Oscar Wilde and the Poetics of Ambiguity*, pp.51–6, for a more detailed discussion of this process.

15. See, for example, 'Oscar Wilde's First Manuscript of *The Picture of Dorian Gray*', in the Norton Critical Edition of *The Picture of Dorian Gray*, pp.423–33.

16. Donald Lawler, *An Inquiry into Oscar Wilde's Revisions of* The Picture of Dorian Gray (New York and London: Garland Publishing, 1988). For a more compressed though extremely scrupulous summary of Wilde's changes, see Joseph Bristow, 'Introduction', *The Picture of Dorian Gray* (Oxford: Oxford University Press, 2006), pp.xxiv–xxvi.

17. Oscar Wilde, *The Picture of Dorian Gray*, ed. Michael Gillespie (New York and London: W.W. Norton, 2007), p.19. All subsequent quotations are taken from this edition and are incorporated in the text. References in the footnotes will direct readers to where these quotes can be found in the edition of *The Picture of Dorian Gray* (1891), published in the Oxford series. *The Complete Works of Oscar Wilde*, Vol. 3, edited Joseph Bristow (Oxford: Oxford University Press, 2005), p.183.

18. Ibid., p.187.

19. Ibid., pp.348–9.

20. Certainly, Wilde conceived Dorian as a romantic figure. He says as much in a 30 June 1890 letter to the editor of the *Daily Chronicle*: 'Dorian Gray has not got a cool, calculating, conscienceless character at all. On the contrary, he is extremely impulsive, absurdly romantic, and is haunted all through his life by an exaggerated sense of conscience which mars his pleasure for him and warns him that youth and enjoyment are not everything in the world'. *Letters*, p.436. Of course, this is both a reference to the Dorian of the novella and not the novel, and it also comes as one of the emotionally charged exchanges between Wilde and a series of critics castigating the first version of the work as immoral. Nonetheless, to my reading, Wilde establishes the early sense of the Romantic hero that he would erode through his revisions as he expanded the work to novel length.

21. See her 'Digging for Darwin: Bitter Wisdom in *The Picture of Dorian Gray* and "The Critic as Artist"', *Irish Studies Review*, 12, 3 (2004), pp.315–27.

22. Ibid., p.316.
23. Wilde, *The Picture of Dorian Gray*, pp.305–11.
24. Ibid., pp.292–4.
25. The Frankfurt School, with its vigorous critique of fascism in the 1930s, highlights this sort of investigation with the starting point for such work being Walther Benjamin's pioneering 1935 essay, 'Das Kunstwerk im Zeitalter seiner technischen Reproduzierbarkeit [The Work of Art in the Age of Mechanical Reproduction]'.
26. Isaiah Berlin, *The Roots of Romanticism* (Princeton, NJ: Princeton University Press, 1999), pp.3–4.
27. For more detailed assessments, see John Carey's *The Intellectuals and the Masses: Pride and Prejudice among the Literary Intelligentsia, 1880–1939* (New York: St Martin's Press, 2002); see also Claude Rawson's *God, Gulliver, and Genocide: Barbarism and the European Imagination, 1492–1945* (Oxford: Oxford University Press, 2001).
28. Gillespie, *Oscar Wilde and the Poetics of Ambiguity*, pp.50–6.
29. A concern for individualism runs throughout Wilde's works. In 'The Critic as Artist,' for example, he says at one point: 'If you wish to understand others, you must intensify your own individualism' (reprinted in the Norton Critical Edition, p.330), and certainly 'The Decay of Lying', 'Pen, Pencil and Poison', and 'The Portrait of Mr. W.H.' do nothing if not celebrate individualism.
30. Isobel Murray, 'Oscar Wilde and Individualism: Contexts for *The Soul of Man*', *Durham University Journal*, 52, 2 (July 1991), pp.195–207.
31. Lawrence Danson, 'The Soul of Man under Socialism', in *Wilde's Intentions: The Artist in His Criticism* (Oxford: Clarendon Press, 1997), pp.148–67.
32. Referenced by Jarlath Killeen in *The Faiths of Oscar Wilde: Catholicism, Folklore, and Ireland* (London: Palgrave Macmillan, 2005), p.110.
33. Ibid., p.119.
34. Ibid., p.120.
35. Moyra Haslett follows a similar approach to analysis in her essay 'A Portrait of Modern Times: Reading *The Picture of Dorian Gray*', in *Marxist Literary and Cultural Theories* (Basingstoke: Macmillan Press Ltd., 2000), pp.233–58. Her view, however, offers a strict, materialist reading of the novel, emphasizing a very different ideological position from the one that I am articulating.
36. Killeen, *The Faiths of Oscar Wilde*, p.109.
37. 'The Soul of Man under Socialism', in *The Complete Works of Oscar Wilde*, Vol.4, Criticism, ed. Josephine Guy (Oxford: Oxford University Press, 2007), p.231.
38. Wilde, *The Picture of Dorian Gray*, p.352.
39. Ibid., p.167.
40. Ibid., p.183.
41. Ibid., pp.186–7.
42. Ibid., p.187.
43. Ibid., pp.172–7.
44. Ibid., p.183.

45. Ibid., p.184.
46. Ibid., p.218.
47. Ibid., p.176.
48. Ibid., p.182. For additional discussion, see B.J. Gold's essay, 'The Domination of Dorian Gray', *The Victorian Newsletter*, 91 (Spring 1997), pp.27–30.
49. Wilde, *The Picture of Dorian Gray*, p.225.
50. Ibid., p.229.
51. Ibid., p.230.
52. Ibid., p.182.
53. Ibid., p.193.
54. Ibid., p.216.
55. Ibid., pp.252–6.
56. Ibid., pp.292–5.
57. Ibid., pp.308–11.
58. Ibid., pp.347–8.
59. Quoted in the *The Picture of Dorian Gray*, Norton Critical Edition, p.374.
60. From 'Character Design in *The Picture of Dorian Gray*', reprinted in the Norton Critical Edition, p.452.

CHAPTER SIX

Oscar Wilde:
The Critic as Dialectician

BRUCE BASHFORD

As this volume indicates, Oscar Wilde's versatile genius enabled him to produce in a variety of genres works that continue to receive close attention from scholars and critics. Indeed, his achievement may be unique measured by an odd but genuine criterion of success: that academic critics can regard Wilde's works in each genre as of the first rank while displaying minimal interest in his works in other genres – as though critics of Shakespeare's drama ignored the *Sonnets*. So critics of fiction regard *The Picture of Dorian Gray* (1890) as one of the major novels in English and drama critics marvel at the originality of *Salome* (1894), with neither group necessarily evincing an interest in the text, and certainly not in the scholarly commentary, that engages the other group.[1] This is also the case with Wilde's critical work. Many of Wilde's works contain criticism in the broad sense of statements about the nature and function of art. If one asks, however, which of his texts have established themselves as important works of literary theory by this unusual criterion, the answer is clearly the two dialogues in *Intentions* (1891), 'The Decay of Lying' (1889) and 'The Critic as Artist' (1890). These works will be the focus of this introduction to Wilde's critical thought. Two assumptions will guide the discussion: first, that the doubts and puzzlement readers of these two works have reported since their publication are clues to difficulties new readers may have as well. Second, that criticism is a genre in which persons reflect or take thought, and so how Wilde is thinking requires analysis in order to determine what he thinks. It will turn out that examining Wilde's two critical dialogues initially by themselves suggests a way of understanding Wilde's literary production as a whole.

We expect critical theorists to present their arguments directly in a discursive form such as the essay. Wilde doesn't meet this expectation. He himself says in a letter that 'The Decay of Lying' 'is meant to bewilder the masses by its fantastic form; *au fond* it is serious of course'.[2] The phrase 'fantastic form' apparently means 'imaginative form', in this case, the dialogue form. It may also refer to the main speaker Vivian's use of paradox to express his doctrines since in another letter Wilde claims, 'The admirable English are still much bewildered by "The Decay of Lying", but even here there are a few who can decipher its paradoxes'.[3] If the contemporary reviewers of *Intentions* weren't 'bewildered', they were at least sometimes puzzled and even a bit annoyed. They noticed the paradoxes, of course, but wondered if they were forced or overstated; as an anonymous reviewer complains, 'To call Mr. Wilde's favourite rhetorical figure by the name of paradox is really too complimentary; he carries his joke too far, and makes paradox ridiculous'.[4] A related form of complaint is that Wilde's critical insights don't really require the use of paradox; thus another anonymous reviewer reports, 'Mannerism apart, there is much excellent matter in Mr. Wilde's dialogues and essays'.[5] Reviewers saw that Wilde forms his paradoxes through contradicting received opinion, which they found facile; as the first reviewer continues, 'His method is this: he takes some well-established truth, something in which the wisdom of centuries and the wit of the greatest men have concurred, and asserts the contrary'.[6] More favourably and more shrewdly, Arthur Symons observes, 'By constantly saying the opposite of sensible opinions he proves to us that opposites can often be equally true'.[7] The reviewers also noticed the dialogue form of the two pieces, and this made them wonder how to connect the views expressed to Wilde. So while Symons believes a remark made by the main speaker in 'The Critic as Artist' would apply to Wilde, he takes care to observe, 'To be precisely accurate, it is one of the characters in a dialogue who makes this remark'.[8]

In the subsequent scholarship, the 'method' that the first reviewer above describes has been recognized, in Hilda Schiff's phrasing, as Wilde's 'deeply ingrained dialectical habit of mind'.[9] In the Commentary accompanying their edition of *Oscar Wilde's Notebooks*, Philip E. Smith and Michael Helfand argue that Wilde is a specifically Hegelian dialectician. Since Wilde plainly absorbed many influences, we have to be careful about interpreting him in the context of any single influence. Still, Smith and Helfand's view is useful for present purposes on several counts: it's explicitly concerned with Wilde's manner of thinking; ample evidence survives as to how Wilde encountered this influence; and Wilde himself calls attention to it. In what respects, then, is Wilde an Hegelian?

Smith and Helfand's edition shows that Wilde was familiar with the thought of the German philosopher Georg Wilhelm Friedrich Hegel (1770–1831), from various sources, but one will suffice here: William Wallace's lengthy and, considering its subject, remarkably clear Prolegomena to *The Logic of Hegel* (1874). That Wilde copied into his notebook passages spanning virtually all of Wallace's commentary indicates that he read it closely. In doing so, he would have met Wallace's exegesis of 'what Hegel termed the dialectical nature in thought – the tendency, by which an idea, when it is carried to extremes, recoils and swings round to the opposite'.[10] And he would have come on Wallace's definition of 'Dialektik':

> the principle of compensation, which shows the other side or negative of things ... It is a negative and destructive action, a swing round in the reverse direction ... The primary aspect of each form of things presents it as an affirmative reality; the second inspection shows that there is contradiction in what we saw, and that it is neither complete nor absolute. The revelation of this undiscerned feature leads to a synthesis ... by which negative and positive are assimilated to each other.[11]

In these passages we see the basis in Hegelian dialectic for Symons's insight above: 'opposites can often be equally true' because a full analysis of concepts shows them to *contain* their opposites.

Wilde helped Symons toward this insight by a passage that he added to the end of 'The Truth of Masks' when he revised the piece for *Intentions*:

> Not that I agree with everything that I have said in this essay. There is much with which I entirely disagree. The essay simply represents an artistic standpoint, and in aesthetic criticism attitude is everything.

For in art there is no such thing as a universal truth. A Truth in art
is that whose contradictory is also true. And just as it is only in
art-criticism, and through it, that we can apprehend the Platonic
theory of ideas, so it is only in art-criticism, and through it, that
we can realize Hegel's system of contraries. The Truths of meta-
physics are the truths of masks.[12]

Evident in this passage is Wilde's grasp of the motor of an Hegelian dialectical method: since 'contradictories' are true, the way to investigate a topic,
to go from one truth to another, is to 'swing round' from a thesis to its
contrary. This is the passage referred to above as Wilde's own indication of
his Hegelianism, and even critics not exploring this influence regularly
cite it as Wilde's most explicit statement about the nature of thought.[13]
Since the statement has assumed this status, it's worth pausing to address
a difficulty: if this is Wilde's view of thought in general, why does he
say 'it is *only* in art-criticism, and through it, that we can realise Hegel's
system of contraries'? Perhaps Wilde regarded nearly everything he wrote
as 'art-criticism' and so 'only' doesn't limit the scope of the statement; he
did after all call *The Picture of Dorian Gray* an 'essay on decorative art'.[14]
More plausible, however, is that 'realise' has the sense of 'Present as real;
bring vividly before the mind' (*Shorter OED*). The objects of criticism are con-
crete works of art; criticism makes claims that go beyond those works but
nevertheless are filled out, given body, through reference to those works.
'The Truth of Masks' (1891) is a defence of historical accuracy
in costume and staging – that's the 'artistic standpoint' Wilde is partially
disowning – developed though detailed discussion of Shakespeare's
practice. Thus while 'Hegel's system of contraries' applies to thought at large,
art criticism has a special capacity to present the system in palpable form.

Wilde's grasp of the motor of a dialectical method is also evident in
his review of Walter Pater's *Imaginary Portraits* (1887) when he says that
Pater 'is always looking for exquisite moments, and, when he has found
them, he analyzes them with delicate and delightful art, and *then passes on,
often to the opposite pole of thought or feeling*, knowing that every mood has its
own quality and charm, and is justified by its mere existence' (emphasis
mine).[15] While Wilde certainly gained some of his acquaintance with
Hegel through Pater, his version of dialectic isn't the same as Pater's. In
the essay 'Coleridge' (1889), Pater states,

The philosophical conception of the relative [Hegel's idea that things are known only in relation to other things] has been developed in modern times through the influence of the sciences of observation. These sciences reveal types of life evanescing into each other by inexpressible refinements of change. Things pass into their opposites by accumulation of undefinable quantities.[16]

This gradual, almost imperceptible process of change isn't how dialectic typically works in Wilde; Wallace's description of a idea taken to 'extremes' that then 'recoils and swings round to the opposite' fits Wilde better. This is why Wilde's characteristic form of expression is the paradox, as it isn't for Pater. A paradox consists of two apparent truths that contradict each other: the extreme, having swung round, faces its opposite directly. The absence in Wilde of the patient tracing of transition that Pater describes, a tracing that justifies the transition, goes a considerable way toward explaining the early reviewers' sense that Wilde's compressed reversals of received wisdom are both facile and outlandish.

Recognizable in Wallace's definition of 'dialectic' are the three stages of an Hegelian method that have passed into common culture: thesis, antithesis and synthesis. Wilde's version of dialectic doesn't quite work this way. Even professional commentators acknowledge the difficulty of construing Hegel, but it seems that for Hegel the ultimate synthesis would be visible only from a transcendent perspective: an undeveloped Spirit externalizes itself into the world of thought and matter as we know it, and through the process of history returns to itself as a synthesis of all that is. While Wilde occasionally sounds like an orthodox Hegelian, the perspective adopted in his works is typically *subjective*: as Vivian will declare in 'The Decay of Lying', 'Things are because we see them'.[17] It's important not to take 'subjective' as merely indicating variety of opinion, as when we say taste in wine is subjective, but as referring to the *subject*, the whole person holding the opinion. Wilde said further of the dialogue in his letters that it 'is written only for artistic temperaments: the public are not allowed a chance of comprehension ...'.[18] The relevant definition of 'temperament' also helps us see the full reference of Wilde's subjectivism: 'Constitution or habit of mind, esp. as determined by physical constitution and affecting behaviour; natural disposition, personality' (*Shorter OED*). Wilde didn't necessarily think our thoughts are determined by our physical constitutions – though it's a notion he played with in *The Picture of Dorian Gray* – but the definition has the value of reminding us that temperaments are housed in actual bodies. The last term in the definition, 'personality', is Wilde's favourite term for his subjectivism, and in this case the relevant definition fits exactly: 'The assemblage of qualities or characteristics which makes a person a distinctive individual' (*Shorter OED*). Wilde's habitual perspective is *person-centred*.[19]

Due to this perspective, Wilde's use of the dialectic method doesn't lead to the same kind of synthesis that Hegel's does; again, for Hegel the ultimate form of this synthesis requires a comprehensive perspective exceeding that of any individual, but for Wilde, the individual's viewpoint remains. To look ahead: while commentators disagree about how we're to align the positions of the main speakers in the two critical dialogues with Wilde himself, those positions do predominate in their respective dialogues, rather than merging with those of their interlocutors. That Wilde's dialectic doesn't lead to an encompassing synthesis prevents his use of dialectic from becoming formulaic. It remains Hegelian in that it proceeds by turning to opposites, but rather than moving neatly through a three-phase process, it has an exploratory quality about it. While Wallace is trying to give us orthodox Hegel, his definition of 'reflection' captures something of this quality. 'Reflection' is the mind's effort to uncover the dialectical process, an effort it makes in part by asking itself questions such as: 'what follows from this? How does this comport itself with other known facts? What would this lead to in such a case?'[20] For Wilde, the dialectical method, rather than resolving intellectual problems once and for all, is an instrument for continually probing the complexity of these issues.

In yet another letter, Wilde says of 'The Decay of Lying' that 'underneath the fanciful form it hides some truths, *or perhaps some great half truths*, about art, which I think require to be put forward, and of which some are, I think, quite new, and none the worse for that' (emphasis mine).[21] On the interpretation of Wilde as dialectician being proposed, 'great half truths' aren't half right and half wrong, so one could simply discard the wrong half; rather they're the *other half* of a more complete truth, and they 'require to be put forward' in order to bring an important aspect of that truth into view. The suggestion is, then, that the critical dialogues be approached as Wilde's swinging round to the opposite pole with respect to certain widely held tenets of aesthetic theory.[22]

In the earlier dialogue, 'The Decay of Lying', this swing round is easiest to see in Vivian's memorable claims that 'Life imitates Art',[23] and that Nature does as well, which clearly reverse venerable critical maxims. The dialogue takes its title from the article Vivian reads from intermittently, and while he subtitles his article 'A Protest', the dialogue is better called 'A Defence of Lying'. This defence is the dialogue's most encompassing turn to the opposite, even if the shape of the reversal isn't immediately apparent. The initial pole in the reversal is the view that telling the truth, including doing so through realistic art, is preferable to not doing so, that is, to lying. The form of lying Vivian will defend is minimally, just making things up; thus the caveman, whom Vivian calls the 'founder of social intercourse', makes up exploits as a hunter 'without ever having gone out to the rude chase'.[24] There's a clue to the final goal of Vivian's defence when he responds to Cyril's opening entreaty that they have their conversation outdoors by saying, 'I prefer houses to the open air. In a house we feel of the proper proportions. Everything is subordinated to us, fashioned for our use and our pleasure. Egotism itself, which is so necessary to a proper sense of human dignity, is entirely the result of indoor life', and concluding, 'Nothing is more evident than that Nature hates Mind'.[25] 'Indoor life' is Vivian's figure for culture, and thus the ultimate goal of making things up is constructing a human environment in the face of an actively hostile Nature.[26]

Vivian also dismisses Cyril's early objection that politicians and lawyers already keep up lying on the grounds that both parties make some appeal to the truth, while a 'fine lie' is 'that which is its own evidence'.[27] He doesn't mean that a 'fine lie' contains fabricated evidence, but rather that it's so satisfying as to be self-justifying. Thus he follows his praise of the cave man later by saying that 'the aim of the liar is simply to charm, to delight, to give pleasure. He is the very basis of civilized society.'[28] The focus of Vivian's essay is 'lying in art', and 'In literature', he states, 'we require distinction, charm, beauty, and imaginative power'.[29] For Vivian, while these qualities appear in the work, they belong ultimately to the author: 'The justification of a character in a novel is not that other persons are what they are, but that the author is what he is'.[30] A fine lie satisfies, apart from its content, because through it we encounter a realm of values only other persons can create. Vivian insists that Art keep 'between herself and reality the impenetrable barrier of beautiful style, of decorative or ideal treatment'[31] because style is the artist's continual shaping of content to his or her expressive purposes. It's actually this sense of control, he claims, that gives us a sense that a work is true: in art, 'Truth is entirely and absolutely a matter of style'.[32] With this reversal, a main strand of dialectic has completed itself. Initially in the dialogue, truth is true to something: what Vivian calls derisively 'a mess of facts'.[33] Style appears to be the contrary to this notion of truth, as the early reviewer above opposes Wilde's 'mannerisms' to his insight. But a fuller understanding of the concept of truth shows it to contain this contrary: indeed, in the realm of the arts, to be its contrary.

When Vivian states, 'Lying and poetry are arts – arts, as Plato saw, not unconnected –'[34] his passing reference to Plato places his defence of lying in the 'Defence of Poetry' tradition.[35] This tradition begins with Plato's attack on the arts in The Republic and runs in its English line through Sir Philip Sidney's Apology for Poetrie (1595 publication), Percy Bysshe Shelley's Defence of Poetry (1821, published 1840), Matthew Arnold's The Study of Poetry (1880) and beyond. Since this is the context in which persons interested solely in Wilde as a literary theorist are likely to examine his critical dialogues, it should be noted that 'The Decay of Lying', whatever its capacity to bewilder, is actually a typical modern defence in two respects. The question that defines the tradition is whether literature improves human life, and the crucial issue in the debate is whether literature tells the truth about the world and human life in it. At a glance, Plato and Vivian seem opposed – one attacking and the other defending – but Vivian's oblique reference may indicate that he realizes the relation is more complicated. While Plato did charge literature with telling lies, his conception of truth was broad enough so that philosophy could attain to the truth, rhetoric could be guided by truth, and even myths could express truth. By the late nineteenth century, a philosopher holding such a broad view of truth would be on the same side of the fence as poets and critics, all defending themselves against the scientific conception of truth as what survives testing against data.

The dialogue is typically modern in that it doesn't try to meet this stricter standard but instead acknowledges the subjectivity of the arts. This is evident in Vivian's argument for the paradox that Nature imitates Art: 'For what is Nature? Nature is no great mother who has borne us. She is our creation. It is in our brain that she quickens to life. Things are because we see them, and what we see, and how we see it, depends on the Arts that have influenced us.'[36] The dialogue is also typical of modern defences in its double movement: Vivian insists on the autonomy of art – 'Art never expresses anything but itself'[37] – but he separates art from life in order to reconnect the two on art's own terms. This is evident in his argument for the paradox that life imitates art, which is the core of his defence: 'Scientifically speaking, the basis of life – the energy of life, as Aristotle would call it – is simply the desire for expression, and Art is always presenting various forms through which this expression can be attained.'[38] Life itself is an expressive process, and art provides the shaping forms that make ongoing acts of expression possible.

These last two arguments provide the occasion to return to the early reviewer's complaint that Wilde 'makes paradox ridiculous'. Vivian's most outlandish statement must be his conclusion that 'the whole of Japan is a pure invention [of artists]. There is no such country, there are no such people.'[39] Surely we're to enjoy Vivian's sheer exuberance, as Harold Bloom does, calling Vivian's claim 'one of the grand critical epiphanies, one of those privileged moments that alone make criticism memorable'.[40] But there's a logical aspect of Vivian's exuberance as well. Julia Prewitt Brown makes the subtle observation that Wilde allows 'Vivian to exaggerate [in this statement] so as to suggest that all general statement invites contradiction', and thus the overstatement implicitly directs the reader to take Vivian's assertion itself as a 'contrary', a necessary contradiction of the view that art imitates life.[41] Vivian's epiphany also reflects Wilde's version of dialectic. Vivian continues by saying 'if you cannot see an absolutely Japanese effect [strolling in Piccadilly], you will not see it anywhere'.[42] This is plausible if things are because we see them and our sight is guided by artistic forms. The entire dialogue could be described as Wilde positing this principle and then asking, in

Wallace's words, 'what follows from this?' How would familiar issues in aesthetics look from this point of view? Unlike the cautious Pater, Wilde turns directly to the opposite pole, or to put this differently, he takes his assumed point of view all the way out: it is by stating the opposite pole in its unqualified form that the 'half truth' of the reversal comes into view. Vivian could stop with the claim that you have to be able to see a 'Japanese effect' everywhere to see it anywhere, but his dialectical momentum carries him further, causing comic disaster for Japan.

Commenting on Plato, Walter Watson notes that 'dialectic' is a term derived from a Greek word meaning 'to talk with', and so the dialectical method has a natural affinity for the dialogue form. In the Platonic dialogue, Watson continues, 'the dialectician asks questions and another answers them. The dialectician must work with whatever answer he gets, and therefore the method of the dialogue depends on both questioner and answerer.'[43] While Wilde's critical dialogues aren't really Platonic dialogues, they do progress through the interaction between main speaker and interlocutor.[44] In 'The Critic as Artist', Gilbert cites as an advantage of the dialogue form its capacity to exhibit 'all the richness and reality of effect that comes from those side issues that are suddenly suggested by the central idea in its progress, and really illumine the idea more completely, or from those felicitous after-thoughts that give a fuller completeness to the central scheme, and yet convey something of the delicate charm of chance'.[45] The dialogues need these sudden suggestions and 'felicitous after-thoughts' because due to Wilde's subjective perspective, there is no free-standing subject whose independent contours could dictate the course of investigation. There are criteria, such as the 'completeness' Gilbert mentions, but they're criteria for the adequacy of an investigation accomplished by the talk itself. Thus in 'The Decay of Lying', in the service of completeness, it's the interlocutor Cyril who, sensing an implication of Vivian's claims, asks him to prove that Nature, like Life, imitates Art, as well as asking Vivian to summarize his theory at the dialogue's close. This dynamic is nicely captured by J.D. Thomas's comments on Cyril's early interjection of the commonplace that a 'return to Life and Nature' would be a 'panacea' for art: by this device, 'Wilde is able to move on to his main thesis, the primacy of art over both life and nature, without the necessity for internal transition and continuity within the article from which his spokesman is supposedly quoting. The logic of expository development is exchanged for dialectic.'[46]

Symons's felt need to acknowledge that a statement he discusses, spoken by 'one of the characters in a dialogue', appears in the subsequent commentary both as the question of how to attach the views expressed by Vivian and Gilbert to Wilde and, more radically, as the doubt that the dialogues express any views at all.[47] Vivian identifies the source of both question and doubt when he rejects Hamlet's 'aphorism' that Art holds the mirror up to Nature on the grounds that the aphorism 'is merely a dramatic utterance, and no more represents Shakespeare's real views on art than the speeches of Iago represent his real views on morals'.[48] But we can recognize that Wilde's dialogues have a dramatic aspect without making them into completely self-referential works of art. Wilde himself doesn't seem to have done the latter: in a letter advising Bosie Douglas to express his feelings in poetry more obliquely, he points out that, 'One can really, as I say in *Intentions*, be far more subjective in an *objective* form than in any other way';[49] that is, he feels easy about taking as his own a statement Gilbert makes in 'The Critic as Artist'. The dialogue form would attract Wilde because of his person-centred subjectivism. As William E. Buckler observes, Gilbert 'is an imaginary character with his own temperament, taste, and talents placed in a certain relationship to life and to another imaginary character'.[50] That the claims in the dialogues are made by developed characters allows Wilde to remind us that ideas are always *someone's*. This does mean that the assertive mode of the dialogues is oblique in comparison to a discursive essay, but Wilde again may provide the best guide in his remarks about the earlier dialogue's being accessible only to readers of 'an artistic temperament', particularly recalling the full sense of 'temperament' relevant here. There has to be a match between the claims and the person: a match aptly described by Hilda Schiff's remark that,

> Ideas for Wilde are neither sacred not absolute; they are to be explored and appreciated and adhered to only so long as they are conducive to illumination and intellectual delight. Always they are to be dominated by a sense of the greater reality of the individual

who holds them and whose richer quality of imagining and understanding they serve.[51]

The purpose of the analysis to this point has been to show that the features of Wilde's criticism that have sometimes puzzled or even put off readers, principally his use of paradox embedded in the dialogue form, result from his dialectical habit of mind modified by his subjectivism. While that analysis has been developed mainly through discussion of 'The Decay of Lying', it applies equally well to Wilde's second dialogue 'The Critic as Artist'. In fact, this approach to Wilde as a critical thinker readily explains why there's a shift in explicit topic between the two dialogues: Wilde is reversing a different proposition, namely, Matthew Arnold's claim in 'The Function of Criticism at the Present Time' (1864), that 'the critical power is of lower rank than the creative'.[52] The swing round to the opposite of Arnold's view has three main strands in Part I of the dialogue, each more ambitious than the other. The first is Gilbert's claim that the 'antithesis between [the creative faculty and the critical faculty] is entirely arbitrary'.[53] He recalls Ernest's assertion that a 'fine spirit of choice and delicate instinct of selection' is essential to creation and observes, 'that spirit of choice, that subtle tact of omission, is really the critical faculty in one of its most characteristic moods, and no one who does not possess this faculty can create anything at all in art'.[54] This is transparently dialectical: one pole of an opposition again turns out to contain its contrary. Ernest readily concedes this point, but still doubts that criticism itself is 'really a creative art'.[55] Gilbert replies, 'Why should it not be? It works with materials, and puts them into a form that is at once new and delightful. What more can one say of poetry?'[56] In fact, Gilbert claims, criticism can be 'more creative than creation' because the critic builds on or extends the turning away from external reality begun in the works of art he criticizes, the assumption being that this turning away is one meaning of 'creative'. Thus Gilbert is once more arguing a dialectical point, the close relation of apparent opposites, but by a different strategy, that the same criteria can be used to judge both poles. To return for a moment to the matter of the dialogue form, while Schiff is certainly right to say that for Wilde ideas find their place in a person's whole intellectual life, this insight shouldn't obscure our task as readers: both dialogues are largely composed of arguments,

arguments that have to be recovered before they can play any role in our intellectual lives.

The third strand consists of Gilbert's effort to show that criticism is not only a creative art but an 'independent' one.[57] It's this effort that produces the dialogue's reversal of Arnold's famous dictum that the object of criticism is to 'see the object as in itself it really is', a dictum that according to Gilbert ignores 'Criticism's most perfect form which is in its essence purely subjective, and seeks to reveal its own secret and not the secret of another. For the highest Criticism deals with art not as expressive but as impressive purely.'[58] Authors express; readers and critics receive impressions. By making the latter the focus of criticism, Gilbert moves criticism in its pure form further into the subjective realm congenial to Wilde. To Wilde's credit, however, Ernest is allowed to ask whether what Gilbert is describing is 'really criticism':[59] a doubt based on our ordinary understanding that criticism is of something. Or to put this in the terms being used here: the dialogue's dialectical method risks breaking down if the critical pole is severed completely from the creativity represented by primary works of art.

In the earlier dialogue, Vivian, challenged by Cyril, declares he 'is prepared to prove anything',[60] by which, flippancy aside, he means he's prepared to see what can be said on behalf of any position, no matter how initially improbable.[61] Ernest's doubt is so sensible Gilbert too seems to cast about to see what can be said for a position hardly intuitively obvious, and this brings to the fore the exploratory feel characteristic of dialectic in Wilde. Gilbert's efforts to dispel Ernest's doubt include not only his analysis of criticism in its freest form, but his discussion of the more restricted interpretive criticism that opens the dialogue's second part. In both places, Gilbert is so resourceful that his arguments call to mind Thomas's conjecture that 'intentions' in the title Wilde chose for his volume has its etymological sense of 'stretchers'.[62] And as 'stretchers', they pose interpretive problems.

In support of his claim that criticism can be an independent art, for instance, Gilbert asserts that, 'Beauty is the symbol of symbols. Beauty reveals everything, because it expresses nothing. When it shows us itself, it shows us the whole fiery-coloured world.'[63] The problem is inferring how beauty accomplishes this. What Gilbert needs for his general claim is a way of keeping criticism tethered to primary art while still leaving the critic free to express his 'own secret'. We should recall from 'The Decay of Lying' that for Wilde form enables expressive energy to realize itself. When Gilbert says that the highest criticism 'criticises not merely the individual work of art, but Beauty itself',[64] he apparently means that criticism can attend to this capacity of form itself. To see beauty as 'the symbol of symbols' is to see it as referring to the symbol-making or expressive process not coupled with any specific content. Beauty 'shows us the whole fiery-coloured world' by revealing how aspects of the world might be expressed. This is why, 'The one characteristic of a beautiful form is that one can put into it whatever one wishes, and see in it whatever one chooses to see'.[65] The beautiful form is the point of contact between artist and critic, enabling the former to shape a content while allowing the latter to put the form to a new use.

When Gilbert admits in the dialogue's second part that a critic can try to interpret an author's expression, he hastens to add that the critic 'will not be an interpreter in the sense of one who simply repeats in another form a message that has been put into his lips to say'.[66] This is the earlier danger seen from the other end: if the interpretive critic 'simply repeats' the primary artist's 'message', then the creative pole, rather than existing in relation to the critical pole, swallows it up. This won't happen, according to Gilbert,

> For, just as it is only by contact with the art of foreign nations that the art of a country gains that individual and separate life that we call nationality, so, by curious inversion, it is only by intensifying his own personality that the critic can interpret the personality and work of others, and the more strongly this personality enters into the interpretation the more real the interpretation becomes, the more satisfying, the more convincing and the more true.[67]

Gilbert has given us a four term analogy, and the problem is deciding what goes with what. One might think the interpretive critic is like the 'art of a country' coming in contact with the 'art of foreign nations', or the works of various artists, but that would make the result of the contact the illumination of the critic's 'nationality' or distinctive character. Apparently, then, the critic is like the art of the foreign nations, and the 'curious inversion' is that by cultivating his own personality, the critic is able to throw into relief the personality and expression of someone else. Through his analogy, Gilbert has found a way to preserve a dialectical relation between art and criticism even in the phase of criticism most focussed on primary art: understanding the artist requires an approach through the distinct perspective of the critic.[68]

'The Critic as Artist' continues the Defence of Poetry begun in the earlier dialogue; Gilbert argues, for instance, that the experience provided by the arts is superior in several respects to real-life experience, including exhibiting a 'fine correspondence of form and spirit'.[69] However, due to its basic dialectical reversal, the swing round from creation to criticism, the dialogue is actually a Defence of Criticism, or more accurately, a Defence of Being a Critic. Gilbert is making this defence when, following his claim that Heredity, as a kind of collective unconscious, makes available to us a vast repository of experience from the past, he asserts that the 'true critic' and the 'true man of culture' are one:

> The culture that this transmission of racial experiences makes possible can be made perfect by the critical spirit alone. For who is the true critic but he who bears within himself the dreams, and ideas, and feelings of myriad generations, and to whom no form of thought is alien, no emotional impulse obscure? And who is the true man of culture, if not he who by fine scholarship and fastidious rejection has made instinct self-conscious and intelligent, and can separate the work that has distinction from the work that has it not, and so by contact and comparison makes himself master of the secrets of style and school, and understands their meanings, and listens to their voices, and develops that spirit of disinterested curiosity which is the real root, as it is the real flower, of the intellectual life, and thus attains to intellectual clarity, and having learned 'the best that is known and thought in the world', lives – it is not fanciful to say so – with those who are the Immortals.[70]

The 'true critic' represents judgment, and the 'true man of culture' content, and Gilbert's point is that each needs what the other has. The man of culture's exercise of judgment must be an expressive process, since the dialogue doesn't recognize any other kind. In the letter to Bosie cited above, Wilde is referring to Gilbert's assertion that 'the objective form is the most subjective in matter. Man is least himself when he talks in his own person. Give him a mask, and he will tell you the truth.'[71] The mask acts back on the person, providing an identity that allows the person to express the truth. Something analogous happens when the man of culture engages the expressions of the past in the encyclopaedic manner Gilbert describes: these forms act back on his capacity for judgment, changing it from an 'instinct' to a 'self-conscious' faculty.

This change distances the man of culture – who is now identical to the true critic – from the objects of his attention: as Gilbert continues,

> the contemplative life, that life that has for its aim not *doing* but *being* merely, but *becoming* – that is what the critical spirit can give us. The gods live thus: either brooding over their own perfection, as Aristotle tells us, or, as Epicurus fancied, watching with the calm eyes of the spectator the tragi-comedy of the world they have made. We, too might live like them, and set ourselves to witness with appropriate emotions the varied scenes that man and nature afford.[72]

Gilbert is defending his ideal critic by placing him in the *viva contemplativa*, or contemplative life tradition. As scholars have noted, while this was a tradition at odds with the prevailing Victorian emphasis on industry and practicality, it also had influential cultural spokesmen like Arnold.[73] This defence allows us to return to the question of what form 'synthesis' takes for Wilde in the critical sphere – a question since Wilde's looser version of dialectic doesn't lead to the neat synthesis associated with Hegel. What gets synthesized are the 'dreams, and ideas, and feelings of myriad generations': these, though not strictly 'contraries', are understood as different enough to be potentially 'alien' to any single perspective. While not a synthesis with the transcendental scope of Hegel's, its amplitude, in principle all extant human expressions, is considerable. Gilbert, having first made the critic creative, is now returning in his fashion to the more usual notion of the critic as someone who looks at rather than produces, but on a much larger scale. The critic leads the contemplative life because his scope is godlike: he, in effect, re-expresses all of human culture. The process of synthesis initially coincides with the critic's self-development, or in Gilbert's terms, the process by which the man of culture becomes a critic. The synthesis itself is maintained by, held together by, the ongoing activity of the mature critic; this is why, self-conscious of his own activity, the critic, like the gods, knows he's watching a world he has made. Rather than being an end of history and process, then, this synthesis remains dynamic. As Gilbert will say shortly, 'Through constant change, and through constant change alone, [the critic] will find his true unity. He will not consent to be the slave of his own opinions. For what is mind but motion in the intellectual sphere?'[74]

When authors produce both works of literary theory and primary literature, we assume the former will apply to the latter, as, say, the writings collected in Henry James's The Art of Fiction (1884) illuminate the purposes and techniques of his novels. As usual, Wilde doesn't conform to our assumptions. If there were such a match between theoretical and primary works, we would expect it in texts treating similar ideas, but as Richard Ellmann says of The Picture of Dorian Gray, 'The book is [Wilde's] parable of the impossibility of leading a life on aesthetic terms'.[75] At a glance, the novel, rather than illustrating the doctrines of the critical dialogues, seems to repudiate them. Approaching Wilde as a dialectician, however, allows us to understand the relation between the dialogues and the novel differently.

The broad difference between the critical dialogues and the novel is similar to that between the two dialogues themselves: Wilde is reversing a different set of ideas. The reversal that shapes the novel's plot transfers the ageless beauty of art to a person and human conscience to a work of art. While the two dialogues have different explicit foci, roughly art in the earlier and criticism in the later, these foci are related closely enough to compose one theoretical statement. The critical dialogues and the novel differ more radically. 'The desire to realise the modern personality in life, not thought', observes Rodney Shewan, is 'responsible for [the character] Dorian Gray': while the critic of the dialogues lives in the contemplative realm, Dorian moves in the actional world.[76] The central aesthetic concept common to the dialogues and the novel is beauty, and borrowing once more from Wallace, it's as though Wilde's project in the novel is to ask, 'what would Beauty be like in such a case'? The case is now the physical beauty of a person. 'Beauty', declares Lord Henry, 'is the wonder of wonders', a phrasing that recalls Gilbert's statement that 'Beauty is the form of forms'. However, while Gilbert is describing beauty's role in enabling expression, Harry is referring to the power physical beauty gives a person to pursue his goals in the face of impediments posed by the presence of other persons in the world: beauty 'cannot be questioned. It has divine right of sovereignty.'[77] Dorian's exemption from the aging process that also comes with the reversal allows him to exercise this power throughout the novel.

Wallace's notion of dialectic as exploring cases has been more fully explicated by Stanley Cavell:

> Very generally, a dialectical examination of a concept will show how the meaning of that concept changes, and how the subject of which it is the concept changes, as the context in which it is used changes: the dialectical meaning is the history or confrontation of these differences. For example, an examination of the concept of silence will show that the word means different things – that silence is different things – depending on whether the context is the silence of nature [or] the silence of shyness ... And the specific meaning of the word in each of those contexts is determined by tracing its specific contrasts with the others – the way its use in one context 'negates' its use in another, so to speak.[78]

While Dorian does come to a bad end, the suggestion here is that the novel 'negates' the dialogues not by repudiating their doctrines, but by placing beauty in another context, the actional world, and exploring how in that context, beauty is, or at least may be, a 'different thing'. The further, and admittedly large, suggestion is that the repetition with a difference of themes so often noted in Wilde is a sign of the dialectical process Cavell describes being played out in Wilde's corpus as a whole. For instance, the recurrent Wildean opposition between pleasure and happiness isn't the same in the context of 'Lord Arthur Savile's Crime' (1887) as it is in the context of 'The Happy Prince' (1888), and to determine what the opposition comes to for Wilde would require juxtaposing its meanings in these and other contexts.

The critical dialogues, on this view, become one instance among others of Wilde's investigating the topics that interest him. But they're also more than that. In his study of dialectic, Nicholas Rescher distinguishes between a 'hermeneutic' form, which seeks to clarify concepts, and dialectic as a technique of disputation.[79] Dialectic in Wilde is clearly of the first type, and so on the suggestion above, Wilde's corpus itself has a contemplative cast. Looking back on his career in *De Profundis* (1905), Wilde says, 'to truth itself I gave what is false no less than what is true as its rightful province, and showed that the false and the true are merely forms of intellectual existence'.[80] This echoes the dialectical addendum to 'The Truth of Masks': the realm of the true 'rightfully' includes its contradictory, the false. Moreover, the claim is implicitly contemplative, since we have to step back and reflect on the concepts of the true and the false to see them as 'merely forms of intellectual existence'. It's because the critical dialogues offer us the opportunity to step back and contemplate Wilde's dialectical mode of thought that they not only present criticism as it might be, but provide a valuable introduction to his works as a whole.

NOTES

1. See Bruce Bashford, 'When Critics Disagree: Recent Approaches to Oscar Wilde', *Victorian Literature and Culture*, 30, 2 (2002), pp.613–25, for an overview of recent critical approaches to Wilde's works in several genres.

2. Oscar Wilde, letter to Violet Fane, 15 January 1889, in *The Complete Letters of Oscar Wilde*, eds Merlin Holland and Rupert Hart-Davis (London: Fourth Estate, 2000), p.386. Wilde is referring to the magazine version of the 'The Decay of Lying' which appeared in the January 1889 edition of *The Nineteenth Century*. 'The Critic as Artist' appeared originally in two numbers of the same journal in July and September 1890 with the title, 'The True Function and Value of Criticism: With Some Remarks on the Importance of Doing Nothing: A Dialogue'. The two other pieces in *Intentions*, 'The Truth of Masks' and 'Pen, Pencil, and Poison', also appeared earlier in magazines. Wilde revised all four pieces for *Intentions*, his only volume of criticism, published in 1891. For publication history, a discussion of Wilde's revisions and the surviving manuscript variants, see Josephine M. Guy (ed.) *Criticism*, the fourth volume of *The Complete Works of Oscar Wilde* (Oxford: Oxford University Press, 2007). All references to the two critical dialogues and to 'The Truth of Masks' are to this volume.

3. Oscar Wilde, letter to Marie-Anne de Bovet, early 1889, in *Letters*, p.393.

4. Karl Beckson (ed.), *Oscar Wilde: The Critical Heritage* (London: Routledge & Kegan Paul, 1970), p.92.

5. Ibid., p.90.

6. Ibid., p.92.

7. Ibid., p.96.

8. Ibid., p.94.

9. Hilda Schiff, 'Nature and Art in Oscar Wilde's "The Decay of Lying"', *Essays and Studies by Members of the English Association*, 18 (1965), p.101.

10. William Wallace, 'Prolegomena' in *The Logic of Hegel*, trans. William Wallace (Oxford: Clarendon Press, 1874), p.xxxiii.

11. Ibid., p.clxxx.

12. Wilde, 'Truth of Masks', p.228.

13. For an insightful comparison of the passage to Mikhail Bakhtin's notion of the 'dialogic', see Jonathan Freedman, *Professions of Taste: Henry James, British Aestheticism, and Commodity Culture* (Stanford, CA: Stanford University Press, 1990), p.72.

14. Oscar Wilde, letter to the Editor of the *St James's Gazette*, 28 June 1890, in *Letters*, p.433.

15. Oscar Wilde, 'Mr. Pater's Imaginary Portraits', in *Oscar Wilde: Selected Journalism*, ed. Anya Clayworth (Oxford: Oxford University Press, 2004), p.22.

16. Walter Pater, 'Coleridge', in *Selected Writings of Walter Pater*, ed. Harold Bloom (New York: Columbia University Press, 1974), pp.143–4.

17. Wilde, 'Decay of Lying', p.95.

18. Oscar Wilde, letter to Amelie Rives Chanler, January 1889, in *Letters*, p.388.

19. For further discussion of Wilde's subjectivism, see Bruce Bashford, *Oscar Wilde: The Critic as Humanist* (Cranbury, NJ: Fairleigh Dickinson University Press, 1999), pp.11–13; 28–31). The Commentary by Philip E. Smith II and Michael Helfand in *Oscar Wilde's Oxford Notebooks: A Portrait of Mind in the Making* (New York: Oxford University Press, 1989), remains the fullest analysis of Wilde as an Hegelian, and I'm indebted to them throughout my discussion. Readers are invited to evaluate the differences in our views of Wilde. They seem to find in Wilde a perspective that would be transcendent in the Hegelian manner, and while there is some evidence for their view, I think the Wilde of the critical dialogues is better read as a subjectivist. I agree with them that Wilde is an 'idealist' in the sense of refusing to reduce our conscious lives – our thoughts, feelings and imaginings – to mere epiphenomena of the material world. I don't think, however, that he is an idealist in another familiar but distinct sense of believing that beyond the world as we encounter it there's a hidden realm with the mode of existence of ideas – in Hegel's case, a realm of pure Spirit. I'm not sure about their position on this point. For other studies that have Wilde rejecting the existence of a transcendent reality connected with this second sense of idealism, see Linda Dowling, *Language and Decadence in the Victorian Fin de Siècle* (Princeton, NJ: Princeton University Press, 1986), pp.96–7; Jürgen Klein, 'Aesthetics of Coldness: The Case of Oscar Wilde', in Uwe Böker, Richard Corballis and Julie A. Hibbard (eds), *The Importance of Reinventing Oscar: Versions of Wilde during the Last 100 Years* (Amsterdam: Rodopi, 2002), pp.67–79.

20. Wallace, 'Prolegomena', p.clxxx.

21. Oscar Wilde, letter to Mrs George Lewis, January 1889, in *Letters*, p.389.

22. For two studies that explore in detail Wilde's dialectical habit of mind as displayed in areas other than his criticism, see Declan Kiberd's discussion of the dialectical shape of Wilde's life in 'Oscar Wilde: The Artist as Irishman', in *Inventing Ireland* (Cambridge, MA: Harvard University Press, 1996), pp.33–50; and Bernard Beatty's analysis of Wilde's style in 'The Form of Oscar: Wilde's Art of Substitution', *Irish Studies Review*, 11, 1 (2003), pp.34–49.

23. Wilde, 'Decay of Lying', p.90.

24. Ibid., p.88.

25. Ibid., p.74.

26. See also Northrop Frye's observation that the dialogue's 'main thesis is that man does not live directly and nakedly in nature like the animals, but within an envelope he has constructed out of nature, the envelope usually called culture or civilization' *Creation and Recreation* (Toronto: Toronto University Press, 1980, p.5). While Frye deeply admires Wilde's critical dialogues, he also makes a remark that could have come from one of the early reviewers: Wilde 'sets up a palisade of self-conscious and rather mechanical wit, which not merely infuriates those who have no idea what he is talking about but often puts off those who do' (p.5).

27. Wilde, 'Decay of Lying', p.74.

28. Ibid., p.88.

29. Ibid., p.79.

30. Ibid., p.79.

31. Ibid., p.84.

32. Ibid., p.88.

33. Ibid., p.82.

34. Ibid., p.76.

35. Vivian's mention of Plato has prompted several discussions of Wilde's reply to Plato; see, for instance, Wendell Harris, 'Arnold, Pater, Wilde, and the Object as in Themselves They See It', *Studies in English Literature*, 11 (1971), p.743; Edward Watson, 'Wilde's Iconoclastic Classicism: "The Critic as Artist"', *English Literature in Transition, 1880–1920*, 27, 3 (1984), pp.225–35.

36. Wilde, 'Decay of Lying', p.95.

37. Ibid., p.102.

38. Ibid., p.94.

39. Ibid., p.98.

40. Harold Bloom, 'Introduction', in Harold Bloom (ed.), *Modern Critical Views: Oscar Wilde* (New York: Chelsea House, 1985), p.4.

41. Julia Prewitt Brown, *Cosmopolitan Criticism: Oscar Wilde's Theory of Art* (Charlottesville, VA: University of Virginia Press, 1997), p.70. Brown reads Wilde largely in the context of Kant's philosophical legacy, rather than Hegel's.

42. Wilde, 'Decay of Lying', p.98.

43. Walter Watson, *The Architectonics of Meaning* (Albany, NY: State University of New York Press, 1985), p.85.

44. As Edouard Roditi points out, in the Platonic dialogues, 'Socrates rarely expresses any opinion of his own', which is hardly true of Vivian and Gilbert (*Oscar Wilde* [New York: New Directions, 1986], p.62).

45. Wilde, 'Critic as Artist', in *Complete Works*, Vol.4, pp.186–7.

46. J.D. Thomas, 'The Intentional Strategy in Oscar Wilde's Dialogues', *English Literature in Transition, 1880–1920*, 12 (1969), p.13.

47. For the argument that the dialogues make no assertions, see Herbert Sussman, 'Criticism as Art: Form in Oscar Wilde's Critical Writings', *Studies in Philology*, 70 (1977), pp.108–22.

48. Wilde, 'Decay of Lying', p.89.

49. Oscar Wilde, letter to Lord Alfred Douglas, 2? June 1897, in *Letters*, pp.873–4.

50. William E. Buckler, 'Building a Bulwark Against Despair: "The Critic as Artist"', *English Literature in Transition: 1880–1920*, 32, 3 (1989), p.279.

51. Schiff, 'Nature and Art', p.101.

52. See Isobel Murray's head note to the dialogue in *Oscar Wilde: The Major Works*, ed. Isobel Murray (Oxford: Oxford University Press, 2000), p.589.

53. Wilde, 'Critic as Artist', p.142.

54. Ibid., p.142.

55. Ibid., p.153.

56. Ibid., p.154.

57. Ibid., p.153.

58. Ibid., p.155.

59. Ibid., p.158.

60. Wilde, 'Decay of Lying', p.95.

61. Vivian's flippant tone may also make readers doubt that Wilde and his spokesmen are really 'serious'. To assuage this doubt, it helps to recall that one especially astute contemporary reader, Walter Pater, found no incompatibility between Vivian's tone and the intellectual value of his remarks, calling 'The Decay of Lying' 'all but unique in its *half-humorous*, yet wholly convinced presentment of certain valuable truths of criticism' ('A Novel by Mr. Oscar Wilde', in *Selected Writings of Walter Pater*, p.263 [emphasis mine]). Wilde's lifelong rejection of seriousness may itself be seen dialectically as an effort to complement our normally serious approach to intellectual issues by taking an 'unserious' perspective on them.

62. Thomas, 'The Intentional Strategy', 18.

63. Wilde, 'Critic as Artist', p.158.

64. Ibid., p.158.

65. Ibid., p.159.

66. Ibid., p.164.

67. Ibid., p.164.

68. See Suzy Anger for a high estimate of Wilde's interpretive theory. *Victorian Interpretation*

(Ithaca, NY: Cornell University Press, 2005), pp.141–65. A difference readers can evaluate: for Anger, as 'The Critic as Artist' progresses, 'the conversation moves from subjectivist to objectivist views without marking the shifts' (p.151). In my view, when Gilbert acknowledges that the critic may attend to the intention of the author he becomes more inventive to maintain his subjectivist perspective.

69. Wilde, 'Critic as Artist', p.173.

70. Ibid., p.178.

71. Ibid., p.185.

72. Ibid., pp.178–9.

73. Clyde De L. Ryals, for instance, observes that in Victorian 'industrial society which valued production above almost everything else, that which was not obviously useful was suspect'. 'The Nineteenth-Century Cult of Inaction', *Tennessee Studies in Literature*, 4–6 (1959–61), p.56. See Ryals for a placement of Wilde in the *vita contemplative* tradition as it existed in the nineteenth century. See Smith and Helfand's Commentary in *Oscar Wilde's Oxford Notebooks* for Wilde's specific acquaintance with the tradition. Since the tradition remains as beleaguered in our time as it was in Wilde's, readers might want to consult the direct defence of it in Josef Pieper, *Leisure: The Basis of Culture*, trans. Gerald Malsbary (South Bend, IN: St Augustine's Press, 1998), pp.3–60. Though Pieper never mentions Wilde, his description of the contemplative life matches Gilbert's in several respects, suggesting that while Gilbert's claims may sound overstated, Wilde again is being '*au fond*' 'serious'.

74. Wilde, 'Critic as Artist', p.189.

75. Richard Ellmann, 'Introduction', in *The Picture of Dorian Gray and Other Writings by Oscar Wilde* (New York: Bantam, 1982), p.ix.

76. Rodney Shewan, *Oscar Wilde: Art and Egotism* (London: Macmillan, 1977), p.104.

77. Oscar Wilde, *The Picture of Dorian Gray* (1891), in *The Complete Works of Oscar Wilde*, Vol.3, edited Joseph Bristow (Oxford: Oxford University Press, 2005), p.186.

78. Stanley Cavell, *Must We Mean What We Say?* (Cambridge, MA: Cambridge University Press, 1976), pp.169–70.

79. Nicholas Rescher, *Dialectics: A Controversy-Oriented Approach to the Theory of Knowledge* (Albany, NY: State University of New York Press, 1977), p.52.

80. Oscar Wilde, *De Profundis*, in *The Complete Works of Oscar Wilde*, Vol.2, *De Profundis*, 'Epistola: In Carcere et Vinculis', ed. Ian Small (Oxford: Oxford University Press, 2005), p.95.

CHAPTER SEVEN

Performance and Identity in the Plays of Oscar Wilde

SOS ELTIS

In 'The Soul of Man under Socialism' (1891) Oscar Wilde envisaged a utopia free from authority, law, social morality, institutions and obligations, in which the 'true personality of man' can finally be realized.[1] Self-sufficient and self-delighting, this true personality will not argue or dispute or meddle with others, but will develop organically, pleasing all with its beauty: 'It will grow naturally and simply, flowerlike, or as a tree grows.'[2] Self-realization is the ultimate goal for all individuals and the essay proposes an anarchic rejection of all authority as the means to achieve this ideal. This organic model of the self, coherent and self-contained, remains a vision and not a reality, however, for the actual conditions of society render it questionable whether the full expression of a personality has ever been achieved outside 'the imaginative plane of art'.[3] At best societies are brutal and inspire self-assertion through rebellion and protest, or at worst they disguise their authority in kindness and rewards:

> People, in that case, are less conscious of the horrible pressure that is being put on them, and so go through their lives in a sort of coarse comfort, like petted animals, without ever realising that they are probably thinking other people's thoughts, living by other people's standards, wearing practically what one may call other people's second-hand clothes, and never being themselves for a single moment.[4]

Scripted and costumed by others, these unrealized personalities remain unaware that they are acting out a role written by others. A coherent organic self remains a utopian dream, while a performed identity – whether conscious or not – is the inevitable corollary of social existence.

Critics from Jonathan Dollimore onwards have identified Wilde's model of self as non-essentialist, multiple, fluid and unfixed.[5] Wilde presents the self as unstable, constantly forming and re-forming in, as Walter Pater describes it, a 'strange, perpetual weaving and unweaving of ourselves'.[6] But, unlike Pater's, Wilde's model of self is not walled in, confined to 'the narrow chamber of the individual mind'.[7] Instead Wilde's concept of the self is one which can access multiple identities, whether through the medium of art which, as Gilbert observes in 'The Critic as Artist' (1890), 'creates for one a past of which one has been ignorant', or through imagination which 'enables us to live the lives of the dead' so that 'our soul is no single spiritual entity'.[8] Performance itself becomes a means of realizing alternate selves, as Gilbert explains: 'What people call insincerity is simply a method by which we can multiply our personalities.'[9]

Wilde's model of a non-essential, performative self has proved influential and attractive to modern critics, in particular in his anticipation of Judith Butler's theories of the performativity of gender. But the notion of identity expressed and realized through performance was not necessarily antithetical to extant nineteenth-century notions of selfhood. As Lynn Voskuil has recently argued in *Acting Naturally: Victorian Theatricality and Authenticity*, the influential acting theories of William Hazlitt and George Henry Lewes conceptualized the most effective acting as rooted in the recollection and recreation of genuine emotion, and, in the actress Alchiarisi, George Eliot portrayed the trained artist as one whose spontaneous emotions are instinctively expressed in theatrical gesture.[10] Furthermore, the stylized gestures and positions detailed in Victorian acting manuals were rooted in ideas of the physiology of expression and emotion in mankind so that the very adoption of prescribed positions was supposed to awaken the associated emotion. As William Archer opined, 'No one denies, I think, that the primary emotions of an imagined character do in fact tend to communicate themselves to the nerve centres of the actor, and to affect his organs of expression'.[11]

Though such notions of the interrelation of representation and experience could sit comfortably alongside Wilde's notions of the performative self, his theories stood in direct and confrontational opposition to influential scientific theories of pathology and sexology, which used evolutionary notions of inherited characteristics to pathologize and categorize human character-types. Criminologist Cesare Lombroso in *L'Uomo Delinquente* (1876) and sexologist Richard von Krafft-Ebing in *Psychopathia Sexualis* (1886), for example, exhaustively anatomized and listed the various types and variations of criminals and sexual 'perverts', arranged into sets and subsets, accompanied by lists of distinctive features and distinguishing patterns of behaviour. Heredity was destiny, according to Lombroso's anatomizing of the inherited characteristics of the children of drunkards, prostitutes and thieves, unless the state intervene to control and re-direct these degenerate types. Wilde's model of the fluid, multiple, self-creating and ever-shifting personality, as expounded in the essays in *Intentions* (1891), challenged the central premises on which this science of character types was based.

A consistent admirer of Charles Darwin, Wilde was well versed in the science of evolution and natural selection. He drew on the ideas of Herbert Spencer and William Kingdon Clifford among others, in order to argue that individuation was the key to development in both nature and thought.[12] As he wrote in his Oxford Notebook:

> Progress in thought is the assertion of individualism against authority, and progress in matter is the differentiation and specialization of function: those organisms which are entirely subject to external influences do not progress any more than a mind entirely subject to authority.[13]

Wilde used evolutionary theory to validate individualism, where criminologist Max Nordau raised the bugbear of evolutionary degeneration to argue for the necessity of policing those who vary from the healthy norm and threaten to pass their deformities on to future generations. Wilde was well aware of the potential for ideas of biological inheritance to be co-opted in support of taxonomies and typologies of human character, but he evaded such limiting implications by introducing a multiform and unlimited inheritance of the mind and emotions. Thus heredity, as theorized by Wilde's Gilbert, is not a diagnostic tool but a portal to past worlds and lives. In the sphere of the soul, Gilbert opines, heredity manifests itself as imagination, which is 'simply concentrated race-experience' with the power to grant the individual access to 'countless lives':

> And so it is not our own life that we live, but the lives of the dead, and the soul that dwells within us is not a single spiritual entity, making us personal and individual ... It can help us to leave the age in which we were born, and to pass into other ages ... It can teach us how to escape from our experience, and to realise the experiences of those who are greater than we are.[14]

Wilde's celebration of the multifarious, self-inventing individual, in opposition both to notions of an objectively recognized and fixed 'reality' and to the authority of organized society, raised the particular ire of conservative commentator Max Nordau. Degeneration, the English translation of Nordau's Entartung (1892), was hugely popular and went through eight editions in the three years following its publication in 1895, and its readers were treated to a long diatribe against both Wilde's theories and person. Nordau dedicated some twenty pages to repudiating Wilde's celebration of the supremacy of the imagination and the doctrine of self-realization, and above all his proposition that Life imitates Art. On the basis of such theories and his idiosyncratic dress, Nordau confidently categorized Wilde as an Ego-Maniac, subset Aesthete.[15] In Nordau's view, the feelings of the majority were sacrosanct, and the purpose of education was to teach the individual 'to repress many manifestations of opinions and desires out of regard for his fellow-creatures'; anyone who had not learned this self-restraint was either, like Wilde, a 'deranged ego-maniac' or simply a 'blackguard'.[16]

Wilde's very lowest ebb, appealing to the Home Secretary for early release from Reading Gaol, is marked by his, at least outward, submission to this pathologized model of identity. So he describes, in the third-person, the 'terrible offences of which he was rightly found guilty' as 'forms of sexual madness ... diseases to be cured by a physician, rather than crimes to be punished by a judge'.[17] Handing himself over whole-sale to the theorists he had repudiated, Wilde humbly submitted that,

In the works of eminent men of science such as Lombroso and Nordau, to take merely two instances out of many, this is specially insisted on with reference to the intimate connection between madness and the literary and artistic temperament, Professor Nordau in his book on 'Degenerescence' published in 1894 having devoted an entire chapter to the petitioner as a specially typical example of this fatal law.[18]

Wilde's capitulation, however tactical, was fruitless: his petition was refused.

Wilde rescinded his submission to the pathologizing of character in his long prison letter, best known by the title *De Profundis*.[19] Jonathan Dollimore finds in *De Profundis* 'a conscious renunciation of his transgressive ethic and a reaffirmation of tradition as focussed in the depth model of identity', located in Wilde's emphasis on the spiritual growth and self-knowledge which come with suffering.[20] Far from being a purely 'confessional narrative', as Dollimore describes it, however, *De Profundis* (first published, in partial form, 1905), offers multiple models of the self, staging self-created and performed identities alongside the confessional, growth model. Theatrical images recur throughout: Wilde thought life a 'comedy' and found it a 'tragedy'; first stage-managed by Lord Alfred Douglas as a pawn in his feud with his father, he is then staged by the prison authorities, he and his fellow convicts are dressed as 'the zanies of sorrow', and in ultimate humiliation he is made a spectacle for a baying crowd at Clapham Junction. History 'with that grotesqueness of effect that is as it were a Gothic element' has cast him alongside the Marquis de Sade and Gilles de Retz, while Douglas farcically plays the role of the 'infant Samuel'.[21] Wilde concludes with a determination to transform his life, to refashion it as a work of art, transforming its meaning to fit his own narrative arc, to make its 'two great turning-points' when his father sent him to Oxford and when society sent him to prison.[22] The transformative imagination remains supreme, as he echoes the terms of *Intentions*:

Time and space, succession and extension, are merely accidental conditions of Thought. The Imagination can transcend them, and move in a free sphere of ideal existences. Things, also, are in their essence what we choose to make them. A thing is, according to the mode in which one looks at it.[23]

Like the manuscript of the letter, sent to Robert Ross with instructions for it to be typed up with 'a wide rubricated margin ... left for corrections', self is a work in progress, its author free to make further revisions in his own wide rubricated margin.[24]

In his prose fiction Wilde further explored these alternative models of selfhood, exploiting the fantastical possibilities of fairy tale and the gothic to construct literally split and doubled selves. In 'The Fisherman and his Soul' (1891), the soul is no sooner divided from the fisherman's body than it embarks upon an odyssey of its own, becoming a fully articulate and independent protagonist who seeks to seduce the fisherman away from his mermaid lover and blames its deviousness on its enforced separation from the heart. In *The Picture of Dorian Gray* (1890), a portrait becomes a double of its subject, absorbing the physical effects of Dorian's experiences and enabling him to lead a double life, safe from detection. Dorian's face becomes a living embodiment of Vivian's idea in 'The Decay of Lying' (1889) that Life imitates Art, and the intrinsic relation between art and life runs as a *leitmotif* through the novel, as, for example in the following much-quoted passage:

> For the canons of good society are, or should be, the same as the canons of art. Form is absolutely essential to it. It should have the dignity of a ceremony, as well as its unreality, and should combine the insincere character of a romantic play with the wit and beauty that make such plays delightful to us. Is insincerity such a terrible thing? I think not. It is merely the method by which we can multiply our personalities.
>
> Such, at any rate, was Dorian Gray's opinion. He used to wonder at the shallow psychology of those who conceive the Ego in man as a thing simple, permanent, reliable, and of one essence. To him, man was a being with myriad lives and myriad sensations, a complex multiform creature that bore within itself strange legacies of thought and passion, and whose very flesh was tainted with the monstrous maladies of the dead.[25]

Artificial and natural merge here, as do texts and voices: the apparent voice of the third-person narrator merges with what is belatedly identified as that of Dorian himself, while the whole passage echoes and quotes the dialogues of *Intentions*. Textual and narrative identities are as fluid and multiform as Dorian's model of the Ego.

The splitting, doubling and fluidity of identity which Wilde theorizes in his essays and enacts in his fiction stand in stark contrast to the conventional dynamics of Victorian theatre which were deeply rooted in fixed character types and notions of revelation and truth. The mid-Victorian repertory system and its popular staple, melodrama, were both structured around familiar types – the young female and young male leads, villain, comic servant, and so forth – all of whom were instantly recognizable to audiences on first appearance. Melodramatic plots commonly climaxed with the unmasking of the villain and the public recognition of the hero's or heroine's virtue. Melodrama, in Peter Brooks's influential analysis, enacts a Manichaean battle between good and evil in which essential moral truths are made manifest. As Brooks defines it, melodrama is a mode in which surface and depth are in complete accordance, essential types are instantly recognizable, and all is expressed:

> Nothing is spared because nothing is left unsaid; the characters stand on stage and utter the unspeakable, give voice to their deepest feelings, dramatize through their heightened and polarized words and gestures the whole lesson of their relationship. They assume psychic roles, father, mother, child, and express basic psychic conditions. Life tends, in this fiction, toward ever more concentrated and totally expressive gestures and statements.[26]

The fundamental trope of villainy's unmasking and virtue's public vindication is recognizable throughout the long life of the genre, stretching right through the century, from Guilbert de Pixérécourt's *Coelina, ou l'Enfant du mystère* (1800), to Tom Taylor's *The Ticket-of-Leave Man* (1863), G.R. Sims's *The Lights o' London* (1881) and Henry Arthur Jones's *The Middleman* (1889).

By the 1890s the lingering influence of melodrama had been met by the unsettling impact of Henrik Ibsen's plays. The first professional production of one of Ibsen's dramas to catch widespread notice was

A Doll's House (1879), which opened at the Novelty Theatre on 7 July 1889, produced by and starring Janet Achurch and her husband Charles Charrington. By 1891 Ibsen had become an established part of the theatrical landscape, with productions of *Rosmersholm* (1886), *Ghosts* (1881), *Hedda Gabler* (1890) and *The Lady from the Sea* (1888) all opening in a ten-week period between the end of February and the beginning of May. Though never big box-office, Ibsen's plays had a huge critical impact, acting, as playwright H.A. Jones commented, like 'an emetic or liver pill' forcibly purging the stage of 'stock dummies ... our master-pieces of impossible virtue and impossible vice'.[27] As Gay Gibson Cima has noted, Ibsen's characters demanded new naturalistic, psychologized acting styles.[28] His characters were not fixed, but multi-layered, unstable, mutable and impossible to categorize into types. His plays do not reveal an ultimate 'truth' about their protagonists or deliver a final verdict, but instead imply the artificiality of socially sanctioned roles. Nora Helmer realizes she has been playing the role of a doll in a doll's house, but who she may become, as she shrugs off the part of 'song-bird' and 'squirrel' and steps out into a public world she does not comprehend, is unanswered at the end of the play.[29] Mrs Alving realizes the damage done by her dutiful maintenance of a respectable front in her marriage to a philandering husband, and shrugs off the 'ghosts' of dead ideas and ideals, but it remains uncertain who she now is and what she now believes and, most crucially, whether she can bring herself to administer to her son the merciful death he desires. The damage inflicted by false roles, social expectation and constrictive morality on women such Nora Helmer, Mrs Alving and Hedda Gabler is clear, but no 'true self' is unveiled beneath these roles; the individual, baffled and thwarted by social morality, is necessarily a complex compound of instinct, education and circum-stance, and can never exist free of social pressures to conform.

Late-Victorian playwrights, such as Henry Arthur Jones, Arthur Wing Pinero and Sydney Grundy, responded to Ibsen's innovative theatre by marrying elements of his revolutionary technique to the familiar structures of melodramatic revelation. Where plays like *A Doll's House*, *Ghosts* and *Hedda Gabler* anatomize the distortion of the individual under the pressure of false social roles, Pinero, Jones and Grundy wrote plays which tackled questions of social morality but ultimately declared society's laws to be natural and inevitable. In Jones's *The Case of Rebellious Susan* (1894), for example, a wife refuses to accept her husband's adultery as 'a respectable average case' and embarks on an affair herself, while her cousin leads a militant feminist attack on a post office. But both are duly humiliated and punished, their rebellions proving a fruitless protest against the inescapable truth delivered by the play's *raisonneur* that, 'Nature's darling is a stay-at-home woman, a woman who wants to be a good wife and a good mother, and cares very little for anything else.'[30] Similarly, the eponymous heroine of Pinero's *The Notorious Mrs Ebbsmith* (1895) rejects the laws of marriage to live in free union with her lover, but her feminist ideals crumble to dust and her true feminine nature asserts itself when she dons a low-cut dress and feels her lover's sexual admiration. 'My sex has found me out', she declares, duly retiring to a vicarage and wondering at her former foolish belief that 'laws made and laws that are natural – may be set aside or slighted'.[31] In such plays, the struggle to maintain social reputation may turn social interactions into artificial performances, but in the end the truth will out and society's conventions are confirmed as necessary restraints upon human weakness. So, for example, in H.A. Jones's *The Liars* (1896), Lady Jessica's indiscreet *rendez-vous* with an admirer involves all her friends and relations in an escalating farce of evasion and deceit, until her would-be lover proves his mettle by confessing the truth. The lover's honesty and integrity show him to have the necessary moral backbone to survive in the depths of the Empire, whereas the morally frail Lady Jessica is sent back to her husband and the necessary support of strict social custom. Characters are sorted into the worthy and the weak, and society's laws provide a vital sustaining structure for the latter.

In contrast, George Bernard Shaw, an early champion of Ibsen, declared his disgust with theatre such as Pinero's which deployed surface naturalism to depict a version of reality which Shaw judged grossly unrealistic. Shaw pursued a contrasting pre-Brechtian path; eschewing surface naturalism, he deployed hyper-articulate character types, extravagant plots and comic exaggerations in order to depict the economic and political imperatives underlying the falsely idealized mask of social morality. In Shaw's *Widowers' Houses* (1892), for example, the ruthless rent collector Lickcheese and the smoothly complacent slum-landlord Sartorius initially appear to be the villains responsible for the horrific housing and living conditions of the poor off whom they live. But, as the underlying economic system is anatomized, it is the sympathetic and apparently clean-handed gentleman, Trench, who is identified as the primary mover; the poor are milked to drive the system which pays interest on his unearned income. The Dickensian names and melodramatic trappings of character are no guide to the social realities beneath.

At first glance, Wilde's plays seem to adhere to melodrama's traditional structure of revelation and truth. As Richard Ellmann remarked, 'While the ultimate virtue in Wilde's essays is in make-believe, the dénouement of his dramas and narratives is that masks have to go. We must acknowledge what we are.'[32] Wilde's society plays unearth past sins, though with an added appeal to Christian charity not to exclude the sinner, but to offer redemption and forgiveness. In *Lady Windermere's Fan* (1892), for example, Mrs Erlynne is identified as Lady Windermere's errant mother, and redeems her past delinquencies by sacrificing her own reputation to save her daughter's marriage. *A Woman of No Importance* (1893) sees Mrs Arbuthnot unmasked as an unmarried mother, but she wins her son's forgiveness, and dismisses her former seducer as 'a man of no importance'. In *An Ideal Husband* (1895), Sir Robert Chiltern faces disgrace for selling a cabinet secret for money but is forgiven by his sternly moral wife and given a second chance for political glory. Such plot lines seem to buy into an essentialist model of self, stripping off layers of pretence to disclose innate character.[33] But these revelations crucially do not reveal a fixed inner truth; beneath one performance lies another. Mrs Erlynne sacrifices her own reputation to save her daughter, but the maternal role, which she describes in significantly theatrical terms, is then discarded in favour of self-determination:

> I have no ambition to play the part of a mother. Only once in my life have I known a mother's feelings. That was last night. They were terrible – they made me suffer – they made me suffer too much. For twenty years, as you say, I have lived childless – I want to live childless still. (*Hiding her feelings with a trivial laugh*) Besides, my dear Windermere, how on earth could I pose as a mother with a grown-up daughter? ... I thought I had no heart. I find I have, and

a heart doesn't suit me, Windermere. Somehow it doesn't go with modern dress.[34]

However genuine her maternal feelings, Mrs Erlynne declines the role of mother, and similarly scorns to 'retire into a convent, or become a hospital nurse ... as people do in silly modern novels'. Repentance is too unbecoming a role to play, requiring as it does 'a bad dressmaker' to supply the requisite costume to win credibility (p.54). Mrs Erlynne may don a mask to conceal her true feelings, but all roles, she implies, are performed. Lord Windermere believes he now knows the 'true' Mrs Erlynne, based on her presence in a bachelor's rooms at night, and he reproaches her with an image of her former innocence, a picture of her youthful self which his wife kisses every night before she prays: 'It's the miniature of a young innocent-looking girl with beautiful dark hair.' But Mrs Erlynne simply deconstructs innocence as another carefully rehearsed pose: 'Dark hair and an innocent expression were the fashion then, Windermere!' she coolly replies (p.53). Nor is Mrs Erlynne the only one keeping a front up at the finale of the play; when Lord Augustus re-enters to announce his engagement to Mrs Erlynne, on the basis that 'she has explained everything', Lord and Lady Windermere respond with comic horror (p.58). Husband and wife are lying to each other, their marital happiness dependent on mutual deception.

Revelations about the past do not fix Wilde's characters, as the past bears an uncertain relationship to both present and future. This is explicitly debated in an *An Ideal Husband*, where differing views are expressed on the relation between Sir Robert's crime and his 'true self'. Lady Chiltern at first believes firmly that 'One's past is what one is', but her decision to stand by her husband both in their marriage and his political career suggests a change of heart on this count – though her train of thought on the matter is significantly never given (p.185). Mrs Cheveley and Lord Goring hold equally certain but opposing views:

MRS CHEVELEY: As if anything could demoralize Robert Chiltern! You seem to forget that I know his real character.

LORD GORING: What you know about him is not his real character. It was an act of folly done in his youth, dishon-ourable, I admit, shameful, I admit, unworthy of

> him, I admit, and therefore ... not his true
> character. (pp.225–6)

In an off-stage speech to the House of Commons Robert Chiltern condemns the Argentine canal scheme, despite believing that he is thereby inviting public disgrace. This could be taken as his moment of redemption, an indication of his true character – and film versions of the play by Alexander Korda (1947) and Oliver Parker (1999) introduce scenes which are explicitly framed as delivering the 'true' Robert Chiltern, in which he delivers a parliamentary speech demonstrating a deep commitment to a reformed moral self. But the play's only information on the speech is offered in the highly ironized form of The Times's glowing praise, read out by the arch-conservative Lord Caversham:

> 'Sir Robert Chiltern ... most rising of all our young statesmen ...
> Brilliant orator ... Unblemished career ... Well-known integrity of
> character ... Represents what is best in English public life ...
> Noble contrast to the lax morality so common among foreign
> politicians.' (p.230)

Whatever the unknown content or intention of Robert Chiltern's speech, its effect is to reinforce his long-rehearsed public exhibition of virtue. With a seat in the Cabinet, Sir Robert's moral persona is recruited to enhance the government's and the nation's image. Performance is not purged at the end of the play, but reinforced. Lady Chiltern's acceptance of her husband's ambition is delivered in a word-for-word parroting of Lord Goring's speech to her, producing an effect which is inevitably self-consciously theatrical; the exact repetition both strains credibility and undercuts the notion of a heartfelt conversion. Language itself is unsettlingly performative, its meaning less intrinsic than dependent on context and reception. Lady Chiltern's letter to Lord Goring – 'I want you. I trust you. I am coming to you. Gertrude.' – shifts its meanings repeatedly: to Lord Goring it signifies that she has learnt the truth about her husband's crime; to Mrs Cheveley it signifies an affair; to Sir Robert it is a declaration of forgiveness (p.213). Re-addressed, with or without an envelope, it is open to re-inscription and re-interpretation, until Lady Chiltern writes her husband's name on it in a belated attempt to freeze its troubling fluidity.

Wilde's dandies, from *Intentions'* Gilbert and Vivian, to Lord Henry Wotton, Lord Darlington, Lord Illingworth and Lord Goring, are, of course, entirely aware of the performative nature of life and manners, and their deliberate artificiality acts as a critical commentary on the rituals and morals of society. The central idea of the dandy, as Peter Raby has explained, 'is the fulfilment of the individual, within a hostile society, by his elevation to the status of a thing, an elevation in which his perfect exterior becomes symbolic of his true value'.[35] The cult of the dandy, from Beau Brummell to Charles Baudelaire and Jules Barbey D'Aurevilly, was rooted in a philosophy of appearance, idleness and aesthetic values, which repudiated contemporary valuations according to usefulness, class or commerce. The dandy presents the perfect outward appearance of the gentleman, detached from the ethics of duty, utility, family and power which traditionally accompanied and defined him. As Ellen Moers noted in her 1960 study, *The Dandy, Brummell to Beerbohm*, the dandy tradition in both its social and literary incarnations is rooted in parody, a calculated reproduction of the behaviours and gestures of society and the 'gentleman' which knowingly highlights their inauthenticity.[36] Regenia Gagnier led the way with her influential 1987 study of Wilde, *Idylls of the Marketplace: Oscar Wilde and the Victorian Public*, in highlighting the political implications of the dandy's philosophy of artificiality, triviality, inactivity, style and surface, as in essence a critical challenge to social doctrines of duty, utility, competition, commerce and social responsibility.[37] The male dandy's emphasis on aesthetic appearance and fashion and rejection of industry and productivity further destabilized gender categories, displacing essentialist notions of gender with a stress on surface, manners and mimicry.

Wilde's *dramatis personae* can often be divided into dandies and puritans, with the former teaching the latter to question their 'hard and fast rules' of moral absolutism and judgement.[38] Yet, just as Wilde's essays challenge any clear divide between the artificial and the natural, the sincere and the insincere, so the plays blur the lines between dandyesque performance and puritan honesty. In the case of Mrs Erlynne, for example, the dandy's pose is not the negation of emotion, but stands in complex and uncertain relation to feeling. The dandies stand to gain or lose as much as the puritans in the course of the plays, and their detachment is repeatedly suspended as they enter the fray and take up morally serious and committed positions, while the sincere puritans are inextricably implicated in the deceptions, rituals and displays of social existence.

Lord Darlington abandons his dandyesque detachment to confess his sincere love to Lady Windermere, offering her his 'whole life' and imploring her not to become a mask for her husband's supposed affair with Mrs Erlynne. His appeal is for sincerity and truth rather than empty public performance:

> But there are moments when one has to choose between living one's own life, fully, entirely, completely – or dragging out some false, shallow, degrading existence that the world in its hypocrisy demands ... Be brave! Be yourself! (pp.28–9)

The dandy's abandonment of pretence for a heartfelt appeal for self-realization is here further complicated by the fact that it is based on false assumptions: Lord Windermere is devoted to his wife, and to run away with Lord Darlington would hardly be the fulfilment of Lady Windermere's true feelings. Deep emotion sits problematically with the dandy's detachment, and can force the dandy into social compliance: Lord Illingworth agrees to marry Mrs Arbuthnot to maintain a relationship with Gerald; *An Ideal Husband*'s perfect dandy; Lord Goring, who devotes his energies to changing his clothes at least five times a day, preaches self-sacrifice to Lady Chiltern, in a bid to secure his friend's position in the heart of government. When Robert Chiltern propounds his belief that power over other men is 'the one supreme pleasure worth knowing', Lord Goring condemns it '*with great deliberation*' as 'A thoroughly shallow creed' (p.193). Yet, as Chiltern points out, Goring was born on the inside of an establishment which demands birth and wealth, so his condemnation of his friend's ambition is compromised by his unearned possession of what the politician craves. Goring's speech urging Lady Chiltern to stand by her husband is not only sincere but validated in a stage direction added to the 1899 published edition of the play as '*showing the philosopher that underlies the dandy*' (p.241). The speech is premised on gender essentialism – 'A man's life is of more value than a woman's ...' – and validates the very ambition and love of power that he had previously condemned (pp.241–2). Parroted by Lady Chiltern, Goring's philosophy secures Sir Robert's recruitment to the public performance of morality for a society founded on wealth, privilege and hypocrisy. Embedded in inherited privilege and ultimately shoring up the establishment's reputation for moral superiority, Goring's status as a dandy is fundamentally compromised.

Conversely, the sincerity and integrity of Wilde's morally-serious puritans is compromised by performance. Lady Windermere proposes to correct society's 'lax' standards, and 'make an example' which every good woman in London will applaud, by striking Mrs Erlynne publicly across the face with her fan. Her moral stand is effectively an act of public theatre, her drawing room is to be the platform for Mrs Erlynne's ritual humiliation. In the event Lady Windermere finds herself unable to overcome her social training and the pressures of decorum, and drops her fan, leaving Mrs Erlynne to stage her social comeback with wit and skill. Lady Windermere believes social ritual can embody moral values, but her party reveals social morality to be nothing more than empty role-playing. Mr Dumby's greetings to arriving guests are clearly pre-scripted, emphasizing the artificiality of the social rite long before Mrs Erlynne's entrance, and the fallen woman is quickly assimilated into society's act of respectability, as Lady Plymdale urges Dumby to introduce her to Lord Plymdale in order to absorb his uxorious attentions. In the course of the play, Lady Windermere's moral education in the complexities of her own and others' identities embeds her deeper in a series of deceptions; first in the sacrificial disgrace of Mrs Erlynne, and then by keeping the secret of her abortive flight from home. Performance and sincerity are complexly interwoven; the puritan wife justifies leaving husband and home with a well-turned epigram: 'It is he who has broken the bond of marriage – not I! I only break its bondage' (p.33).

In *A Woman of No Importance*, sincerity is even more unsettlingly immersed in performance. Lord Illingworth and Mrs Allonby are supremely aware of the theatrical nature of their flirtation:

> LORD ILLINGWORTH: You fence divinely. But the button has come off your foil.
> MRS ALLONBY: I have still the mask.
> LORD ILLINGWORTH: It makes your eyes lovelier. (p.112)

Mrs Allonby's 'ideal man' is one willing to play out an extravagant drama of rejection, heartbreak, confession and forgiveness, 'always ready to have a perfectly terrible scene', and never tired of playing the entire drama 'all over again from the beginning, with variations' (p.117). The self-conscious theatrics of the play's dandies stand in apparent contrast to the sincerity of the 'simple' characters, as they are repeatedly described (p.100; p.121). Yet, however unconscious their performances might be, the puritans' moral seriousness is as histrionic as the dandies' flirtation. When Hester holds forth on social injustice and calls for an equally punitive Old Testament condemnation of both men and women, Lady Caroline coolly highlights her soap-boxing: 'Might I, my dear Miss Worsley, as you are standing up, ask you for my cotton that is just behind you' (p.120). Lady Hunstanton's comment that 'there was a great deal of truth, I dare say, in what you said, and you looked very pretty while you said it, which is much more important', both frames Hester's speech a picturesque self-staging and pinpoints the irony of a millionaire's daughter speaking of the iniquities of poverty while dressed, as Julia Neilson was in the first production, in a luxurious gown of white satin, entirely veiled by silver-spangled tulle.[39] The casting of the statuesque Julia Neilson in the role of Hester Worsley further undermined expectations of simplicity and spontaneity. So playgoer Kate Terry Gielgud could only describe Neilson's performance as a failure to achieve the unself-conscious naturalness which she saw as the essential expression of virtue. Gielgud believed Hester typified 'the goodness that overcomes evil', and as such should be artless:

> It is essentially an unconventional part, it demands absolute sim-
> plicity in its representation, the words should not suggest any
> attempt at producing an effect upon her listeners, they should
> come pell-mell from a heart overflowing with pitiful indignation,
> she should speak because she cannot help speaking and be covered
> with confusion almost before her tirade is at an end. Hester Worsley
> would be an infinitely more effective character, her influence
> would be far more comprehensible, were her attitude throughout
> intense lovableness rather than dignified loveliness.[40]

Gerald is an equally problematic embodiment of 'simple' character, his spontaneous outbursts delivered in the most hackneyed language of moral cliché and melodramatic excess, as in his wonderfully extravagant response to Lord Illingworth's attempt to kiss Hester: 'you have insulted the purest thing on God's earth ... As there is a God in Heaven I will kill you!' (p.143).

The plot of A Woman of No Importance was itself a theatrical staple, giving the play an air of theatrical self-consciousness which Wilde himself emphasized:

> I took the plot of this play from The Family Herald, which took it – wisely, I feel – from my novel The Picture of Dorian Gray. People love a wicked aristocrat who seduces a virtuous maiden, and they love a virtuous maiden for being seduced by a wicked aristocrat. I have given them what they like, so that they may learn to appreciate what I like to give them.[41]

Just as in Dorian Gray, Wilde confounds distinctions between authenticity and pretence, between the mask and the self. The novel's actress, Sybil Vane, finds emotional reality in playing Shakespeare's heroines, and, when she commits suicide, Dorian can only see her death as 'a wonderful ending to a wonderful play'.[42] Lord Henry encourages Dorian to welcome the 'artistic elements' of Sybil's death because they have the power to convert life into art and its inhabitants into aesthetic consumers of their own existence, simultaneously actors and audience: 'We watch ourselves, and the mere wonder of the spectacle enthrals us.'[43] Moral outrage on the reader's part at the aristocrats' lack of empathy for the betrayed actress is, however, problematized by the fact that she and her family are less fictionally 'real' off-stage than on: she knows her fiancé only as 'Prince Charming', and her mother constantly strikes poses, self-consciously staging herself as a tragic figure. James Vane dislikes his mother's artificiality, but his own passionate threats to avenge any harm done to his sister read as pure melodrama, though paradoxically their theatricality makes life more real to his mother: 'The exaggerated folly of the threat, the passionate gesture that accompanied it, the mad melodramatic words, made life seem more vivid to her.'[44] Moreover, the mother is delighted by her son's vehemence, since it compensates for the relatively poor theatrical effect of her own forced confession that she is the unmarried, abandoned lover of a gentleman: 'The situation had not been gradually led up to. It was crude. It reminded her of a bad rehearsal.'[45]

Though ironically unaware of the theatrical nature and effect of his utterances, A Woman of No Importance's Gerald expresses himself in the same mixture of over-inflated melodramatic rhetoric and trite cliché. Mrs Arbuthnot similarly stages herself as the archetypal figure of seduced maiden, led astray and betrayed by a wicked aristocrat. In her Act II encounter with Lord Illingworth, the former lovers inhabit two contrasting dramatic genres, Mrs Arbuthnot speaking in the moral absolutes of melodrama, while Illingworth offers the pragmatic language of post-Ibsenite naturalism. Rejecting Gerald's morally conventional (and conveniently self-serving) demand that she marry his father, Mrs Arbuthnot describes her past life as a long performance of the role of repentant magdalen, a role she felt obliged to act out, but, contrary to theories of natural acting, without experiencing the inner emotions consonant with outward gesture:

> And you thought I spent too much of my time in going to Church, and in Church duties. But where else could I turn? God's house is the only house where sinners are made welcome, and you were always in my heart, Gerald, too much in my heart. For, though day after day, at morn or evensong, I have knelt in God's house, I have never repented of my sin (p.150).

Both actor and spectator of herself in the role of repentant magdalen – for who else is there who knows what she has to repent? – it is impossible to locate a 'true' Mrs Arbuthnot, or to deduce whether her adoption of the role is deliberate and tactical, or the unconscious result of the sexual morality she has imbibed but which her own desires contravene.

Neil Sammells, writing on the performative nature of all Wilde's characters, describes his characterization as 'bricolage', constituted of style and language, and devoid of depth, and identifies Mrs Arbuthnot's speech as an exercise in 'kitsch'.[46] Yet to do so is to empty Wilde's plays of their Ibsenite demonstration of the damage done by social laws and absolute morality. A Woman of No Importance is not just a play which ironises moral positions and sends up theatrical styles, emptying them of meaning; the play also highlights the cost of such moral positioning and role playing for those who enact them, whether consciously or unconsciously. Where *Dorian Gray* challenges notions of the real, playing games with the reader's putative moral indignation, *A Woman of No Importance* recycles plot and situations from the novel but in a game which is necessarily played for higher emotional stakes. The play challenges notions of the natural while displaying the human cost of lives deformed by moral absolutes, of living as 'The Soul of Man' puts it, 'by other people's standards' and wearing 'other people's second-hand clothes'.[47]

Gerald Arbuthnot never achieves independent adulthood and ends the play still mouthing moral platitudes, his putative career swapped for the role of husband and son; Lord Illingworth loses his son and is reduced to the villainous role he vainly resisted; and Mrs Arbuthnot clings to her hatred, though it has become a weapon turned outward rather than in on herself. In the utopian society of 'The Soul of Man under Socialism' the individual can develop an organic and coherent self, but, as Wilde's essays make clear, selfhood cannot exist outside of culture – they shape and create each other – so under the strictures and morals of Victorian society, the organic self does not exist; instead identity is *always* a series of performances, conscious or unconscious, interleaved and inextricable. Unlike the society plays of Pinero and Jones, there is no authentic self to be revealed, no stripping off of layers of performance and deceit to disclose a moral truth; in Wilde's plays morality itself is revealed as a performance.

No one can avoid becoming a player in this social comedy; the best to be hoped for is artistic self-creation, a conscious awareness of roles chosen and enacted. Wilde's dramas enact this self-consciousness, reifying social ceremonies and turning rituals and rites into absurd theatrical displays. As Francesca Coppa has observed, Jack's entrance in mourning for his fictional brother Ernest, in *The Importance of Being Earnest*, is a self-conscious performance of grief which emphasizes the performative nature of all public rituals, even those rooted in supposedly the most intimate emotions.[48] Wilde de-familiarizes and de-naturalizes them: Lady Agatha's fourteen 'Yes, Mama's showcase the meticulous production and marketing of the dutiful daughter and bride; the merciless logic of Lady

Bracknell's arbitrary qualifications for the status of eligible bachelor does the same for prospective husbands; the tea and cake used as weapons in a tea-party skirmish between the politely trained Cecily and Gwendolen are an absurd parody of good manners. Society is a self-perpetuating and self-sustaining theatre, its purpose being, as Wilde observed, 'to ensure its own continuance'.[49]

To further denaturalize performance and defy attempts to read a stable truth, each play has its own theatrical mode. *An Ideal Husband* is political power-play, rooted in class and money, and validating itself in the language of morality and idealism. In *Salome* (1894) each character is actor and spectator in their own private play, projecting their own desires onto others, and using language not to describe or express but to create and transform. In *The Importance of Being Earnest* there is no stable reality or truth to confine the self-creative performances of its characters. Life imitates art, and fiction becomes fact; self-creation is the only possibility in a world where deceit transforms into the authentic, whether in the form of Cecily's fantasy engagement, or Jack's invention of a younger brother. *Earnest's* is a world of self-conscious theatricality and self-invention, where there is no punishment for falsehood and fantasy. From Lane's confirmation that there were no cucumbers to be had in the market, even for ready money, to Algy's embodiment of Jack's imaginary brother, lies are corroborated and accepted. Effect and style, not truth, are the currency of value in this performative world, as its inhabitants freely acknowledge; when Algy declares that he only pretended to be Ernest in order to meet Cecily, she does not believe him:

CECILY: But that does not affect the wonderful beauty of his answer.

GWENDOLEN: True. In matters of grave importance, style, not sincerity, is the vital thing. (p.295)

Character is not fixed by fact or revelation. Reality bends gymnastically to realise the self-creative fictions of the play's characters, who themselves embrace the mutability and multiplicity of self-invention: as Gwendolen says, when Jack asks if she can forgive him for having told the truth, 'I can. For I feel that you are sure to change.' (p.307)

Wilde's dramatic characterization thus reflects the mutability, complexity and multiplicity of his theoretical models of identity, embodying the merging of truth and artifice, sincerity and insincerity, self and masks. Where Pinero and Jones naturalize social laws and morality, Wilde reifies them into subversively stylized rituals, from which no one can exit like Nora Helmer by simply slamming the door behind them; knowing how to play the game is the only option, as Mrs Allonby observes, in *A Woman of No Importance*: 'The one advantage of playing with fire ... is that one never gets even singed. It is the people who don't know how to play with it who get burned up' (p.102). This self-conscious stylization and undermining of notions of revealed truth and sincere identity have been a key element in successful productions of Wilde's plays since their premieres in the 1890s. Eschewing the increasingly popular naturalistic acting styles, often described as 'being' a character – a term consistently used of Ellen Terry's apparently spontaneous charm and the emotional immediacy of the relatively untrained newcomer Mrs Patrick Campbell in the role of Pinero's Paula Tanqueray, for example – the casting of Wilde's leads deliberately raised false expectations and confounded simple associations between actor and role.[50] The casting of Herbert Beerbohm Tree as Lord Illingworth, for example, would have raised misleading expectations of the dandy's ultimate repentance and sentimental self-disclosure, given his strong association with the previously hugely successful role of H.A. Jones's the Duke of Guisebury, a cynical aristocrat who discovers his moral foundations and proposes marriage to his mistress.[51] The stately Julia Neilson would never deliver an artless Hester Worsley, and Marion Terry, who played the first Mrs Erlynne, was famous for playing 'good' women, a stage repertoire that, matched with a spotless off-stage reputation, thus raised and confounded audience expectations that Wilde's fallen woman would cast off her wicked ways and reveal her sentimental core in the final act. The tension between actors and roles thus echoed and enacted the complexities of character central to the plays.[52]

The multiplicity and fluidity which Wilde ascribed to selfhood applies equally to the plays which embody it. Every dramatic text offers a plethora of potential performances, multiple future enactments each of which realize different interpretative possibilities. Just as Wilde's plays refuse to fix their characters within final judgements or revealed truths, so the texts offer an extraordinary openness to dramatic interpretation. In 'The Critic as Artist', Wilde noted that,

> People sometimes say that actors give us their own Hamlets, and not Shakespeare's; and this … is a fallacy … In point of fact, there is no such thing as Shakespeare's Hamlet. If Hamlet has something of the definiteness of a work of art, he has also all the obscurity that belongs to life. There are as many Hamlets as there are melancholies.[53]

Wilde's own dramas remain true to this maxim. There are as many Salomes as there are dances: the stage direction, '*Salome dances the dance of the seven veils*' (p.85), sounds deceptively specific, as though the dance were as familiar as the waltz or the polka rather than Wilde's own invention. No precedent or further description limits the actor's delivery of the princess's dance, inspiring the extraordinarily rich and diverse stage history of Wilde's play. From the 'slow, free dance of ecstatic joy' of Alisa Koonen's dance in the Kamerny Theatre's Cubist production in 1917, to the 'explicit carnal desire' of Maud Allan's free modernist dance in J.T. Grein's 1918 production, or Olwen Fouere's mimed striptease in which she removed her clothes only in the audience's imagination in Steven Berkoff's 1989 production, the performance possibilities of the dance alone can embody an infinite number of Salomes, each with varying degrees of innocence, grace, savagery, skill and passion.[54] Crucial issues, such as whether Sir Robert Chiltern retains his ruthless ambition, whether Lady Chiltern has abandoned her moral rigour for an unquestioning wifely devotion or holds the morally dominant role, watching his every future move with a careful eye, are open to the actors' interpretation: an unspoken gesture or the hesitancy with which Sir Robert asks if his wife loves him can speak volumes about their future.

The highly stylized surface of Wilde's plays does not dissolve to reveal inner truths, and it is left to audiences, directors, actors and readers to posit what possible, mutable, fluid, inchoate or multiple selves inhabit their imagined psyches. Denied unfettered self-development in a socialist utopia, his characters act out the rituals and roles of their society, knowing or unknowing performers whose identity remains in unfixed and unjudgeable relation to their inescapably performed exterior.

NOTES

1. 'The Soul of Man under Socialism', in *The Complete Works of Oscar Wilde*, Vol.4, Criticism, ed. Josephine Guy (Oxford: Oxford University Press, 2007), p.239.

2. Ibid.

3. Ibid.

4. Ibid., p.244.

5. See Jonathan Dollimore, *Sexual Dissidence, Augustine to Wilde, Freud to Foucault* (Oxford: Clarendon Press, 1991), and see, for example, Lizzie Thynne, 'Surely You Are Not Claiming to Be More Homosexual Than I?', in Joseph Bristow (ed.), *Oscar Wilde and Modern Culture* (Athens, OH: Ohio University Press, 2008), pp.180–208; Kerry Powell, *Acting Wilde: Victorian Sexuality, Theatre, and Oscar Wilde* (Cambridge: Cambridge University Press, 2009).

6. Walter Pater, *The Renaissance* (Oxford: Oxford University Press, 1986), p.152.

7. Ibid., p.151.

8. Wilde, 'The Critic as Artist', in *The Complete Works of Oscar Wilde*, Vol.4, Criticism, p.177.

9. Ibid., p.189.

10. Lynn M. Voskuil, *Acting Naturally: Victorian Theatricality and Authenticity* (Charlottesville, VA and London: University of Virginia Press, 2004). See also Joseph Roach, *The Player's Passion: Studies in the Science of Acting* (Newark, NJ: University of Delaware Press, 1985); William Hazlitt, 'Madame Pasta and Mademoiselle Mars' (1825); George Henry Lewes, *On Actors and the Art of Acting* (1875); George Eliot, *Daniel Deronda* (1876).

11. William Archer, 'Masks or Faces? A Study in the Psychology of Acting' (1880), quoted in Jane Goodall, *Performance and Evolution in the Age of Darwin: Out of the Natural Order* (London: Routledge, 2002), p.178.

12. See *Oscar Wilde's Oxford Notebooks: A Portrait of Mind in the Making*, eds Philip E. Smith II and Michael S. Helfand (New York and Oxford: Oxford University Press, 1989), and John Wilson Foster, 'Against Nature? Science and Oscar Wilde', in *Wilde the Irishman*, ed. Jerusha McCormack (New Haven and London: Yale University Press, 1998), pp.113-24.

13. Wilde, Commonplace Book, in Smith and Helfand (eds), *Oscar Wilde's Oxford Notebooks*, p.121.

14. Wilde, 'The Critic as Artist', pp.177–8.

15. Max Nordau, *Degeneration*, translated from the second edition of *Entartung*, (London: Heinemann, 1895), pp.317–37.

16. Ibid., p.318.

17. Oscar Wilde, letter to the Home Secretary, 2 July 1896, in *The Complete Letters of Oscar Wilde*, eds Merlin Holland and Rupert Hart-Davis (London: Fourth Estate, 2000), p.656.

18. Ibid.

19. For a history of the manuscript's composition and publication, and for discussion of its liminal and multiple status as public autobiography, literary work, personal

letter with several addressees, see *De Profundis*, 'Epistola: In Carcere et Vinculis', in *The Complete Works of Oscar Wilde*, Vol.2, ed. Ian Small (Oxford: Oxford University Press, 2005).

20. Dollimore, *Sexual Dissidence*, p.95.
21. Wilde, *De Profundis*, pp.64, 127–8, 44.
22. Ibid., p.99.
23. Ibid., p.155.
24. Oscar Wilde, letter to Robert Ross, 1 April 1897, in *Letters*, p.781.
25. *The Picture of Dorian Gray* (1891), in *The Complete Works of Oscar Wilde*, Vol.3, ed. Joseph Bristow (Oxford: Oxford University Press, 2005), pp.287–8.
26. Peter Brooks, *The Melodramatic Imagination: Balzac, Henry James, Melodrama, and the Mode of Excess* (New York: Columbia University Press, 1985), p.4.
27. Report in the *Era* (2 May 1891), p.10, in Michael Egan (ed.), *Ibsen: The Critical Heritage* (London: Routledge & Kegan Paul, 1972), pp.233–4.
28. Gay Gibson Cima, *Performing Women: Female Characters, Male Playwrights, and the Modern Stage* (New York: Cornell University Press, 1993), Chapter 1.
29. Symbolically, before the final conversation with her husband in which she confronts him with the artificiality of her role as wife, Nora declares she is 'Taking off this fancy dress' (Henrik Ibsen, *A Doll's House* in Ibsen, *Four Major Plays*, trans. James McFarlane [Oxford: Oxford University Press, 1981], III, p.78).
30. Henry Arthur Jones, *The Case of Rebellious Susan*, in *Plays by Henry Arthur Jones*, ed. Russell Jackson (Cambridge: Cambridge University Press, 1982), III, pp.153–4.
31. Arthur Wing Pinero, *The Notorious Mrs Ebbsmith* in *The Social Plays of Arthur Wing Pinero*, Vol.1, ed. Clayton Hamilton (New York: E.P. Dutton and Co., 1917), III, pp.316, 361.
32. Richard Ellmann, *Oscar Wilde* (London: Penguin, 1987), p.xiv.
33. For interpretations rooted in revelation and punishment, see, for example, Keith Miller, *Oscar Wilde* (New York: Ungar, 1982); Philip Cohen, *The Moral Vision of Oscar Wilde* (London: Associated University Press, 1978); Anne Margaret Daniel, 'Wilde the Writer', in Frederick S. Roden (ed.), *Palgrave Advances in Oscar Wilde Studies* (Basingstoke: Palgrave Macmillan, 2004), pp.36–71.
34. Wilde, *Lady Windermere's Fan*, in Oscar Wilde, *The Importance of Being Earnest and Other Plays*, ed. Peter Raby (Oxford: Oxford University Press, 1995), p.54. All further references to Wilde's plays are to this edition and are incorporated in the text.
35. Peter Raby, *Oscar Wilde* (Cambridge: Cambridge University Press, 1988), p.35.
36. Ellen Moers, *The Dandy, Brummell to Beerbohm* (London: Secker and Warburg, 1960).
37. Regenia Gagnier, *Idylls of the Marketplace: Oscar Wilde and the Victorian Public* (Aldershot: Scolar Press, 1987).
38. Wilde, *Lady Windermere's Fan*, p.10.
39. See Joel Kaplan and Sheila Stowell, *Theatre and Fashion: Oscar Wilde to the Suffragettes* (Cambridge: Cambridge University Press, 1994), p.25.
40. Haymarket Theatre, 19 April 1893, Kate Terry Gielgud, *A Victorian Playgoer*, ed. Muriel St Clare Byrne (London: Heinemann, 1980), p.8.

41. Quoted in Hesketh Pearson, *Beerbohm Tree: His Life and Laughter* (London: Methuen, 1956), p.67.

42. Wilde, *The Picture of Dorian Gray*, p.253.

43. Ibid., p.254.

44. Ibid., p.230.

45. Ibid.

46. Neil Sammells, *Wilde Style: The Plays and Prose of Oscar Wilde* (Harlow: Longman, 2000), pp.88, 98.

47. Wilde, 'The Soul of Man', in *Criticism*, p.244.

48. Francesca Coppa, 'Performance Theory and Performativity', in Roden (ed.), *Palgrave Advances in Oscar Wilde Studies*, pp.75–6.

49. Wilde, 'The Critic as Artist', in *Criticism*, p.174.

50. See, for example, George Bernard Shaw, Preface, in Christopher St John (ed.), *Ellen Terry and Bernard Shaw: A Correspondence* (London: Constable, 1931), p.xix; Shaw, letter to Charles Charrington, quoted in Margot Peters, *Mrs Pat: The Life of Mrs Patrick Campbell* (London: Hamish Hamilton, 1984), p.107.

51. Jones, *The Dancing Girl*, first performed Haymarket Theatre, London, 15 January 1891.

52. For analysis of how modern productions of Wilde have emphasized the performative nature of both dandies and puritans, see, for example, Robert Gordon, 'Wilde's "Plays of Modern Life" on the Contemporary British Stage' (pp.156–66) and Joel H. Kaplan, 'Wilde in the Gorbals: Society Drama and the Citizens Theatre' (pp.214–23), both in George Sandalescu (ed.), *Rediscovering Oscar Wilde* (Gerrard's Cross: Colin Smyth, 1994).

53. Wilde, 'The Critic as Artist', pp.165–6.

54. Oliver M. Sayler on Kooner, and *The Stage* on Maud Allan, quoted in William Tydeman and Steven Price, *Wilde, Salome* (Cambridge: Cambridge University Press, Plays in Production, 1996), pp.73, 84.

CHAPTER EIGHT

Victorian or Contemporary? Wilde and Questions of Heredity and Inheritance

ANNE VARTY

The past is the key of the future.[1]

What lies before me is my past.[2]

In the most literal sense Wilde belongs to the Victorian age. Not only did he aspire to marry Queen Victoria, she was the only British monarch to reign during his short life.[3] Culturally, Wilde was thoroughly of the age in which he lived. Bourgeois family man, secret lover, hack writer, Greek scholar, Irish expatriate, flâneur, criminal, his modes of identity are Victorian. Despite his contempt for his own era ('ours is certainly the dullest and most prosaic century possible'),[4] the readers and audiences he wrote to engage were *his* contemporaries, not ours. Even his rebellions against the age are conditioned precisely and absolutely by his cultural context. He asserted, for example, 'modernity of form and modernity of subject-matter are entirely and absolutely wrong',[5] rejecting the fashionable trend of realism which dominated the culture of his day. But in what he achieved through these rebellions Wilde ushers new arguments into the field of cultural debate and anticipates, perhaps fashions, our own areas of cultural contest.

For this reason alone, it can be asserted that Wilde is our contemporary. His work is never off the stage or screen; his life is a magnet for biographers; his status as a martyr to his sexuality assures his currency; his riddling national identity claims attention in our era which is at once post-colonial and imperial. Wilde's image, epigrams, characters have been commodified and are in constant circulation around the globe. They have become ironic tokens emptied of meaning for an age no less acquisitive than his own which 'knows the price of everything and the value of nothing'. Wilde is woven into the fabric of our cultural lives; the mere mention of his name provokes a set of expectations. John Stokes has provided the finest and most extended investigation of Wilde's afterlives, demonstrating how '[o]n stage, as in life, he stalks us still' and exploring his astonishing achievement in bridging scholarly and popular culture.[6] But perhaps the cultural stratum Wilde occupies is one of nostalgia. Does he invite anything more than a backward glance, a yearning desire for the wit, grace and polish of late Victorian style? Where, then, do we situate Wilde? How, if at all, does his work interact with our own era? What do we inherit from him? Smith and Helfand conclude their analysis of his Oxford Notebooks with the statement: '[w]e think we have painted a faithful portrait of Wilde as the last Victorian sage'.[7] At the same time they argue:

> Wilde's essential contribution to the present is not the anticipation of any particular critical system (as critics from the beginning of this century to the present have claimed) but rather a basic position about the necessity of a dialectical view which complicates and enriches the production and reception of art and criticism and recognizes its place and relation to other institutions.[8]

A number of critics or theorists, as Smith and Helfand note, have found in Wilde's work anticipations of their own or other people's methods. Wilde's most authoritative biographer Richard Ellmann, for example, states that, 'Wilde sounds like an ancestral Northrop Frye or Roland Barthes'.[9] This view is shared by Terry Eagleton who writes of his sense of how 'astonishingly Wilde's work prefigured the insights of contemporary cultural theory':

> [L]anguage as self-referential, truth as a convenient fiction, human identity as an enabling myth, criticism as a form of creative writing, the body and its pleasures pitted against a pharisaical ideology: in these and other ways, Wilde looms up for us more and more as the Irish Roland Barthes.[10]

An account of some particular schools of theory claiming Wilde as a forefather is provided by Zhang Longxi's 'The Critical Legacy of Wilde' (1988).[11] Regenia Gagnier argues that Wilde's work exhibits aspects which we can recognize as strands of postmodernity in Victorian culture.[12] A compelling view of Wilde's legacy is offered by Neil Sammells's *Wilde Style*, in which he asserts 'Wilde substitutes style for authenticity, and it is his fascination with style that marks him as our contemporary, as well as Manet's'.[13] Sammells closes the study with the claim that 'Wilde seems close to us partly because he grapples with contradictions we have yet to resolve ... insofar as Wilde anticipates and articulates these contradictions we should see him not as simply reflective of his historical moment but as formative of our own'.[14] But if we subscribe to these contemporizing views, is there a danger that we read Wilde anachronistically, engaging with his work as he claims William Wordsworth engaged with the lakes, finding in the stones of his landscape 'the sermons [we] had hidden there'?[15] Equally, it has to be remembered that Wilde's work did not meet a full response from his own contemporaries and immediate successors because the scandal of his trial in 1895 removed it from wide circulation. His early twentieth-century rehabilitation was interrupted by the outbreak of the First World War. *Intentions*, for example, first published in 1891, was reissued in 1904 after a nine-year suppression following the trial. From then it remained in print until 1913, but did not appear again in Britain until 1947. These contingencies served to propel Wilde's work into the mid-twentieth century before its mature assimilation in its own time, and contribute to the dynamism of its interventions in twentieth-century culture.

This essay sets out to explore Wilde's view of the individual's position in history, from which he builds a picture of personal identity which is both temporally conditioned and yet free from the burdens of time. The exploration draws on aspects of his aesthetic theory and its relations to Victorian ideas about heredity. It examines in particular his responses to two Victorians, Pater and Ruskin, and suggests that he revolutionizes their work to suit his own liberating vision of inherited, conditioned identity.

Wilde himself was acutely aware of the temporal positioning of art and the artist, and of the value of historical scholarship for interpretation. After all, he insisted that 'he who desires to understand Shakespeare truly must understand the relations in which Shakespeare stood to the Renaissance and the Reformation'.[16] But for the critic as artist, this is not enough. Wilde does not believe that there is a true, complete or finished view of the artwork which the critic can excavate or recover. At the end of the labours of historical interrogation, the critic 'will look upon Art as a goddess whose mystery it is his province to intensify, and whose majesty his privilege to make more marvellous in the eyes of men'.[17] Wilde's radical aestheticism, which holds that 'Art never expresses anything but itself',[18] places his pronouncements on historicizing methods in apparent conflict with his ideas of art and aesthetic criticism as acts of vatic revelation:

> So far from being the creation of its time, [Art] is usually in direct opposition to it, and the only history it preserves for us is the history of its own progress. Sometimes it returns upon its footsteps, and revives some antique form ... At other times it entirely anticipates its age, and produces in one century work that it takes another century to understand, to appreciate, and to enjoy. In no case does it reproduce the age. To pass from the art of a time to the time itself is the great mistake that all historians commit.[19]

This is at once an invitation and a warning to historical scholars of Wilde's own work: no matter what position you adopt on Wilde's Victorianism or contemporaneity, disappointment is guaranteed. Art, on Wilde's terms, necessarily eludes exegesis, and stands in conflicted relation to the era in which it was conceived. However, Wilde articulates his sense of the monumental cultural significance of his own era in 'The Critic as Artist. II': '[t]he nineteenth century is a turning point in history, simply on account of the work of two men, Darwin and Renan, the one the critic of the Book of Nature, the other the critic of the books of God'.[20] Both Darwin and Renan challenged, in different ways, conventional ideas about the existence of God, the divine origins of humanity, the assurance of an afterlife and the immortality of the soul. Wilde's sense of Darwin's stature is based on his reading of The Origin of Species (1859) and The Descent of Man (1871).[21] His knowledge of the French historian of religion Ernest Renan was based on his reading of the first volume, La Vie de Jésus (1863) of the eight volume Histoire des origins du

Christianisme (1863–83), in which Renan questioned the divinity of Christ, by writing a kind of biography, an account of historical documents about the life of 'Jesus', rather than a holy book about the life of 'Christ'.[22] Wilde occupies a pivotal position at the turning point he identifies. And he made no secret of the fact that he was sufficiently self-aware to know it: 'I was a man who stood in symbolic relations to the art and culture of my age'.[23] It is the way in which he responded to certain conditions of his own culture which allows him to intervene in our own. His responses to the biological determinism represented by Darwin and to the clash of secular with sacred represented by Renan form, it can be argued, the central engine of his lasting innovation. Intolerance of the naturalist schools of art, which is nevertheless coupled with an equally powerful respect for Darwin's work, governs Wilde's yearning for metaphysical and spiritual freedom. Regard for Renan's historiography intensifies rather than inhibits Wilde's desire to find some way in which a man can still be a god. Wilde seeks transcendence and immortality rather than abasement and extinction, as they are poised at the end of 'The House of Judgement':

> And God said to the Man, 'Wherefore can I not send thee unto Heaven, and for what reason?'
> 'Because never, and in no place, have I been able to imagine it', answered the Man.
> And there was silence in the House of Judgement.[24]

He stakes out the ground for his combat with determinism and his quest for immortality in the three dialogues, 'The Decay of Lying' (*The Nineteenth Century*, January 1889) and its companions 'The Critic as Artist' Part I (*The Nineteenth Century*, July 1890) and Part II (*The Nineteenth Century*, September 1890).[25] Here he yokes theories about art with theories about nature and develops a view of what may best be termed 'Aesthetic Determinism' to rescue humanity from the traps and trappings of biology and unbelief. At the centre of this vision is the well-known assertion about the relationship between Art and Nature made in 'The Decay of Lying':

> For what is Nature? Nature is no great mother who has borne us. She is our creation. It is in our brain that she quickens to life.

Things are because we see them, and what we see, and how we see it, depends on the Arts that have influenced us. To look at a thing is different from seeing a thing. One does not see anything until one sees its beauty. Then, and only then, does it come into existence.[26]

Wilde's first step in elaborating upon the view that art determines the created world and frames the limits of perception is to collapse the traditional hierarchy and distinction between Art and Nature: 'she is our creation'. With this move he is out of line with Goethe ('Art is Art because it is not Nature'), but surprisingly in line with J.S. Mill, who had also refused the distinction in his 1874 essay 'On Nature', where he declared: 'Art is as much Nature as anything else; and everything which is artificial is natural – Art has no independent powers of its own: Art is but the employment of the powers of Nature for an end.'[27] Unlike Mill, Wilde reverses the conventional primacy of one creative process over another. 'One does not see anything until one sees its beauty. Then and only then does it come into existence.' Vision, perception, or, to use the term derived from the Greek for perception, 'aesthetics', are empowered to generate 'existence'. Nature becomes secondary to Art. 'Being natural is simply a pose' asserts the aristocratic lord of creation, Lord Henry Wotton in *The Picture of Dorian Gray* (1890).[28] This paradox captures Wilde's ambition for Aesthetic Determinism in which the cultivated mind controls identity; nurture, not nature, predominates.

Throughout the three dialogues Wilde frames his discussion of aesthetics in the language of naturalism. The Darwinian principle of natural selection is given a new definition in 'The Decay of Lying': 'Art itself is really a form of exaggeration; and selection, which is the very spirit of Art, is nothing more than an intensified mode of over-emphasis.'[29] He deliberately chooses the language of scientific discourse to destabilize the traditional dichotomy he is addressing. In doing this Wilde alters the trajectory of Aestheticism. Walter Pater, for example, just one month earlier, in December 1888, developed a similar point about the means by which artistic expression is fashioned, but his deployment of the discourse of evolution is latent rather than intrusive: '[y]our historian ... amid the multitude of facts presented to him must needs select, and in selecting assert something of his own humour, something that comes not of the world without but of a vision within'. Pater continues: '"The artist", says [Friedrich] Schiller, "may be known rather by what he omits"; and in literature, too, the true artist may be best recognised by his tact of omission.'[30] Wilde takes his cue from Pater and emphasizes the part played by 'selection' by the artist, moving towards a powerful assertion about what it can achieve. He flamboyantly declares: 'It is style that makes us believe in a thing – nothing but style.'[31] Selection is a mark of style and style creates belief or ideological consensus. In 'The Critic as Artist' Wilde extends his metaphor of genesis to language, declaring 'language is the parent, not the child, of thought'.[32] Again, he responds to Pater, who had written of things in the 'solidity with which language fixes them'.[33] But Pater, grappling with Heraclitean flux, seeks transcendence only in art, while Wilde rephrases the Paterian insight in Darwinian terms. He conceives of the relationship between language and conception in familial terms, invoking a sense of heredity and with it, determinism, through the use of the term 'parent', the source of inheritance.

Throughout the three dialogues under discussion here, Wilde systematically glosses the discourse of aestheticism with the language of evolution. While the 'Decay of Lying' is concerned primarily with the poverty of Realism as a method in art and the promotion of Aestheticism as an enriching alternative, 'The Critic as Artist' offers more detailed responses to various schools of naturalism. Wilde's handling of the French critic Hippolyte Taine's trinity 'race, milieu, moment' merges with Darwin's emphasis on heredity and environment as shaping factors in the process of evolution. The value of these elements in the material world is given its due by Wilde. It is precisely because he acknowledges their force that he is compelled to think beyond them, to look beyond the physical to the metaphysical. Again he adopts the language of evolutionary discourse and transposes it to the realm of aesthetic theory:

> Aesthetics, in fact, are to Ethics in the sphere of conscious civilization, what, in the sphere of the external world, sexual is to natural selection. Ethics, like natural selection, make existence possible. Aesthetics, like sexual selection, make life lovely and wonderful and fill it with new forms, and give it progress, and variety and change.[34]

Smith and Helfand argue that Wilde's use of this analogy demonstrates his belief that:

> only sexual selection was progressive, while natural selection and the ethics which it generated simply continued to make existence possible. They were a stabilizing, inertial force, like the artistic realism he decried in 'The Decay of Lying'. Therefore Wilde believed it was time to invert the previous order, to emphasise aesthetics rather than ethics in conscious civilization and sexual rather than natural selection in the external world.[35]

As part of a programme of changing emphasis, Wilde addresses each of the major tenets of naturalism in the course of 'The Critic as Artist'. Taine's notion of the determining factors contained by the influence of *moment* he simply turns on its head: 'It is not the moment that makes the man, but the man who creates the age.'[36] This is in line with his championing of individualism, and as John Wilson Foster notes, found expression in his Commonplace Book as the statement, 'Progress in thought is the assertion of individualism against authority'.[37] The influence of *milieu* or, in more Darwinian terms 'environment', he depicts in the context of Platonism:

> But to be purified and made perfect, this sense requires some form of exquisite environment … You remember that lovely passage in which Plato describes how a young Greek should be educated, and with what insistence he dwells upon the importance of surroundings, telling us how the lad is to be brought up in the midst of fair sights and sounds, so that the beauty of material things may prepare his soul for the reception of beauty that is spiritual.[38]

It is the Greek scholar in Wilde's Victorian identity which allows him to draw on this Platonic reference to offer a cultural counterpoint to biological genetics, and he found the view corroborated in the fiction of a fellow Greek scholar, Pater's 'The Child in the House' (1878). In that story Pater describes the early development or 'brain-building' of his boy protagonist Florian and dwells in slow detail on how his environment seemed 'actually to have become part of the texture of his mind'. The narrative voice notes that 'the sense of harmony between his soul and its physical environment became ... like perfectly played music'.[39] Wilde's claim for the cultural impact of environment on the spiritual development of the individual was radical but not unique.

His grandest eloquence is reserved for the discussion of heredity, which for Wilde embraces both *moment* and *milieu*, in the realms of the physical and the metaphysical:

> By revealing to us the absolute mechanism of all action, and so freeing us from the self-imposed and trammelling burden of moral responsibility, the scientific principle of Heredity, has become, as it were, the warrant for the contemplative life. It has shown us that we are never less free than when we try to act ...
>
> And yet, while in the sphere of practical and external life it has robbed energy of its freedom and activity of its choice, in the subjective sphere, where the soul is at work, it comes to us, this terrible shadow, with many gifts in its hands, gifts of strange temperaments and subtle susceptibilities, gifts of wild ardours and chill moods of indifference, complex multiform gifts of thoughts that are at variance with each other, and passions that war against themselves. And so it is not our own life that we live, but the lives of the dead, and the soul that dwells within us is no single spiritual entity, making us personal and individual, created for our service and entering into us for our joy ... Do you think that it is the imagination that enables us to live these countless lives? Yes; it is the imagination; and imagination is the result of heredity. It is simply concentrated race-experience.[40]

Wilde ascribed to the contemporary scientific view that culturally acquired characteristics were inherited and passed on.[41] Changing scientific theory has not negated the significance of Wilde's thinking here, since he moves beyond biology, to a coherent and self-sustaining celebration of form, style, imagination and multiplicity of identity.

Pater too had been working on a fusion of ancient and modern in his understanding of 'race', blending the Pythagorean myth of metempsychosis with the tenets of naturalism. But where Wilde's vision is buoyant and liberating, Pater's is bleak, defeated, contemplating personal extinction as the price of advancing humanity:

For in truth we come into the world, each one of us, 'not in naked-ness', but by the natural course of organic development clothed far more completely than even Pythagoras supposed in a vesture of the past, nay, fatally shrouded, it might seem, in those laws or tricks of heredity which we mistake for our volitions; in the language which is more than one half of our thoughts; in the moral and mental habits, the customs, the literature, the very houses, which we did not make for ourselves; in the vesture of a past, which (so science would assure us) is not ours, but of the race, the species: that Zeit-geist, or abstract secular process, in which, as we could have had no direct consciousness of it, so we can pretend to no future personal interest. It is humanity itself now – abstract humanity – that figures as the transmigrating soul, accumulating into its 'colossal manhood' the experience of ages; making use of, and casting aside in its march, the souls of countless individuals, as Pythagoras supposed the individual soul to cast aside again and again its outworn body.[42]

This is Pater's voice in the 1890s, in his lectures on *Plato and Platonism* (1892–3). It is radically different in tone from his passage on the Mona Lisa in which, twenty years earlier, he had voiced similar views. Where in the 1890s Pater finds death, in 1869 he had found life, and Wilde answers to the call of the younger Pater, his imagination animated by the transmigrations Pater finds etched on the face of La Gioconda. Wilde famously rehearses as liturgy Pater's prose in 'The Critic as Artist. I':

> I murmur to myself, 'She is older than the rocks ... and all this lives only in the delicacy with which it has moulded the changing lin-eaments ...' And I say to my friend, 'The presence that thus so strangely rose ...' and he answers me, 'Hers is the head ...'[43]

Wilde uses the passage as the founding example of what he means by the 'critic as artist': 'the criticism I have quoted is criticism of the highest kind. It treats the work of art simply as a starting-point for a new creation.'[44] He embeds it as an imaginary exchange within the dialogue form to enact the idea that the critical spirit is in constant process, always 'becoming', evolving, never static.[45] While this reported act of repetition could be seen as static, an arresting, even backward-looking moment, Wilde overcomes the potential stasis in two ways. First, he animates it by scripting it as ritualized, almost religious, dialogue, turning it into a kind of meditative exchange, a transmission between presence and absence, past and present, written and spoken, interior and exterior; secondly, he leaves the quotation incomplete, inviting response, recognition, memory from the reader. The deliberate incompletion of Pater's Mona Lisa passage allows the invisible, the unheard, the implied and imagined to come into play. The concluding sentences which Wilde does not quote are those by which Pater situates his vision on the borderlands between the supernatural and the naturalist:

> The fancy of a perpetual life, sweeping together ten thousand experiences, is an old one; and modern philosophy has conceived the ideas of humanity as wrought upon by, and summing up in itself, all modes of thought and life. Certainly Lady Lisa might stand as the embodiment of the old fancy, the symbol of the modern idea.[46]

But that Wilde acknowledges their force is evident from the recurrence of these ideas two months later when Part II was published, at the fitting interstice, in his account of the gifts granted by the terrible shadow 'heredity':

> [the soul that dwells within us] is something that has dwelt in fearful places, and in ancient sepulchres has made its abode. It is sick with many maladies and has memories of curious sins. It is wiser than we are and its wisdom is bitter ... It can help us leave the age in which we were born, and to pass into other ages and find ourselves not exiled from their air.[47]

Syntax, lexis and cadence are all inherited from Pater. The words 'ancient', 'sepulchres', 'maladies', 'curious', 'sins' reveal the genetic coding of Wilde's prose, pointing back to Pater's account of the Mona Lisa, invoking the punningly iconic 'father' of British Aestheticism. He embodies in prose the twinned doctrines of heredity and metempsychosis which are being thematically considered, to act out the dynamic relationship between past, present and future which is being proposed. It is a paradox that in the moment when Wilde celebrates the liberating gifts of heredity for the imagination, exploring the 'warrant for the contemplative life', the prose deployed is a deliberate palimpsest, layered with repetition, not original, therefore potentially charged with inauthenticity and insincerity.

The family resemblance of Wilde's prose is one thing, but the differences are equally vital for Wilde's quest to assert the liberating, vivifying force of inheritance, influence, heredity, for the imagination. He returns to his paradoxical idea of aesthetic determinism in which Art and Heredity are fused and joined with the conception of 'soul', held together by the rather over-determined pronoun 'it':

> It can teach us how to escape from our experience, and realise the experiences of those who are greater than we are. The pain of Leopardi crying out against life becomes our pain ... We can see the dawn through Shelley's eyes, and when we wonder with Endymion the Moon grows amorous of our youth. Ours is the anguish of Atys, and ours the weak rage and anguish of the Dane. Do you think that it is imagination that enables us to live these countless lives? Yes ...[48]

The life of the mind triumphs over the life of the body. While the body is single, the mind is multiple, mobile, ahistorical. Identity, fashioned by the imagination, becomes 'countless', 'mulitiform'. If there is slippage in Wilde's work between his denotation of art and the artist, it is because the artist's (or the critic's) identity is made up of the art he selects. Determinism is yoked to aesthetics and becomes an agent of liberation. Wilde spells this out:

> The culture that this transmission of racial experience makes possible can be made perfect by the critical spirit alone ... and, having learned 'the best that is known and thought in the world', lives ... with those who are the Immortals ... the contemplative life, the life that has for its aim not doing but being, and not being merely, but becoming – that is what the critical spirit can give us. The gods live thus ...[49]

For Wilde even the realm of the inner life is conceived in terms of evolution, constant self-refining process, 'becoming'. Paradoxically, by applying the vocabulary of biology associated with change, death and even extinction, to the 'inner life', Wilde argues that to cultivate the life of the mind in this way becomes equivalent to living 'with … the Immortals'. Immortality itself is not a stasis, but also changing. This is Wilde's version of Paterian 'renaissance' or rebirth. He has answered Renan and Darwin together; he has found a way in which a man can be a god even in the last decade of the nineteenth century. It is a vision of immortality which is by no means fitting with conventional Christianity, or any other organized religion, but is fashioned by Wilde to answer the specific crises of his era.

Wilde also scrutinizes the principle of aesthetic determinism in his fictions. The Picture of Dorian Gray is a sustained disquisition on the competing claims of Art and Nature, the plot notoriously blurring the distinctions between them. The man and his portrait are co-extensive, the portrait yielding Dorian the means for self-understanding: 'Ah! In what a monstrous moment of pride and passion he had prayed that the portrait should bear the burden of his days, and he keep the unsullied splendour of eternal youth! All his failure had been due to that.'[50] Dorian's crime is not the litany of murders or deaths that follow in his wake, nor the catalogue of tawdry offences against conventional morality his actions incur. His great crime is that he seeks to arrest his own development, to stifle change or growth. And Lord Henry's crime is to encourage him: 'You're quite perfect. Pray, don't change.'[51] The correlative aesthetic crime is that Basil's portrait of Dorian, having represented an ideal form, turns into a grossly realist work, which directly imitates life, shrunken here to the sordid world of Dorian's conventional crimes and conscience. Just as Dorian is capable of identifying his own culpability in daring to defy the laws of art and nature, so too, he has the imagination to recognize the complexity of his identity in terms which reiterate Wilde's voice in 'The Critic as Artist'. These are Dorian's reported thoughts from Chapter 11 of the novel, which represents the phase of his life where his mental life is most at liberty:

> Yet one had ancestors in literature, as well as in one's own race, nearer perhaps in type and temperament, many of them, and certainly with an influence of which one was more absolutely conscious. There were times when it appeared to Dorian Gray that

the whole of history was merely the record of his own life, not as
he had lived it in act and circumstance, but as his imagination had
created it for him, as it had been in his brain and in his passions
... It seemed to him that in some mysterious way their lives had
been his own.[52]

Imagination brings Dorian freedom which is not matched in the
gothic world of action within the novel.[53] The more Dorian struggles to
liberate himself through action, the more he is constrained. He is forced
to experience the negative power of Wilde's vision of 'Heredity':

It has hemmed us round with the nets of the hunter, and written
upon the wall the prophecy of our doom. We may not watch it, for
it is within us. We may not see it, save in a mirror that mirrors the
soul. It is Nemesis without her mask.[54]

The novel establishes a dominant background of the annihilating effects
of action and the sense of the individual as a product. Dorian is shown
to be a naturalist product of his environment, genetic and social inheritance; his ever-youthful appearance and its value are produced by a
work of art. As a product, Dorian becomes an object for consumption,
both by himself and others.

The generative power of language comes under particular scrutiny.
Dorian states, seeking to suppress discussion of Sybil Vane's suicide: 'If
one doesn't talk about a thing, it has never happened.'[55] Yet the power of
silence to extinguish is matched by the power of language to create.
Gossip, rumour, idle talk, draw Basil back to Dorian and culminate in the
artist's murder. Basil warns Dorian: 'I think it right that you should know
that the most dreadful things are being said against you in London ... I
don't believe these rumours at all. At least, I can't believe them when I
see you.'[56]

It may seem surprising that despite Wilde's view that the laws
of heredity exposed human agency and moral choice as chimeras,
he nevertheless devoted the last three years of his creative life to the
composition of drama, a form traditionally concerned with the representation of agency and choice. But theatre is also most obviously the
realm of the artificial, in which speech is scripted and action prescribed.
Theatre is the house of illusion in which heredity is simultaneously most

profoundly concealed and intensely revealed. Characters are puppets, and the audience knows it but chooses to suspend disbelief; it is only in the suspension of disbelief that theatre differs from a life in which heredity has 'revealed the absolute mechanism of all action'.[57] The authors of the 1892 burlesque *The Poet and the Puppets*, about Wilde and his relationship with the characters of *Lady Windermere's Fan* (1892), may have been responding not simply to what they perceived as the egotism of celebrity or to the methods of symbolist drama, but to a profound and far-reaching dimension of his work.[58]

Despite the conventional aspects of Wilde's social comedies, he was constantly experimenting with form, seeking a drama of inaction and theatre for puppets, as if to demonstrate the validity of his claims for heredity as the 'warrant for the contemplative life'[59] where it seemed most difficult. He declared with punning triumph of Act I of *A Woman of No Importance* (1893), that it was 'a perfect Act' because 'there was absolutely no action at all',[60] and of *An Ideal Husband* that it was 'for ridiculous puppets to play'.[61] With his last play, *The Importance of Being Earnest* (1895), he embarks on farce, technically the most mechanical of theatrical genres, and throws into formal, generic relief his ambitions for 'being' and 'becoming' rather than 'doing'. In that play life literally imitates art. Characters are shown to be the 'slaves of words',[62] a book is mistaken for a baby, and the resolution is only achieved when the 'Army Lists' are consulted to verify Jack's name, 'christened after your father'.[63] Jack's name Earnest is both authentically his own and somebody else's, old and new, inherited and original. The resolution of *Importance* confirms the epigram from *A Woman of No Importance*, that 'the Peerage ... is the best thing in fiction the English have ever done'.[64] It fulfils the insight of *An Ideal Husband*, that 'as a rule, everybody turns out to be somebody else'.[65] Epigram itself is the hallmark of Wilde's highly stylized dramatic dialogue. It is a technique which impedes the flow of action, and compels an eddying of thought for the audience. Laughter, the audience response, is a physical reflex of an intellectual engagement, a step towards the contemplative life, encouraged by the technique of Wilde's dialogue which lies at the heart of his theatre.

An Ideal Husband is stylistically Wilde's most varied play and, as Sammells has argued, the juxtaposition of styles emphasizes the artificiality of each.[66] Stylistic variation occurs both at the level of dialogue and in the composition of scenes, while the structure of the whole conforms to that of the traditional, inherited 'well-made-play' with its exposition, complication, crisis and resolution. The exposition of Act I consists of a sequence of aphorisms delivered by unimportant characters; it creates an aristocratic social milieu, a drama of inaction, into which the mechanism of plot is neatly and tantalisingly dropped. Act II, the complication, is a dramatized critical dialogue, a conversation between self and soul, a contest between the claims of private and public life. Act III, the crisis, is by contrast a farce, almost a play within a play, tightly constructed and hilarious, designed to demonstrate action as a trap and talk, here always thwarted by action or the threat of action, as liberating. The resolution of Act IV is achieved by Lord Goring's sententious delivery of ideas Wilde inherited, or borrowed, from John Ruskin's doctrine of the separate spheres properly inhabited by men and women, expounded in *Sesame and Lilies* (1865). Ruskin asserts:

> The man's power is active, progressive, defensive. He is eminently the doer, the creator, the discoverer, the defender. His intellect is for speculation and invention; his energy for adventure, for war, and for conquest ... But the woman's power is for rule, not for battle, – and her intellect is not for invention or creation, but for sweet ordering, arrangement and decision. She sees the qualities of things, their claims, and their places. Her great function is Praise ...[67]

In Goring's précis this becomes:

> A man's life is of more value than a woman's. It has larger issues, wider scope, greater ambitions. A woman's life revolves in curves of emotions. It is upon lines of intellect that a man's life progresses.[68]

But the authenticity of these words is immediately subverted by Gertrude Chiltern's repetition of them to her husband, as though they were her own, in her efforts to justify her new-found enthusiasm for silence and lies:

> A man's life is of more value than a woman's. It has larger issues, wider scope, greater ambitions. Our lives revolve in curves of emotions. It is upon lines of intellect that a man's life progresses. I

have just learnt this, and much else with it, from Lord Goring.[69]

These lines mark her *volte face* from her excessively moralistic and archaic speech in Act I: 'To the world, as to myself, you have been an ideal always. Oh! Be that ideal still. That great inheritance throw not away – that tower of ivory do not destroy.'[70] The artificiality of her language underlines the artificiality of her husband's virtuous pose. Wilde's use of the term 'inheritance' here is double. It refers both to the outmoded, bankrupt, bourgeois notion of the 'ideal' husband, and to the financial fortune Chiltern will lose if he confesses his insider dealing. The satire has a double target: acquisitive materialism and the bourgeois morality which shores it up. Ironically, within the constraints of the blackmail plot, Chiltern can only remain the 'ideal' husband if Gertrude adopts the pose of the ideal wife as expounded by Goring's Ruskinian doctrine. Against the background of Gertrude's high moral tone her sudden surrender appears glib, comically opportunist and insincere. Her repetition of Goring's inherited ideas exposes the sentiments as simply a form of words. As Wilde had stated in 'The Critic as Artist', '[c]reeds are believed not because they are rational but because they are repeated'.[71] Gertrude Chiltern's rapid conversion is an example of aesthetic determinism or 'form' and 'style' in action. Wilde had asserted in 'The Decay of Lying' that '[i]t is style that makes us believe in a thing – nothing but style'.[72]

This deployment of 'form' is one of the dark gifts of heredity and asserts the power of the imagination. The dramatized use of quotation as repetition in *An Ideal Husband* brings imagination and insincerity into dangerous but compelling kinship. Suggesting that there are no originals, only copies, Wilde sends us back to his account of vision and sensibility afforded by a full understanding of heredity in 'The Critic as Artist'. On the one hand it is by quotation, the reaching for a form of words, the articulation of another's experience from another era that 'imagination enables us to live these countless lives': 'we sicken with the same maladies as the poets … [d]ead lips have their message for us'.[73] But, from another perspective, the deployment of a form of words is straightforward insincerity: 'All art is immoral.'[74] For Wilde, the result is the same: 'What people call insincerity is simply a method by which we can multiply our personalities.'[75] Restated in *The Picture of Dorian Gray*, this becomes 'is insincerity such a terrible thing? I think not. It is simply a method by which we can multiply our personalities.'[76] 'Insincerity' is the ethical term, used by 'honest beaming folk'[77] for what in Wilde's aesthetic discourse is called 'imagination'. The convergence of imagination with insincerity in their twinned ability to generate 'countless lives' or the multiplication of personality reflects Wilde's toying with aesthetic and ethical categories, sexual and natural selection. His hybridizing of aesthetics with heredity licences a revolutionizing, provocative and flamboyant theory of personal identity, totally at odds with the prim, monological versions of determinism we accept today, but as appealing for its bravado as for its sustained intellectual coherence.

Wilde's place in our popular culture is marked by the currency of his epigrams. Often they float free of their original context, but they are always identified as quotations. Our celebration of his wit through repeated quotation is a trivial emblem of a serious philosophy, under-written by Wilde's engagement with ideological challenges of his own day. Certainly, as many have argued, the topics Wilde addresses anticipate, and even shape, areas of cultural debate today. In drawing out a history of ideas those topics can be multiplied and complicated, looking both before and after Wilde. But our quotation of Wilde, coupled with an understanding of what he argued quotation could achieve, cuts across historicizing urges yet at the same time reinforces them.

Wilde's interpretation of heredity enables him to see identity and experience as being at individual disposal, self-selecting, assembled and composed. 'There is no mood of passion that Art cannot give us, and those of us who have discovered her secret can settle beforehand what our experiences are going to be.'[78] Despite the sense that these forms of inheritance always position the individual as a late-comer, heredity is also the principle by which the burden of the past is overcome and Wilde uses it to articulate his own modernity:

> It seems to me that with the development of the critical spirit we shall be able to realize, not merely our own lives, but the collec-tive life of the race, and so to make ourselves absolutely modern, in the true meaning of the word modernity. For he to whom the present is the only thing present, knows nothing of the age in which he lives. To realise the nineteenth century, one must realise

every century that has preceded it and that has contributed to its making.[79]

On Wilde's terms, he is contemporary because he is Victorian.

NOTES

1. Oscar Wilde, 'The Rise of Historical Criticism', in *The Complete Works of Oscar Wilde*, Vol.4, *Criticism*, ed. Josephine Guy (Oxford: Oxford University Press, 2007), p.28.

2. Oscar Wilde, 'Epistola: In Carcere et Vinculis', in *The Complete Works of Oscar Wilde*, Vol.2, *De Profundis*, ed. Ian Small (Oxford: Oxford University Press, 2005), p.155.

3. Hesketh Pearson, *The Life of Oscar Wilde* (London: Methuen, 1954 [1946]), p.339.

4. Oscar Wilde, 'The Decay of Lying', in *Criticism*, p.99.

5. Ibid., p.82.

6. John Stokes, *Oscar Wilde. Myths, Miracles, and Imitations* (Cambridge: Cambridge University Press, 1996), p.22.

7. *Oscar Wilde's Oxford Notebooks: A Portrait of Mind in the Making*, ed. Philip E. Smith II and Michael S. Helfand (Oxford: Oxford University Press, 1989), p.104.

8. Ibid., p.105.

9. Richard Ellmann (ed.), 'Introduction', in *The Artist as Critic: Critical Writings of Oscar Wilde* (Chicago: University of Chicago Press, 1968), x.

10. Terry Eagleton, *Saint Oscar and Other Plays* (Oxford: Blackwell Publishers, 1997), p.3.

11. Zhang Longxi, 'The Critical Legacy of Wilde', in Regenia Gagnier (ed.), *Critical Essays on Oscar Wilde* (New York: G.K. Hall & Co., 1991), pp.157–71.

12. Regenia Gagnier, 'Wilde and the Victorians', in Peter Raby (ed.), *Cambridge Companion to Oscar Wilde* (Cambridge: Cambridge University Press, 1997), pp.18–33.

13. Neil Sammells, *Wilde Style. The Plays and Prose of Oscar Wilde* (Harlow: Longman, 2000), p.4.

14. Ibid., p.127.

15. Oscar Wilde, 'The Decay of Lying', p.83. Smith and Helfand also entertain this view, *Oscar Wilde's Oxford Notebooks*, p.104. Wilde's afterlife, in various guises, is the subject of Uwe Böker, Richard Corballis and Julie A. Hibbard (eds), *The Importance of Reinventing Oscar: Versions of Wilde during the Last 100 Years* (Amsterdam and New York: Rodopi, 2002), and Stefano Evangelista (ed.), *The Reception of Oscar Wilde in Europe* (London: Continuum, 2010).

16. Oscar Wilde, 'The Critic as Artist', in *Criticism*, p.163.

17. Ibid., p.164.

18. Wilde, 'The Decay of Lying', p.102.

19. Ibid., p.102.

20. Wilde, 'The Critic as Artist', p.205.

21. Smith and Helfand, *Oscar Wilde's Oxford Notebooks*, pp.76–7.
22. *The Complete Works of Oscar Wilde*, Vol. 4. Criticism. ed. Josephine M. Guy (Oxford: Oxford University Press, 2007), p.474, note 148.
23. Wilde, '*Epistola*', p.94.
24. Oscar Wilde, 'The House of Judgement', in *The Complete Works of Oscar Wilde*, Vol.1, *Poems*, eds Bobby Fong and Karl Beckson (Oxford: Oxford University Press, 2000), p.172.
25. The title 'The Decay of Lying' invokes Wilde's classical scholarship. It alludes to 'A True Story. I' by Lucian, in which the ancient Greek author declares of his method: 'as I had nothing true to tell, not having had any adventures of significance, I took to lying'. Lucian, *Works*, The Loeb Classical Library Vol.I, trans. A.M. Harmon (London: William Heinemann, 1913), p.253.
26. Wilde, 'The Decay of Lying', p.95.
27. J.S. Mill, 'On Nature' (1874) in *Nature, The Utility of Religion and Theism* (London: Watts & Co., 1904), p.8.
28. Oscar Wilde, *The Picture of Dorian Gray* (1891), in *The Complete Works of Oscar Wilde*, Vol.3, ed. Joseph Bristow (Oxford: Oxford University Press, 2005), p.172.
29. Wilde, 'The Decay of Lying', p.85.
30. Walter Pater, 'Style' (1889), in *Appreciations* (London: Macmillan, 1895, 3rd edn), pp.9, 18. This essay was first published in the *Fortnightly Review*, December 1888.
31. Wilde, 'The Decay of Lying', p.99.
32. Wilde, 'The Critic as Artist', p.147.
33. Walter Pater, 'Conclusion' (1873), in *The Renaissance. Studies in Art and Poetry*, ed. Donald Hill (Berkeley, CA: University of California Press, 1980), p.187.
34. Wilde, 'The Critic as Artist', p.205.
35. Smith and Helfand, *Oscar Wilde's Oxford Notebooks*, p.77.
36. Wilde, 'The Critic as Artist', pp.143–4.
37. John Wilson Foster, 'Against Nature? Science and Oscar Wilde', in Jerusha McCormack (ed.), *Wilde the Irishman* (New Haven, CT and London: Yale University Press, 1998), p.119.
38. Wilde, 'The Critic as Artist', p.191.
39. Walter Pater, 'The Child in the House', in *Miscellaneous Studies* (London: Macmillan & Co., 1895), pp.184, 176, 180.
40. Wilde, 'The Critic as Artist', pp.176–7.
41. Pater, 'The Child in the House', p.67.
42. Walter Pater, *Plato and Platonism* (London: Macmillan, 1895, 2nd edn), pp.72–3.
43. Wilde, 'The Critic as Artist', p.156.
44. Ibid., p.157.
45. This argument links very well to that found in Bruce Bashford's analysis of the critical dialogues in Chapter 6.
46. Walter Pater, *Renaissance*, p.99.
47. Wilde, 'The Critic as Artist', p.177.

48. Ibid., pp.177–8.

49. Ibid., p.178.

50. Wilde, *The Picture of Dorian Gray*, p.354.

51. Ibid., p.346.

52. Ibid., p.289.

53. For further discussion of this aspect of the novel see Heather Seagroatt, 'Hard Science, Soft Psychology, and Amorphous Art in *The Picture of Dorian Gray*', *Studies in English Literature*, 38 (1998), pp.741–59.

54. Wilde, 'The Critic as Artist', p.177.

55. Wilde, *The Picture of Dorian Gray*, p.258.

56. Ibid., pp.292–3. For a compelling politicized reading of Wilde's engagement with Darwin in this novel, see Mary C. King, 'Digging for Darwin: Bitter Wisdom in *The Picture of Dorian Gray* and "The Critic as Artist"', *Irish Studies Review*, 12, 3 (2004), pp.315–27.

57. Wilde, 'The Critic as Artist', p.177.

58. Charles Brookfield and Charles Hawtrey, *The Poet and the Puppets*, opened at the Comedy Theatre, London, in May 1892. Wilde was deeply angered by the play, which was a savage parody of himself and his theatrical style. His attempt to have it censored was unsuccessful, which enraged him further since it coincided with the censorship of his own play *Salome*.

59. Wilde, 'The Critic as Artist', p.177.

60. Cited in Katherine Worth, *Oscar Wilde* (London: Macmillan, 1983), p.99.

61. Ellmann, *The Artist as Critic*, p.387.

62. Wilde, 'The Critic as Artist', p.148.

63. Wilde, *The Importance of Being Earnest and Other Plays*, ed. Peter Raby, (Oxford: Clarendon Press, 1995), III, ll.434–5.

64. Oscar Wilde, *A Woman of No Importance*, in Raby (ed.), *The Importance of Being Earnest and Other Plays*, III, ll.127–30.

65. Oscar Wilde, *An Ideal Husband*, in Raby (ed.), *The Importance of Being Earnest and Other Plays*, I, ll.109–10.

66. Sammells, *Wilde Style*, pp.98–104.

67. John Ruskin, 'Of Queen's Gardens', *Sesame and Lilies, The Works of John Ruskin*, Vol. XVIII, ed. E. T. Cook and Alexander Wedderburn (London: George Allen, 1905), pp.121–2.

68. Wilde, *An Ideal Husband*, IV, ll.454–7.

69. Ibid., ll.484–8.

70. Ibid., I, ll.806–8.

71. Wilde, 'The Critic as Artist', p.196.

72. Wilde, 'The Decay of Lying', p.99.

73. Wilde, 'The Critic as Artist', p.172.

74. Ibid., p.174.

75. Ibid., p.189.

76. Wilde, *The Picture of Dorian Gray*, p.288.

77. Wilde, 'The Critic as Artist', p.174.
78. Ibid., pp.167–8.
79. Ibid., p.176.

CHAPTER NINE

Oscar Wilde: Caught in the Web

D.C. ROSE

INTRODUCTION

At 14.45 GMT on 25 October 2008, using the search engine AlltheWeb, which is more sophisticated than Google, I tapped in 'Oscar Wilde' and was informed that there were 17,500,000 results. I then narrowed this to English and scored 11,600,000 results. French gave 744,000; German, 1,140,000; Spanish 807,000; Italian 883,000. I became gamesome, and tried Farsi: 2,450 results; Slovenian – 13,100; Icelandic – 19,500; Catalan – 46,600; Bulgarian – 6,140. Unfortunately, the system cannot search for Welsh or Basque or Esperanto or Braille. Trying again at 13.30 GMT on 12th February 2010 the following numbers were given, in the same order: 17,800,000 – 9,900,000 – 1,030,000 – 1,030,000 – 1,560,000 – 1,460,000; then 2,320 – 10,200 – 11,400 – 85,900 – 8,130.

By the time these lines are being read, these numbers will have changed. Although it is not possible to place any reliance upon them, a survey carried out annually might be of interest, if not of value. Be that as it may, here is fame beyond any imaginable to Wilde when he told David Hunter Blair that he intended to be famous; beyond any, when his name was removed from theatre posters and his books from bookshops; infinitely beyond the fifteen minutes of fame that pop artist Andy Warhol thought everyone might, or should have. What can one make of all this? To check seventeen million websites – to check seventeen hundred websites – would be a task that only those monkeys with type-writers essaying to write Shakespeare might regard as fruitful. To reduce the quest so that there is a recognizable beast in view demands its own discipline. I have chosen, therefore, to examine and comment upon

- Websites that republish the works of Wilde
- Society sites
- 'Fan' sites
- Further sites that offer scholarly information about Wilde
- Miscellaneous sites that have something to offer
- Miscellaneous sites that have nothing to offer
- Some general conclusions

I will also revisit Fritz-Wilhelm Neumann's 'Wilde – Renaissance on the Internet', which is the best scholarly examination of Wilde's presence in cyberspace.[1]

Beyond what Neumann offers, there are few guidelines offering a methodology of critical analysis of such Internet sites, and much of what there is concerns technicalities. Few websites conform to the criteria of Ryerson University's Yellow Book project, where texts:

> will be transcribed and encoded in XML to permit complex searches and the aggregating of related content ... To enhance interoperability, we intend to maintain protocol in harmony with archives supported by NINES ... We intend to enhance this particular section of The 1890s Online by taking advantage of the 'Temporal Modeling Project' in the Spec Lab at the University of Virginia by developing a time-sensitive map of London's Yellow Book community. We would also like to explore the possibility of using the IVANHOE model to develop interactive critical exploration on the site. The Yellow Book Project could encourage researchers to use gaming tools to explore points of confluence, sites of friction, and patterns of formulation that would be recognizable when different variables are brought into mutual consideration. These signs of pattern or disorder would then encourage the modification of existing theoretical/critical approaches or perhaps suggest new theoretical models or hybrids.[2]

Even understanding this, let alone enacting it, would tax most Wilde scholars, and indeed anyone save a professional webmaster.

This survey is therefore subjective (for the criteria of interest are mine) and unscientific (for ultimately the data can only be random) and limited (for who knows what may develop in the wake of YouTube,

Facebook, Twitter and other new media). To be amplified, it needs to be read at a computer – an inescapable irony. There is also an irony in writing for students who may be better versed in information technology than the writer. One can only propose a departure point for future speculation, grounded in the terminal irony of its own immediate obsolescence.

WILDE WORKS

The most important engagement with Wilde has been the various attempts to publish his works on the Web, and these will be familiar to anyone interested at all in using the Internet for Wilde. Wilde's works can be found on Project CELT, Gutenberg and others, some with scholarly intention, others again the work of enthusiasts, this not always being the same thing. Few of the former (unlike most of the latter) sport any beauty of design; few of the latter (unlike most of the former) contain any information about their origination. Neumann remarked, 'The expensive equipment we are employing when we surf the Net carries machine-readable Wilde, which consists of different versions of respectable editions alongside undergraduate and high-school "stodge" in the dreariest manner imaginable'.[3] At time of writing (spring 2010) plans are advancing for a fully annotated, illustrated, hyperlinked and interactive complete edition of Wilde on Line on the Web (Project WILLOW), compiled by a team of scholars, which will also contain surveys of websites, and most importantly, concordances, of which only one seemingly has ever been compiled: www.public.iastate.edu/~spires/Concord/earnest.html created by Rosanne G. Potter and Joe Struss of Iowa State University. News of Project WILLOW will be published regularly at groups.yahoo.com/group/oscholarship/; and the verdict will come as to which of Neumann's categories it will be classed under.

It would be otiose to try and assess the Web editions of Wilde work by work, but by taking one of these – 'Lord Arthur Savile's Crime' (1887) – as a guide, a survey can be attempted. On-line editions of this text include the following:

- www.besuche-oscar-wilde.de/werke/englisch/stories/lord_arthur_chapter1.htm. This is an unsourced, unannotated edition on an excellent and long-standing German site dedicated to Wilde.

- www.bibliomania.com/0/5/57/309/16461/1/frameset.html. Part of an enormous programme of putting texts on line, this is an unsourced and unannotated edition, somewhat irritatingly divided into short pages that have to be downloaded one at a time.
- en.wikisource.org/wiki/Lord_Arthur_Savile's_Crime. A straight forward and highly legible text version, similarly unsourced and unadorned.
- etext.lib.virginia.edu/toc/modeng/public/WilSavi.html. This is part of a collection on the University of Virginia website, and has been taken from *The Picture of Dorian Gray and Selected Stories* (New York: Oscar Wilde Signet Classic; New American Library of World Literature, Inc., 1962) with 'Lord Arthur Savile's Crime' from *Lord Arthur Savile's Crime and Other Stories* (Methuen & Co., 1909). 'Spell-check and verification made against printed text using WordPerfect spell checker.' This follows the pagination (but not the lines) of the Signet Classic, which one would hardly choose for citations, and italics have been replaced by plain text. 'Portière' is given once as 'partiere' and once as 'portiere'. According to this website's conditions of use:

  Users are not permitted to download our ebooks, texts, and images in order to mount them on their own servers for public use or for use by a set of subscribers. Individuals and institutions can, of course, make a link to the copies at UVa, subject to our conditions of use. It is not in our interest or that of our users to have uncontrolled subsets of our holdings available elsewhere on the Internet. We make corrections, add tags, add images, etc. on a continual basis, and we want the most current text to be the only one generally available to all Internet users.

  This may be compared with the Penn State version (below).

- www.classicbookshelf.com/library/oscar_wilde/lord_ arthur_savile _s_crime_and_other_stories/ This edition is remarkable for its use of Javascript applet technology which allows the reader to choose and change the combination of text size, spacing and colour on the page. This makes it technically the most advanced of the editions under review.
- www.eastoftheweb.com/short-stories/UBooks/LorArt.shtml. A straightforward text, paginated but with no bibliographical details.

There is some embryo attempt to make the text interactive – that is to say that there are links to a page of teaching materials (which was blank at 12th July 2009); to one for comments, where about twenty people in the last six years have left rather unilluminating remarks of three or four lines each; and to one for discussion, which leads to a notice that it has been discontinued. Missable.

- ebooks.nypl.org/1E854BFC-DC13-41A2-BA94-9CA375564146/10/225/en/ContentDetails.htm?ID=94A0828D-73AE-4061-8AB5-0B88F3817CDD. This leads to an 'eNYPL Mobipocket eBook': Mobipocket "PID"' required to open the eBook usable on up to 3 supported devices (PC or PDA). 127 kb.

- www.ebooktakeaway.com/lord_arthur_saviles_crime_oscar_wilde. Unsourced and with no critical apparatus, this straightforward text can be downloaded without problem in html (89.61 kb), pdf (325.71 kb) and text (87.41 kb) formats.

- www.gutenberg.org/etext/773. This is typographically most unattractive, with italics lost in a plain text typeface (ASCII), flushed left, but not paginated. The text of origin is given as 'Transcribed from the 1913 Methuen and Co. edition'. There is an advantage if Gutenberg is used, as there is a search engine which allows users to perform full-text searches on its entirety – that is, the reader can search all of the books on gutenberg.org at once and find all instances of a particular word, phrase, name, place, &c. This is the 'Anacleto' – Project Gutenberg Search Engine bookmine.tesuji.eu/gutenberg/. After typing the keyword into the search box, the 'qualified search' option allows one to refine and filter the search by subject and language. The result brings up the book's page on the Gutenberg website. It is then necessary to open up the text file and search for the word/phrase again to find the specific reference.[4]

- www.kingkong.demon.co.uk/gsr/savile.htm. This a straightforward reproduction of the work as a continuous text, created in 1994 by Philip Harper. Unfortunately, when contacted in July 2009 about origination, Mr Harper no longer remembered.

- manybooks.net/titles/wildeoscetext97ldasc10.html. The chief interest of this edition is that it can be downloaded in many different formats. Unsourced, unannotated.

- www.online-literature.com/view.php/lord-arthur-saviles-crime/ 1?term=lord%20arthur%20savile. A rather unattractive plain text version, divided by chapter.
- www.oscarwildecollection.com/. Although it contains typographical eccentricities (some italicized words appearing in capitals), this is a well designed and easily read version, visually the most attractive of those under review.
- www.scribd.com/doc/896098/Lord-Arthur-Saviles-Crime-and-Other-Stories-by-Oscar-Wilde. This uses the Project Gutenberg text, but has re-paginated it and offers the choice of either of scrolling down the text or reading it page by page in 'slideshow' form. It contains typographical eccentricities, italicized words appearing in normal script but in capitals. I liked this version the least.
- www.ucc.ie/celt/published/E850003-003/index.html. Edition used in the digital edition: Oscar Wilde Lord Arthur Savile's Crime in Lord Arthur's Savile's Crime, The Portrait of Mr. W. H. and other stories (London: Methuen & Co. Ltd., 1912), pp.3–61 (and respecting the pagination, giving it a very jerky appearance). No reason is given for preferring this over the Osgood, McIlvaine 1891 edition; it is not even the original Methuen edition, published in 1909. There are also typographical oddities: opening single quotation marks are diagonal, but closing ones are straight (I myself favour curly ones), long dashes are indicated by three hyphens, and the text is justified left, which surely is not best practice. We are also told 'Compound words have not been hyphenated after CELT practice'. This is an unwelcome editorial intervention, especially as it then goes on to use words like proof-read and hard-copy. My feeling is that the CELT edition is an interesting way of looking at the Methuen edition, but that by attaching itself so firmly to the conventions of print publication it loses value as a Web text.
- www.wilde-online.info/lord-arthur-saviles-crime.html. This website declares on its home page: 'Welcome to Oscar Wilde online, a website dedicated to one of the most successful playwrights of the late Victorian era and one of the greatest celebrities of his day.' This is another anonymous, unsourced, unannotated text, split into twenty-one separate pages, no better and no worse than its congeners. As its address indicates, it is part of a larger project to put Wilde on line in

this unadorned fashion, and there are links on a sidebar to the other texts, a modest biography and a bibliography – although the latter is a blank page – and the list of websites related to Oscar Wilde offers only three. No information is given about the owner or webmaster of this site.

- www.worldwideschool.org/library/books/lit/shortstories/Lord ArthurSavilesCrimeandOtherStories/chap1.html. A highly legible version, split into chapters, without sources or notes. The site introduction optimistically reads:

> Welcome to the World Wide School. The best place on the Internet to learn just about anything. Just read, click and learn. We wish you the best. This site is dedicated to the collection, preservation and presentation of educational material. To participate in the World Wide School all you need to do is to invest your time. For whatever reason, many people may find it difficult to broaden their education by traditional means; attending high school or college can seem like an impossible dream. That is why we are offering an education via the Web. Enjoy.

- www2.hn.psu.edu/faculty/jmanis/oscar-wilde/Lord-Arthur-stories6x9.pdf. This is an unsourced and unannotated text version published on a Pennsylvania State University site. It helpfully warns that:

> This Portable Document file is furnished free and without any charge of any kind. Any person using this document file, for any purpose, and in any way does so at his or her own risk. Neither the Pennsylvania State University nor Jim Manis, Faculty Editor, nor anyone associated with the Pennsylvania State University assumes any responsibility for the material contained within the document or for the file as an electronic transmission, in any way. *Lord Arthur Savile's Crime and Other Stories* by *Oscar Wilde*, the Pennsylvania State University, Electronic Classics Series, Jim Manis, Faculty Editor, Hazleton, PA 18202-1291 is a Portable Document File produced as part of an ongoing student publication project to bring classical works of literature, in English, to free and easy access of those wishing to make use of them.

Assuming that these editions of 'Lord Arthur Savile's Crime' are representative of all of Wilde's work, even *mutatis mutandis*, this should be sufficiently comprehensive to give a critical view of the strengths and weaknesses of Web editions.

CHATTING ABOUT WILDE

The first acquaintance with Wilde on the Web for many would have been the discussion groups by fans that sprang up in the wake of the preparations for the Wilde centenary of 2000. A survey of these can be found at: www.oscholars.com/TO/Appendix/Strange_webs/Strange_Webs3. htm which was last updated in March 2010. The groups have been supplemented by groups.yahoo.com/group/oscholarship/ as an attempt to restore scholarly discussion on Wilde to the Internet, and in this it has failed, although it has a value as a noticeboard. Of the many discussion groups dating to 2000, only one – groups.yahoo.com/group/oscarwilde/ founded in 1999 – remains active (although 'torpid' might describe it better) and has some credibility: it attracted seventy messages in 2009 (nineteen of these discussing the future of the group), but this compares badly to 1,460 in 2000. None of these sites have the academic following that Patrick Leary has generated for VICTORIA with a subscription list not far short of 2,000; and some have been captured by the purveyors of curious personal services, imaginary wealth and quack medicines. One can list a sampling of these, not for their current or recent content, but because the earliest messages indicate the interest in Wilde that was there and is no longer, the sites having been allowed by their owners and moderators to decay or be highjacked:

- groups.yahoo.com/group/Oscar_Wilde_1800s, begun in March 2000;
- groups.yahoo.com/group/wilde-ones begun in June 1999;
- authorsdirectory.com/cgi-bin/search2000/iforum.cgi?forum= Oscar_Wilde&action=list (no longer extant);
- groups.yahoo.com/group/thegreencarnation/ (begun 1999);
- jollyroger.com/zz/ychildrend/OscarWildehall/shakespeare1.html will take you to the 'Oscar Wilde Forum Frigate', where you will be enjoined to:

> Post yer opinion, a link to some of yer work, or yer thoughts
> regarding the best books and criticisms concerning Oscar Wilde.
> We'd also like to invite ye to sail on by the Oscar Wilde Live Chat,
> and feel free to use the message board below to schedule a chat
> session. And the brave of heart shall certainly wish to sign their
> souls aboard The Jolly Roger.

This rather uneasy identification of Oscar Wilde with Long John
Silver seems to be aimed at middle school level.

How long these sites will remain on the Web is open to question; and
I suspect that even as a format they have been superseded by Facebook.
A similar initiative, 'MSN Groups', has been discontinued and its con-
tents removed from the Internet.

THE OFFICIAL WILDE

One other site deserves a longer look as its history contains many of the
issues raised in discussing the Internet Wilde: www.cmgww.com/historic/
wilde/, begun in 1996, is self-described as the 'The official Web site of
Oscar Wilde'. There was a biography of Wilde, which ran to all of 1,074
words; a list of works published in Wilde's lifetime, including a play
apparently called 'The Duchess of Padue', which list, together with one
of six scholastic honours, was described as 'accomplishments'; nine
photographs, with either the name of the photographer or of the owner
as caption, which gave the rather odd effect of an otherwise unidentified
picture of Constance Wilde having the label 'Merlin Holland' (Wilde's
grandson) – clearly some future biographer is going to decide that this
is Mr Holland dressed as Gwendolen Fairfax. Originally, this meagre
offering was distinguished only by a short essay by Merlin Holland.

By January 2003 the site had been updated by being marked '©
1996–2002 Oscar Wilde c/o CMG Worldwide'. Clicking on the internal
links yielded rather more information about CMG ('CMG Worldwide is
the exclusive business and licensing representative for many celebrities
including: Marilyn Monroe, James Dean, Bill Elliott, Babe Ruth and
many more': one notices that 50% of those named came to untimely
ends) than it does about Oscar Wilde. The bibliography does not even

list Merlin Holland's edition of the letters; Ellmann is not mentioned; and the only 'critical works' listed are George (here called Geroge) Woodcock, *The Paradox of Oscar Wilde* (1950); St. John Ervine, *Oscar Wilde* (1951); and Arthur Ransome, *Oscar Wilde: A Critical Study* (1912). Her Grace remained The Duchess of Padue.

By January 2007 this unpromising site had been considerably revamped. It was, however, rather startling to read that

> CMG Worldwide is the exclusive business representative for Oscar Wilde. We work with companies around the world who wish to use his name or likeness in any commercial fashion ... The names and the signatures of our clients are trademarks owned and protected by the estates. In addition, the image, name, and voices of our clients are protectable property right owned by the estates. Any use of the above, without the express written consent of the estate is strictly prohibited. We will consider your request to use the name, voice or image of our clients. Please e-mail us with your proposed use and we will promptly respond to you.

– doubtless having faxed Oscar in the meantime.

The site (last updated on 16 May 2006) is still headed 'The Official Website of Oscar Wilde'. The Duchess of Padua had now been given her correct title, and although the essay by Merlin Holland has vanished away and the bibliography is now called 'Shopping', we do learn that 'the Victorian era swept through London in the late nineteenth century' and that Wilde had three middle names 'at his birth', pretty remarkable, really. According to Merlin Holland, this company was engaged to collect such small US royalties as the Wilde Estate still yields, and the rest is the company's own inflation. By 2010, the news section had become blank and the shopping section corrupt.

SCHOLARLY WILDE

The next development, which grew out of groups.yahoo.com/group/oscarwilde/, was THE OSCHOLARS (Oscar+Scholars), an attempt to reflect and stimulate interest in Wilde and his circles in all aspects: in academe, on stage, in exhibitions and so on, through the medium of a monthly on-line journal. This too has had its ups and downs, but is now part of a family of journals covering different aspects of the *fin-de-siècle* at www.oscholars.com. Although 'hits' on websites are not in any sense a good guide to readership, the total of these in 2008 and 2009 was 712,836. These journals are produced by volunteers, operate on a no income/no expenditure basis, and have no institutional support save the webspace provided free by Rivendale Press. There is a certain patchiness in consequence, although a decent standard of academic quality is maintained and the general feeling among the great majority of Wilde scholars has been favourable. The site includes regularly updated Wilde bibliographies, discographies and scenographies. Project WILLOW originated within THE OSCHOLARS team, and, like it, is committed to open access without charge.

SITES AND SOCIETIES

Of other sites that include Wilde in their coverage, there is no end. These vary from the Oscar Wilde Reading Group (groups.yahoo.com/group/OscarWildeReading/), which in six years has gathered eleven members, via the website of The Oscar Wilde Society (www.oscarwildesociety.co.uk/) with an undisclosed but probably significant readership, to the 168,406 fans of the leading Oscar Wilde Facebook page (there are a great many of these). The website https://www.deviantart.com/ shows 4,894 images of Wilde; eBay consistently offers Wilde related material for sale. Wilde is a man for all ages.

The Oscar Wilde Society's website came late in the Society's development, and, while carrying only a small amount of material on Wilde, is a useful introduction to the Society, the prime scholarly endeavours of which are its biannual journal *The Wildean* and its bulletin *Intentions*, published every other month. Contrariwise, the website of the Oscar Wilde Society of America (www.owsoa.org/) has much useful information, but the Society itself is dormant. The Société Oscar Wilde en France has no website but its journal, *Rue des Beaux Arts*, is published at www.oscholars.com. No other Oscar Wilde society maintains a Web presence. After that come the sites established by a single enthusiast, which wax and wane with the enthusiast's enthusiasm, but only three of these have demonstrated any quality: users.belgacom.net/wilde, which sadly has been discontinued, www.oscarwilde-lys.com/ (in French), which is of extraordinary beauty but incomplete, and www. besuche-oscar-wilde.de/ (in German, with an English sister site www.mr-oscar-wilde.de/) which has changed little over the years. Many other sites are devoted to those who interacted with Wilde at some stage, and these also naturally vary in size, quality and commitment to uploading new material. A number of these are the websites of hero societies. Surveys may be found at www.oscholars.com/TO/Society/Society.htm, www.oscholars.com/RBA/Appendix/Liaisons.htm, www.oscholars.com/RBA/Appendix/Liens.htm, and www.oscholars.com/TO/Appendix/Strange _webs/Strange_Webs2.htm.

This must give a sufficient overview of Wilde's appearance as a star in the galaxies of cyberspace; but does not yet engage with how this experience of Wilde mediates our understanding of him, as Marshall McLuhan would have to be alive to explain. The way we read a text on paper differs experientially from how we read it on a screen, and indeed differs according to the sort of screen on which we read it.[5] Without even touching on the necessity to verify the information that appears on the Internet, from typographical faults to misattributed quotations to the endless repetition of errors, Wilde's œuvre, through the nature of his epigrammatic and aphoristic style, and our reception of this on T-Shirts, fridge magnets, coffee mugs, carrier bags and even scarves, is readily decontextualized. Moreover, Wilde's work is simultaneously recontextualized on the Web in ways that were once confined to the view of his texts afforded either by his illustrators or by the composers of settings of his work. Project WILLOW, by insisting on hyper- or meta-textuality, will be deliberately challenging in this regard, a challenge that Fritz-Wilhelm Neumann anticipated in his extended discussion of John d'Adderio's website *Oscariana* (www.oscariana.net).[6] Neumann concludes: 'By means of a technology that has become ideally accessible, d'Adderio has produced what he calls a "virtual and subjective biography", which is embedded in his personal webpage. This can be seen in itself as an attempt at Wildean eccentricity and self-display.' Or, rather, it cannot: for www.oscariana.net is no longer to be found on the Internet, giving Neumann's tribute an unintended significance by becoming not merely an historical trace of a vanished facility, but providing a commentary on the mutable nature of Web-based information. Curiously, the same fate has overtaken the second website that Neumann discusses at length,[7] Aubrey Husted's *Wilde: Eccentricity at its Best* (www.geocities.com/athens/thebes/6952/) as the whole GeoCities website has been shut down. There is some inwardness in the fact that the ephemeral nature of virtual intelligence has rendered equally pointless these citations from Neumann's solid, or real, paper essay.

There is a last comment to be made on the frailty of all this. The following appears on The Victorian Research Web (victorianresearch.org/other.html) over Patrick Leary's signature:

The 19th-Century London Stage: An Exploration

A remarkable feat of research organized in imaginative hypertext form, this site was created by PhD students at the University of Washington School of Drama, working under the direction of Professor Jack Wolcott.

UPDATE: When Professor Wolcott retired in 2004, he expected that the University of Washington would leave these webpages on the university's server, much as a library book would remain on the shelf. Instead, all of the files associated with this much admired and widely referenced collaborative resource, which had been in progress since 1995, were simply deleted. A few bits and pieces of the site may be salvaged from the Internet Archive's Wayback Machine, but for most practical purposes this valuable project has been destroyed forever. I leave the description here as a reminder of the extreme fragility of online scholarly resources.

Lest this be a self-fulfilling prophecy, this threnody can now appear in print.

NOTES

1. Conference paper, Dresden, 2000; published as Fritz-Wilhelm Neumann, 'Wilde's Afterlife in Cyberspace', in Uwe Böker, Richard Corballis and Julie Hibbard (eds), *The Importance of Reinventing Oscar, Versions of Wilde during the Last Hundred Years* (Amsterdam and New York: Rodopi, 2002), pp.295–303.

2. www.ryerson.ca/1890s/yellowbookintro.htm.
3. Neumann, 'Wilde's Afterlife in Cyberspace', p.295.
4. Acknowledgments for the information about Anacleto to Bob Nicholson, victoria@listserv.indiana.edu, 28 January 2010 14:20:32.
5. For much learned debate on this, the reader is referred to the listserv SHARP (The Society for the History of Authorship, Reading, and Publishing), www.sharpweb.org.
6. Neumann, 'Wilde's Afterlife in Cyberspace', pp.296–7.
7. Ibid., pp.297–9.

Select Bibliography

WORKS BY OSCAR WILDE

The Complete Works of Oscar Wilde, general editor Ian Small (Oxford: Oxford University Press, 2000–):
> *Poems*, eds Bobby Fong and Karl Beckson (2000), Vol.1.
> *De Profundis*, ed. Ian Small (2005), Vol.2.
> *The Picture of Dorian Gray*, ed. Joseph Bristow (2005), Vol.3.
> *Criticism*, ed., Josephine M. Guy (2007), Vol.4.

The Collected Works of Oscar Wilde, ed. Robert Ross (originally published as *The First Collected Edition of the Works of Oscar Wilde* [London: Methuen, 1908–1922]), (London: Routledge, 1993), 15 vols.

Collins' Complete Works of Oscar Wilde, ed. Merlin Holland (London: HarperCollins, 1999).

Lady Windermere's Fan, Salome, A Woman of No Importance, An Ideal Husband, and The Importance of Being Earnest, ed. Peter Raby (Oxford: Clarendon, Oxford Drama Library, 1995).

The Picture of Dorian Gray, ed. Isobel Murray (Oxford: Oxford University Press, Oxford English Novels, 1974).

The Picture of Dorian Gray, Authoritative Texts, Backgrounds, Reviews and Reactions, Criticism, ed. Donald L. Lawler (New York and London: Norton, 1988).

The Picture of Dorian Gray, Authoritative Texts, Backgrounds, Reviews and Reactions, Criticism, ed. Michael Patrick Gillespie (New York and London: Norton, 2007).

Complete Shorter Fiction, ed. Isobel Murray (London: Oxford University Press, 1979).

The Importance of Being Earnest, ed. Russell Jackson (London: Ernest Benn Limited, 1980).

Oscar Wilde: The Major Works, ed. Isobel Murray (Oxford: Oxford University Press, 2000).

Oscar Wilde: Selected Journalism, ed. Anya Clayworth (Oxford: Oxford World's Classics, 2004).

The Complete Letters of Oscar Wilde, eds Merlin Holland and Rupert Hart-Davis (London: Fourth Estate, 2000).

Oscar Wilde's Oxford Notebooks: A Portrait of Mind in the Making, eds Philip E. Smith II and Michael Helfand (New York: Oxford University Press, 1989).

Oscar Wilde: Interviews and Recollections, ed. E.H. Mikhail (London: Macmillan, 1979), 2 vols.

Table Talk, ed. Thomas Wright (London: Cassell, 2000).

BEGINNING WILDE STUDIES

When starting research on Oscar Wilde, the first thing I recommend is reading through the *Collins' Complete Works*. This will give the reader a clear sense of Wilde's range, and discourage any tendency to simplify a writer who worked in such a variety of genres and forms. Once this is done, the following should help guide the reader through the critical maze.

Bashford, Bruce, 'When Critics Disagree: Recent Approaches to Oscar Wilde', *Victorian Literature and Culture*, 30, 2 (2002), pp.613–25.

Guy, Josephine M. and Ian Small, *Studying Oscar Wilde: History, Criticism and Myth* (Greensboro, NC: ELT Press, 2006).

Knox, Melissa, *Oscar Wilde in the 1990s: The Critic as Creator* (Rochester, NY: Camden House, 2001).

Mason, Stuart, *Bibliography of Oscar Wilde* (London: T. Werner Laurie, 1914).

Small, Ian, *Oscar Wilde Revalued: An Essay on New Materials and Methods of Research* (Greensboro, NC: ELT Press, 1998).

Small, Ian, *Oscar Wilde: Recent Research, A Supplement* to Oscar Wilde Revalued (Greensboro, NC: ELT Press, 2000).

BOOKS ABOUT OSCAR WILDE

There is a huge body of work on Wilde, from biographical and critical studies, to those which place him in intellectual and cultural history, available to the contemporary student – so much, indeed, that the student is liable to get lost in the jungle. I have decided to include here only book-length studies (including essay collections) which have Wilde as a major focus and that I think particularly important for gaining a foothold on this most appealing of Victorian writers.

Alderson, David, 'Mansex fine': Religion, Manliness and Imperialism in 19th Century British Culture (Manchester: Manchester University Press, 1998).

Anger, Suzy, Victorian Interpretation (Ithaca: Cornell University Press, 2005).

Bartlett, Neil, Who Was That Man? A Present for Mr. Oscar Wilde (London: Serpent's Tale, 1988).

Bashford, Bruce, Oscar Wilde: The Critic as Humanist (Cranbury, NJ: Fairleigh Dickinson University Press, 1999).

Beckson, Karl (ed.), Oscar Wilde: The Critical Heritage (London: Routledge & Kegan Paul, 1970).

Behrendt, Patricia Flanagan, Oscar Wilde: Eros and Aesthetics (New York: St Martin's Press, 1991).

Bloom, Harold (ed.), Modern Critical Views: Oscar Wilde (New York: Chelsea House, 1985).

Böker, Uwe, Richard Corballis and Julie A. Hibbard, (eds) The Importance of Reinventing Oscar: Versions of Wilde during the Last 100 Years (Amsterdam and New York: Rodopi, 2002).

Bristow, Joseph (ed.), Wilde Writings: Contextual Conditions (Toronto, Buffalo, NY and London: Toronto University Press in assn with the UCLA Center for Seventeenth- and Eighteenth-Century Studies and the William Andrews Clark Memorial Library, 2003).

—— (ed.), Oscar Wilde and Modern Culture: The Making of a Legend (Athens, OH: Ohio University Press, 2008).

Brown, Julia Prewitt, Cosmopolitan Criticism: Oscar Wilde's Theory of Art (Charlottesville, VA: University of Virginia Press, 1997).

Coakley, Davis, Oscar Wilde: The Importance of Being Irish (Dublin: Town House and Country House, 1994).

Cohen, Ed, Talk on the Wilde Side: Towards a Genealogy of a Discourse on Male Sexualities (New York and London: Routledge, 1993).

Cohen, Philip, The Moral Vision of Oscar Wilde (London: Associated University Press, 1978).

Craft, Christopher, Another Kind of Love: Male Homosexual Desire in English Discourse, 1850–1920 (Berkeley, CA and London: University of California Press, 1994).

Danson, Lawrence, Wilde's Intentions: The Artist in his Criticism (Oxford: Clarendon Press, 1997).

Dollimore, Jonathan, Sexual Dissidence, Augustine to Wilde, Freud to Foucault (Oxford: Clarendon Press, 1991).

Dowling, Linda, *Language and Decadence in the Victorian Fin de Siècle* (Princeton, NJ. Princeton University Press, 1986).

———— *Hellenism and Homosexuality in Victorian Oxford* (Ithaca, NY and London: Cornell University Press, 1994).

Downey, Katherine Brown, *Perverse Midrash: Oscar Wilde, Andre Gidé, and Censorship of Biblical Drama* (New York: Continuum, 2004).

Dryden, Linda, *The Modern Gothic and Literary Doubles: Stevenson, Wilde and Wells* (London: Palgrave Macmillan, 2003).

Edwards, Owen Dudley, *The Fireworks of Oscar Wilde* (London: Barrie and Jenkins, 1989).

Ellmann, Richard, *Oscar Wilde* (Harmondsworth: Penguin, 1988).

———— (ed.), *Oscar Wilde: A Collection of Critical Essays* (Englewood Cliffs, NJ: Prentice, 1969).

Eltis, Sos, *Revising Wilde: Society and Subversion in the Plays of Oscar Wilde* (Oxford: Clarendon Press, 1996).

Evangelista, Stefano (ed.), *The Reception of Oscar Wilde in Europe* (London: Continuum, 2010).

Frankel, Nicholas, *Oscar Wilde's Decorated Books* (Ann Arbor, MI: University of Michigan Press, 2002).

Freedman, Jonathan, *Professions of Taste: Henry James, British Aestheticism, and Commodity Culture* (Stanford, CA: Stanford University Press, 1990).

———— (ed.), *Oscar Wilde: A Collection of Critical Essays* (Upper Saddle River, NJ: Prentice Hall, 1996).

Gagnier, Regenia, *Idylls of the Market Place: Oscar Wilde and the Victorian Public* (Aldershot: Scolar Press, 1986).

———— (ed.), *Critical Essays on Oscar Wilde* (New York: G.K. Hall & Co., 1991).

Guy, Josephine M. and Ian Small, *Oscar Wilde's Profession: Writing and the Culture Industry in the late Nineteenth Century* (Oxford: Oxford University Press, 2000).

Halpern, Richard, *Shakespeare's Perfume: Sodomy and Sublimity in the Sonnets, Wilde, Freud, and Lacan* (Philadelphia, PA: University of Pennsylvania Press, 2002).

Hanson, Ellis, *Decadence and Catholicism* (Cambridge, MA: Harvard University Press, 1997).

Holland, Merlin, *Irish Peacock and Scarlet Marquess: The Real Trial of Oscar Wilde* (London: Fourth Estate Ltd, 2004).

Holland, Vyvyan, *Son of Oscar Wilde* (Harmondsworth: Penguin, 1957).

Hyde, H. Montgomery, *Oscar Wilde: A Biography* (London: Eyre Methuen, 1976).

Keane, Robert N. (ed.), *Oscar Wilde: The Man, His Writings, and His World* (New York: AMS, 2003).

Kiberd, Declan, *Inventing Ireland* (Cambridge: Harvard University Press, 1996). ———— *Irish Classics* (London: Granta, 2000).

Killeen, Jarlath, *The Faiths of Oscar Wilde* (London: Palgrave Macmillan, 2005). ———— *The Fairy Tales of Oscar Wilde* (London: Ashgate, 2007).

Kingston, Angela, *Oscar Wilde as a Character in Victorian Fiction* (New York, NY: Palgrave Macmillan, 2007).

Knox, Melissa, *A Long and Lovely Suicide* (New Haven, CT and London: Yale University Press, 1994).

Kohl, Norbert, *Oscar Wilde: The Works of a Conformist Rebel*, trans. David Henry Wilson (Cambridge: Cambridge University Press, 1989).

McCormack, Jerusha (ed.), *Wilde: The Irishman* (New Haven, CT and London: Yale University Press, 1998).

McKenna, Neil, *The Secret Life of Oscar Wilde* (New York, NY: Basic, 2005).

Miller, Keith, *Oscar Wilde* (New York: Ungar, 1982).

Nassaar, Christopher S., *Into The Demon Universe: A Literary Exploration of Oscar Wilde* (New Haven, CT and London: Yale University Press, 1974).

Ní Chuilleanáin, Eiléan (ed.), *The Wilde Legacy* (Dublin: Four Courts Press, 2003).

Nunokawa, Jeff, *Tame Passions of Wilde: The Styles of Manageable Desire* (Princeton, NJ: Princeton University Press, 2003).

O'Sullivan, Vincent, *Aspects of Wilde* (London: Constable, 1936).

Ohi, Kevin, *Innocence and Rapture: The Erotic Child in Pater, Wilde, James, and Nabokov* (New York and Basingstoke: Palgrave Macmillan, 2005).

Pearson, Hesketh, *The Life of Oscar Wilde* (London: Methuen, 1954).

Pine, Richard, *The Thief of Reason: Oscar Wilde and Modern Ireland* (Dublin: Gill and Macmillan, 1995).

Powell, Kerry, *Oscar Wilde and the Theatre of the 1890s* (Cambridge: Cambridge University Press, 1990). ———— *Acting Wilde: Victorian Sexuality, Theatre, and Oscar Wilde* (Cambridge: Cambridge University Press, 2009).

Raby, Peter, *Oscar Wilde* (Cambridge: Cambridge University Press, 1988). ———— (ed.), *The Cambridge Companion to Oscar Wilde* (Cambridge: Cambridge University Press, 1997).

Roden, Frederick S. (ed.), *Palgrave Advances in Oscar Wilde Studies* (Basingstoke: Palgrave Macmillan, 2004).

Roditi, Edouard, *Oscar Wilde* (New York: New Directions, 1986).

Sammells, Neil, *Wilde Style. The Plays and Prose of Oscar Wilde* (Harlow: Longman, 2000).

Sandalescu, George (ed.), *Rediscovering Oscar Wilde* (Gerrard's Cross: Colin Smyth, 1994).

Satzinger, Christa, *The French Influences on Oscar Wilde's* The Picture of Dorian Gray *and* Salome (Lampeter: Edwin Mellen Press, 1994).

Schmidgall, Gary, *The Stranger Wilde: Interpreting Oscar* (London: Abacus, 1994).

Schroeder, Horst, *Oscar Wilde, The Portrait of Mr W.H. – Its Composition, Publication, and Reception* (Braunschweig: Technische Universtät Carolo-Wilhelmina zu Braunschweig, 1984).

———— *Additions and Corrections to Richard Ellmann's* Oscar Wilde (Braunschweig: privately published, 2002, 2nd edn).

Sedgwick, Eve Kosofsky, *Tendencies* (Durham, NC: Duke University Press, 1993).

Shewan, Rodney, *Oscar Wilde: Art and Egotism* (London: Macmillan, 1977).

Sinfield, Alan, *The Wilde Century: Effeminacy, Oscar Wilde, and the Queer Movement* (London: Cassell, 1994).

Smith, Philip E., II (ed.), *Approaches to Teaching the Works of Oscar Wilde* (New York: Modern Language Association of America, 2008).

Stokes, John, *Oscar Wilde. Myths, Miracles, and Imitations* (Cambridge: Cambridge University Press, 1996).

Tufescu, Florina, *Oscar Wilde's Plagiarism: The Triumph of Art over Ego* (Dublin: Irish Academic Press, 2008).

Upchurch, David, *Wilde's Use of Irish Celtic Elements in* The Picture of Dorian Gray (New York: Lang, 1992).

Varty, Anne, *A Preface to Oscar Wilde* (Harlow: Longman, 1998).

White, Heather, *Forgotten Schooldays: Oscar Wilde at Portora* (Fermanagh: Principia Press, 2002).

Willoughby, Guy, *Art and Christhood: The Aesthetics of Oscar Wilde* (London and Toronto: Associated University Presses, 1993).

Wood, Julia, *The Resurrection of Oscar Wilde: A Cultural Afterlife* (Cambridge: Lutterworth Press, 2007).

Woodcock, George, *The Paradox of Oscar Wilde* (New York: Macmillan, 1950).

Worth, Katherine, *Oscar Wilde* (London: Macmillan, 1983).

Wright, Thomas, *Oscar's Books* (London: Chatto & Windus, 2008).

Zipes, Jack, *Fairy Tales and the Art of Subversion* (London: Heinemann, 1983).

Index